08/34.

Class

Class

Knowing your place
in modern Britain

STEPHEN BROOK

VICTOR GOLLANCZ

LONDON

First published in Great Britain 1997
by Victor Gollancz
An imprint of the Cassell Group
Wellington House, 125 Strand, London WC2R 0BB

© Stephen Brook 1997

The right of Stephen Brook to be identified as author of
this work has been asserted by him in accordance with
the Copyright, Designs and Patents Act, 1988.

A catalogue record for this book is
available from the British Library.

ISBN 0 575 06195 2

Typeset at The Spartan Press Ltd, Lymington, Hants.
Printed in Great Britain by
St Edmundsbury Press Ltd, Bury St Edmunds, Suffolk.

97 98 99 5 4 3 2 1

CONTENTS

ACKNOWLEDGEMENTS

A large number of people helped me construct this book or gave up much time to discuss some contentious issues with me. I particularly wish to thank Tony Benn MP, Hugh Black-Hawkins, Kristine Black-Hawkins, David Bolton, Sir Toby Clarke, Gillian Dargue, Vera Fleming, Julian Jeffs QC, Lord Jenkins of Hillhead, Dr John Launer, Wendy Lesser, Giles MacDonogh, Lord Mancroft, Lord Pilkington of Oxenford, Graham Parkin, Raef Payne, Felix Pryor, Tom Sharpe QC, Dr Ron Singer, Dennis Skinner MP and Deborah Stuart. I also wish to acknowledge the many individuals who spoke to me candidly but as a consequence did not wish to be identified by name.

I am also grateful to the organizations that took time to respond to my enquiries, in particular the College of Arms, Lieutenant Colonel A. S. R. Groves (Ministry of Defence), the Haberdashers Company, Robert Banfield of the Church Commissioners, the House of Lords Information Office and the Independent Schools Information Service.

INTRODUCTION

Whether we own a tandem or a Rolls,
Whether we Rudge it or we trudge it, still
A single topic occupies our minds.
'Tis hinted at or boldly blazoned in
Our accents, clothes and ways of eating fish,
And being introduced and taking leave,
'Farewell', 'So long', 'Bunghosky', 'Cheeribye' –
That topic all-absorbing, as it was,
Is now and ever shall be, to us – CLASS.
                    John Betjeman, 'Beside the Seaside', 1948

When a young woman with an impeccable county accent screamed at me that I was 'a nasty little oik', I knew that there was still a class system in Britain. The mud gets slung in both directions: readers who persevere will come across the gentleman referred to in a courtroom as 'upper-class scum'. Of course it is not only on the level of abuse that class antagonism is discernible. Indeed, class war as such is a marginal factor in British social relations. But class distinctions and class consciousness – they are both very much with us.

There is little agreement on what class is, or whether the notion continues to have any intellectual content, and yet as a nation we remain obsessed by it. Opinion polls asking people to identify their class produce absurd and conflicting responses, variously reflecting pride in class origins, satisfaction with class mobility (especially when upward), shame and all manner of other reactions. I have come to the conclusion that class identification is so subjective in Britain as to be meaningless, yet the fact that it seems impervious to measurement suggests how much it matters to people.

To some, class is equivalent to caste, a form of destiny into which you are born and from which there is no escape. That might be equally true of the lord and the labourer. Or it can be seen in terms of 'orders', in which occupation and social function merge. Others find a clear link between class and occupation – thus, teaching is widely regarded as a middle-class profession – and it is occupation which defines class position more than birth. A Marxist would opt for a simpler definition, in which socio-economic role – whether owner-capitalist or hired labourer – defines the group in which you play out your struggle for economic survival.

P. N. Furbank, in *Unholy Pleasure*, argues with satisfaction that class ceased to be a useful or relevant concept with the disappearance of domestic service in the 1930s. The presence of a servant class allowed one sector within Britain to feel superior to another. After World War II, he argues, it became unacceptable to believe in social superiority.

This may be broadly true, but growing up in the 1950s I was very much aware of rank and privilege. At my prep school, and even at my enlightened direct-grant school thereafter, we were expected to strive for rank in the form of prefectships or captaincies of Wolf Cub platoons or whatever. This aspect of the great game of life had little appeal to me. It had more to do with leadership qualities, I suppose, than with class rankings, but it still reflected a hierarchical approach to life.

When I arrived in Cambridge I was quite surprised to find a band of mature men who always called me 'sir'. To this day I wince when I am called 'sir' by a college porter; at the age of eighteen it was both discomfiting and wonderfully flattering. To be called 'sir', daily, reinforces class superiority. An undergraduate at Cambridge, by definition, was a gentleman, however loutish his behaviour, and thus he was to be accorded respect by the college servants on all occasions, including reprimands. Bryan Gould, the Labour politician who returned to his native New Zealand in the early 1990s, has recorded his shock, on arriving in England to study at Oxford, at 'the pervasiveness of the class structure'. He found it 'embarrassing', as I did not, to be waited on by college servants, but I shared his puzzlement that at the ancient universities this was perceived as the natural and immutable order of things.[1]

Within the undergraduate body there were distinctions of rank too. Scholars and exhibitioners were admitted by competitive examination, until the system was abolished in the 1980s. Being a scholar conferred privileges: you were entitled to take rooms in college for three successive years, whereas Commoners – well, that's what they were called – had to find lodgings for their second year. Other privileges were essentially trivial: a flashier gown, the right to attend certain college feasts and the right to deposit letters *without stamps* at the porter's lodge. There the porters would affix the stamps and post the letters, charging you at the end of each term for the postage used. The system was meritocratic in that scholars were rewarded for their academic superiority, but the rewards, in addition to a modest annual stipend, were privileges that distinguished Scholars from Commoners.

It's true that most social units, and thus most universities, have their ranks and their rituals. I recall exclusive dining clubs at Harvard, not to mention fraternity houses at all manner of American universities, each with its own snobberies and rites. But at Cambridge the insistence on rank and privilege (fellows had a completely distinct set of privileges, such as walking on the college lawns) was built in and not merely a social adjunct. When one of my tutors scornfully registered his view of left-wing politics with the phrase (still to be heard today in the Shires) 'the politics of envy', I couldn't help reflecting that millions of my compatriots had good reason to envy my extraordinary fortune in not only being educated in an exquisite Tudor palace but in being so pampered in the process. It would be an exaggeration to say that the Cambridge ambience was a corrupting miasma, but class and privilege were in the air one breathed, a quintessentially British air.

Class boundaries may be much more fluid than they were a few decades ago, but it's significant that popular entertainment is still obsessed by class portraiture. It's true that English comedy from Congreve to Coward and beyond has derived substance and laughs from manners, class and accent, but it is the ubiquity of the theme in contemporary light entertainment that is striking. Switch on any British television sitcom and each character will be perfectly defined in terms of class: accent, clothes, house furnishings, car, deference accorded or received, all will have been minutely worked out. This is not snobbery, merely good craftsmanship. Write in the wrong voice or the wrong hat in an episode of *Coronation Street*, and the viewers will notice. Successful television programmes such as *Upstairs, Downstairs* and the Peter Wimsey detective series were entirely predicated on the quirks of the master–servant relationship – which the overwhelming majority of viewers have never experienced. *To the Manor Born* focused on the scheming of a dispossessed chatelaine.

Hollywood concluded long ago that all British behaviour was conditioned by class. This firm belief gave rise to some mild comedy. In the 1940s film *Mrs Miniver*, a heroic portrait is painted of plucky Britain at war. There is a touch of class warfare when the station master dares to enter his prize roses into a competition organized and traditionally won by Lady Belton, the lady of the manor. Lady Belton's granddaughter asks Mrs Miniver, after whom the rebel rose is named, to have the rose withdrawn from the flower show so as not to offend Lady Belton. The Minivers' callow son Vincent, just down from Oxford, upbraids Miss Belton for perpetuating class tyranny. But he does so in such crass terms that it is impossible to take his views seriously, and Miss Belton easily turns the tables on Vincent by pointing out that she does volunteer work in the slums while he sits in his armchair and theorizes.

The participants in the class struggle are caricatured. Local women wittily attack the station master for 'having ideas above his station'. Lady Belton is portrayed initially as a dragon: 'We don't take orders, we give them.' Servants, called Horace and Gladys, twitter and cringe in deferential accents.

Before long this fawning glance at the class system is forgotten. Vincent marries Miss Belton, and Lady Belton overturns the judges' decision (in her favour, of course) at the flower show and awards first prize to the station master.

Thus the spirit of democracy triumphs over the principle of aristocracy. In modern Britain, however, we like to have it both ways: retaining rank, monarchy, aristocracy, costume and precedence, while insisting that we can teach the rest of the world a thing or two about democracy.

The book that follows is a blend of analysis, anecdote, history, reportage and interview. It is not a sociological study and it does not pretend to be definitive. It takes as its starting point the conviction that in Britain class still matters – far less than it used to, but it still matters. It infuses our institutions: the monarchy, Parliament, our schools and universities, our sporting activities. Definitions of class are tricky, as the boundaries keep shifting, but anyone with eyes and ears can read the codes. We may not understand class rationally, but we experience it viscerally. Class is psychological, in that it is our sense, sometimes rooted, sometimes shifting, of where we stand socially in relation to others. Some individuals may lack this kind of class consciousness. Certainly we are not keen to talk about it. But it remains a form of self-identity that can greatly condition how we function in the world.

As a topic it fascinates us. It engages our snobberies, our insecurities, our self-esteem, our envy. It shapes our sense of place in the world. It excites our press. Proclaim any form of class triumphalism, and you will come under fierce attack; proclaim a new era of classlessness in its place, and the satirists will go for your throat.

Class is social quicksand. It keeps us on our toes or buries us. It appalls us, it beguiles us. It brings out the best in us, and the worst. This book is just the latest crawl across this notorious minefield.

ONE

Class, Status and Other Confusions

Everyone was convinced that there was a great impassable line between 'gentlemen' and 'the lower classes' and everyone drew that line
immediately below his own feet.

Evelyn Waugh, *Letters*, letter to Nancy Mitford, 8 January 1952

The question What do you mean by class? is bound to be asked, but is
not easily answered. My own view differs from that of many people –
notably historians and sociologists – who have wrestled with the topic.
For me class can be approached descriptively – that is, by stratifying
society and defining with greater or lesser rigour what the criteria are
for membership within each band – or psychologically.

The descriptive approach has all the fascination, and limitations, of a
parlour game. At its best it can illuminate the history of society itself –
the making of the English working class, as E. P. Thompson has
demonstrated, can be an enthralling topic – but at its worst it becomes
an exercise in snobbery, one more manual in the game of social
positioning.

By 'psychological' I simply mean that there is a strong subjective
element within all considerations of class. Class is only of interest to us
to the extent that we are conscious of it: and class-consciousness is so
pervasive that almost all of us feel touched by it. A sense of class is, I
would suggest, our sense of how we relate socially to the world around
us. An aristocrat is not merely born into a social stratum; he or she is
raised with certain assumptions, certain expectations. When I talk to
ex-miners in the north of England, they speak of 'the gaffer'. It doesn't
matter whether they respect or depise 'the gaffer'; what does matter is

that they are forced into a relationship with someone who occupies a socially superior role, someone who almost certainly has power over them. Having a gaffer in your life positions you psychologically. The landowner (upper-class) or physician (upper-middle-class) has no gaffer.

I don't wish to suggest that class consciousness is like being the filler in an oppressive social sandwich. For some class is a burden, for others simply an irrelevance. I have no doubt that it impinges on British lives far less than it did, say, forty years ago. Class consciousness isn't necessarily pernicious, though to the extent that it can lead to embarrassment, snobbery, cringing, uncertainty and self-consciousness about peripheral matters such as accent and dress it can be crippling. I do believe that societies in which class is a marginal issue are probably the healthier for it. North American social relations can be bedevilled by all kinds of social positioning – regionalism, accent, wealth, location of country club, devotion to leisure pursuits, occupation and so forth – but *class* identification would be largely irrelevant except in certain pockets of the country. Wealth rather than birth determines social eminence.

In this chapter I shall consider other versions of 'class', not because I subscribe to them or, in some cases, have any strong wish to argue against them, but because it is helpful to understand how the term has been used and what theories have been spun from assumptions about class. This is no easy task, as the subject is benighted by imprecision.

We want to be able to talk about class, but a 'class' is by definition a finite band. A class is defined by its members. But this is to suppose that class definitions are rigid, which is hardly ever the case. It is possible to define 'upper class' in such a way – number of generations of landed ownership, number of heraldic quarterings (a very French preoccupation), possession of title and so forth – that its membership can be counted. But that can never be more than a snapshot, and even a rigidly defined upper class will constantly change as a result of marriage, divorce and death. Where a class is rigidly defined, you have a caste rather than a class: Indian brahmins or Jewish cohanim, for example, both priestly castes. However, I defy anyone to come up with a watertight definition of how the Hungarian middle class in the 1860s or the British working class in the 1960s was constituted. Show me a descriptive class definition, and I can guarantee that I can punch holes in it. None the less the term carries sufficient resonance to be historically useful. The fact that one can quibble indefinitely about the point (if any) at which, say, a gifted working-class designer ascends into the middle class does not mean that the concept has no meaning and no utility.

In some respects confusion is unavoidable because of the two very different ways in which class is postulated. For some it is linked to economic role. You do not have to be a Marxist to believe that occupation and economic function have some bearing on class status. For others status itself, which can be acquired through birth, education, social approval and so forth, is far more important in defining someone's place within the class structure. Put baldly, class can be defined as either economic or, in the broadest sense, cultural. Entire debates, such as the nation-engrossing 'What class does John Prescott belong to?' (discussed in greater detail in a subsequent chapter), stem from a confusion between these two sets of assumptions, which provide endless opportunities for talking at cross-purposes. What is more, the two kinds of definition interpenetrate, as in the age-old question of whether class determines occupation or occupation determines class. R. H. Tawney wrestled with this problem in his book *Equality*, but even his noble mind could shed little light on it. Acknowledging that classes could, on the one hand, be regarded as 'composed of a series of economic groups', he also conceded that they could be regarded 'as a series of social groups, distinguished from each other by different standards of expenditure and consumption, and varying in their income, their environment, their education, their social status and family connections, their leisure and their amusements'.[1]

The present Earl Russell got it completely wrong when he was asked by a newspaper to deliberate about class. In the 18th century, he recalled, 'Lord Acton's family had run out of money and he was employed as a second under-cook. What did that make him? His status was aristocracy but his class was working class.'[2] On the contrary, his class was aristocracy but his status was that of a worker.

Even if we could establish satisfactorily who belonged to which class, we would not necessarily be able to take the next step of determining how class membership affects behaviour. In Marxist models, classes struggle; their *raison d'être* is self-assertion. That is a strength of the Marxist vision: it gives a point to class. The weakness of most descriptive models is that they don't tell us how classes behave. For the market researcher class identification can be a clue as to buying habits, a very limited application of this piece of knowledge. Beyond that, there is uncertainty. In Britain, where class consciousness is so deeply impregnated, we do make assumptions based on class identification. We tend to say, with scant logic, 'Lord Justice Fotheringay went to Eton, stood for Parliament as a Conservative candidate, lives in splendour in Kensington and Hampshire' and complete the sentence, with doubtful legitimacy, 'and therefore he has no understanding of life in the inner city/what it's like to be a poor Bangladeshi/why Oasis is better than Blur.' Anthony Giddens makes the same point formally: to show 'that a given proportion of the political élite are from upper-class backgrounds, or even attended public schools, does not *necessarily* entail that they either share a common moral ethos as elite members, or that they maintain close social contacts with one another'.[3]

The point strikes me as self-evident, but it is one that we all constantly ignore. Class may be important and intriguing, but it is not necessarily a determining factor in anything. Nor does class necessarily influence behaviour. The popular image of the millionaire is of an individual who both earns and dispenses large sums. Long ago Thorstein Veblen, with his theories of 'conspicuous consumption', argued that display and expenditure were signals intended to demonstrate the wealth of the spender, a flash of the peacock's tail. With newspapers gorging on stories of the jet-setting rich, it is tempting to assume that if you are rich you flaunt it. However, a recent study of American millionaires concluded that the very rich tend to be savers rather than spenders; one-third buy second-hand cars, half never spend more than $400 on a suit.[4] As lottery winners are fast learning, you don't grow rich by spending money.

'Classes' were only defined as such from the late eighteenth century onwards. Earlier terms such as 'estate' or 'condition' or 'rank' were used instead. When 'class' came into being as an intellectual construct, it had more neutral associations than previous terms and tended to define economic rather than social groupings. Over previous centuries, societal groupings throughout Europe had been defined in terms of orders or caste. Caste is a special case in that it often stems from religious sanctions: secular laws or customs play second fiddle to religious dictates. Heredity enforces caste, so that members of a particular caste have their status confirmed both by descent and by the functions they are required to perform, whether priestly, military or menial. Tension arises when members of low-status castes refuse to accept the supposed logic of the system, and their despised status becomes hard to justify except among those who accept the religious sanctions on which the whole system depends.

Many ancient societies were based on structures that have more in common with orders than classes. Native American communities of north-west America were divided into three strata: chiefs, commoners and slaves. Primogeniture determined status within families, so that each individual had a definable social standing. There was a conflict between property rights and the need for a tightly knit community to share resources, resolved in the following way: all resources, whether fruit bushes or fishing rights along beaches, were privately owned. 'These rights of use were unalienable and were transmitted like social rank through inheritance.' However, 'permission for use was never refused, and ownership is generally expressed in the right to first fruits'.[5] Thus property ownership was not in conflict with a sharing of resources. A rigidly hierarchical and hereditary social system can coexist with concern for communal welfare.

In medieval Europe orders (or estates) rather than classes were the principle of organization in society. Unlike the Native American societies, they were little concerned with resource management; but, like them, they were often hereditary in principle and rigid in application. The religious validation inherent in a caste system was present in the form of an ecclesiastical order. The Middle Ages identified three orders: nobility, priests and labourers. The English monk Aelfric wrote in 1003 to Archbishop Wulfstan, listing 'three orders in the Church of God: the order of the workers who produce food for us, that of warriors who defend our fatherland, that of *oratores* – these are the clerks, the monks and the bishops – who pray for all'.[6] This simple division of society persisted for many centuries. In 1610 Charles Loyseau, in his *Traité des Ordres et Simples Dignitez*, wrote: 'Some are devoted particularly to the service of God; others to the preservation of the State by arms; still others to the task of feeding and maintaining it by peaceful labours. These are our three orders or estates general of France: the Clergy, the Nobility, and the Third Estate.'[7]

The notion of three orders has a long ancestry, and existed in variant forms in ancient Greece and Rome. In any descriptive view of orders, they are seen as contributing harmoniously, if not equally, to society. In doing so they inevitably smooth over the considerable differences that lie within each order. The commonalty, or labourers, were not a monolithic bloc, any more than the nobility were. Nor were their different roles necessarily mutually exclusive in the way that those of a caste system clearly are.

A system of orders is defined by privileges and obligations within each estate. The system tottered once economic function began to play a greater role. At that point orders slowly, clumsily but inexorably shifted towards a class system, with its greater fluidity. Orders were rigid and hierarchical; classes were mobile, jockeying for position, striving for betterment, winning advantages and shoring up against intrusion. It was a transformation that took centuries to complete, and was not seriously analysed in Britain until the eighteenth century. Adam Smith, using economic criteria, divided British society into three classes: landowners, stock owners and labourers.

The term 'the middling class' was current in the late eighteenth century and makes an appearance in Samuel Richardson's *Clarissa* in 1748. It gradually gave way to 'middle class', a term smugly championed by the philosopher James Mill (1773–1836) as 'both the most warm and the most virtuous part of the community'.[8]

It was with Marx and Engels, above all in their *Manifesto of the Communist Party* published in the revolutionary year of 1848, that the concept of 'class' really took off, since it ceased to be merely descriptive. Instead class was seen as an active force within society, as movements rather than memberships, struggle rather than passivity. Class was economic in the most rudimentary way, since membership was determined by the individual's relation to the means of production and access to basic resources. Class was inescapable; you were bound to it by destiny. It was a condition which prompted individuals to act in the same way in defence of their interests. Marx's formulation was a broad one, and it is therefore not surprising that in his writings 'class' does not always denote the same concept: usually the economic aspect is foremost, sometimes the social.

It is this notion of class as a movement that is unsatisfactory. That factory owners have different economic interests from their employees is clear enough. But labourers and factory owners do not engage in struggle without direction or leadership. Direction implies politicization, which can be a distorting process. A working class directed by a Stalin is a very different force from a working class guided by a Mussolini, even though both options involve unpleasantness for nonconformists. So any historical explanation that conceives of class as the primary component in political change will soon run into trouble. None the less, claims Marxist theory, the class struggle was the central force within society's development; moreover, the proletariat was destined to vanquish capitalism, at which point classes themselves would disappear.

Marx neatly sidestepped difficulties in categorization by devising the term 'strata' to deal with groups such as the lumpenproletariat and the intelligentsia, who by definition are divorced from any processes of production and thus not strictly classes at all, while remaining identifiable groupings within society. Groups associated with the middle classes – artisans, small-scale manufacturers, shopkeepers – would, Marx avowed, eventually throw in their lot with the proletariat and help to overcome the capitalist system with which they had flirted. The lumpenproletariat too would be galvanized into action by the advent of proletarian revolution. The major classes – capitalists and workers – can be defined in fairly crude terms by relating them to means of production only if those relationships are relatively straightforward, which they were in the days when mill owners owned the mills and labourers worked in them. But such models are simplistic, especially in the late twentieth century when the economic status of enormous numbers of people is fluid, and when the boundaries between classes (when defined in Marxist terms) are blurred. For instance, to which class should the self-employed be assigned? Furthermore, the Marxist analysis assumed, no doubt justifiably in 1848, that the proletariat was motivated in its struggle by poverty and deprivation. That is hardly the case today, and has not been for some time. Since my plumber earns far more than I do, what motivation does he have to pursue the class struggle against me and my type?

In Marxist and other theories of class, it is easy to confuse 'class' as a theoretical construct and class as a living entity with an existence of its own that is merely observed by the historian. In the latter sense it can surely only function if it is conscious of the fact that it is a class, if the

Kent fisherman, the Hebridean crofter and the Bradford mill worker have a shared consciousness: class consciousness, the ingrained sense that their lives are governed by an understanding that they own nothing but their labour. It was the primary goal of the Labour Party and trade union organizers to instil and foster that consciousness.

A century ago class struggle did seem close to the surface: frequent strikes, demands for further political and electoral reform, the nurturing of socialist movements and the Labour Party, the growth of trade unionism, all signalled a new awareness of the sheer numerical strength of the British working class. However, some contemporary accounts suggest that this class was far from the unified force that revolutionary Marxists yearned for. Robert Roberts, in his finely wrought account of Edwardian Salford, is sceptical:

> The class struggle, as manual workers in general knew it, was apolitical . . . They looked upon it not in any way as a war against the employers but as a perpetual series of engagements in the battle of life itself . . . Marxist "ranters" from the Hall who paid fleeting visits to our street end insisted that we, the proletariat, stood locked in titanic struggle with some wicked master class . . . most people passed by; a few stood to listen, but not for long: the problems of the "proletariat"', they felt, had little to do with them. Before 1914 the great majority in the lower working class were ignorant of Socialist doctrine in any form . . . Generally, those who did come into contact with such ideas showed either indifference or, more often, hostility.[9]

In October 1996 I attended a meeting of the Socialist Workers Party, the closest thing we have in modern Britain to Salford's Marxist 'ranters'. Lindsay German, author of *A Question of Class*, was speaking on the theme 'Does Class Matter?' She began by taking issue with the widely held view that 'We are all middle-class now.' To show that the reality was different she cited low pensions and compared them with the cost of dinners at the Paris Ritz recently enjoyed by a Conservative MP. She mentioned recent surveys in which 76 per cent said there was still a class struggle in progress, and in which 68 per cent identified themselves as working-class. (As we shall see, self-assessment of class status is all but meaningless.) Another 43 per cent, she asserted, believed that Britain would benefit from socialist planning.

She said workers worked for the pittance they earned; the rich tended to inherit their wealth. She attacked the incentive argument sometimes employed to justify high salaries, pointing out that the argument was never applied to the low-paid. Those with the dirtiest jobs and the longest hours, she went on, tended to be the lowest-paid and faced the worst conditions.

Until now little had been said about class, much about the injustice of the gap between rich and poor. Now she defined as working-class those who were forced to sell their labour in order to survive: classic Marxist doctrine. This included office workers as well as manual workers.

She mocked the distinction between manufacturing and service industry, citing the man who intalls exhausts in a car factory (manufacturing industry) and the man who fixes exhausts at Kwik-Fit (service industry). Both were performing essentially the same job. (Not a helpful analogy. Nobody argues that those working in manufacturing and those working in service industries necessarily occupy different class bands.)

Ms German admitted that lifestyles have changed, that you didn't need to wear overalls to be working-class and that there were working-class people who adored opera. But hobbies were irrelevant to the main issue, which was that class is an economic relationship. She then explicitly endorsed Marx's assertion that class is determined by one's relationship to the means of production. In a variation on classic Marxist doctrine, she conceded the existence of a modest (15 per cent) managerial class, but then pitched them into the enemy camp by calling them 'the policemen of the capitalists'.

Since capitalists are competitive, she went on, they unite in exploiting their workers, but also want to outdo their rivals. This leads to class conflict, as capitalists need to impose harsher conditions on their employees in order to remain competitive. (A dubious example, since there are countless instances of capitalist enterprises that offer good working conditions as incentives.) The exploiters can be beaten at their own game, but only if the workers are organized, and they can only be organized if they are able to think of themselves as workers – the standard Marxist line on the necessity for class consciousness.

The Labour Party has failed the workers; hence the need for revolutionary socialism. It won't be possible, she asserted, to get rid of the ruling class without a party that promotes working-class aspirations.

I don't believe I have misrepresented Ms German's address. It was impassioned but sketchy and, apart from some finessing on the subject of service industries, scarcely conceded that the world had changed since 1848.

After she finished, there were questions from the floor. Or there were supposed to be. Instead, sympathetic listeners rose to express outrage at various forms of oppression: costly redecoration of Camden Council's offices and long 'working breakfasts' were cited as particularly vicious blows against the rights of working people. Everyone who spoke had a personal grievance, however trivial (or in some cases incomprehensible), and the audience was invited to share in the sense of outrage. The perorations were standard: the villains of the piece were the 'bosses', yet it was possible to 'fight the boss who's out to get us'. Many speakers expressed disgust at Tony Blair's 'New' Labour Party, primarily for trying to take the struggle out of class relations, thereby strengthening the hand of the bosses. Blairites were portrayed as privileged people using opted-out schools and advocating binding arbitration in industrial disputes.

The rhetoric suggested that the SWP feels marginalized. Labour's resurgence has diminished its effectiveness. Marxist groups such as the SWP and Militant flourished when Labour was split during the 1980s. Now that Labour has got a grip on itself organizationally and politically, nobody greatly cares what the Marxist groups have to say. So perhaps it was not surprising that the note sounded at the meeting I attended was one of paranoia. Perhaps it should have been dismay at the poverty of its own rhetoric.

Class consciousness, it was supposed, would lead to class solidarity and the spirit of revolution. Indeed, it happened from time to time, if not with the regularity that Marxist theory predicted. Class consciousness is a contributing factor to revolutionary change but other factors – e.g. nationalism, inspired leadership – also have an important part to play. That is why revolutionary movements, at least in fairly sophisticated societies, strike us increasingly as antiquated and outmoded. We simply know they are not telling part of the story, that a purely Marxist analysis rooted in class is not sufficiently complex to deal with the inadequacies of modern societies and economies. Hence too the very limited appeal of such movements, which remain far off on the fringes of politics.

Their rhetoric no longer rings true; our relation to the means of production is not the dominant factor in most people's daily lives. If our class is determined by our economic role, but that role no longer fits 19th-century models, then the Marxist analysis loses pertinence.

I find it significant that even the left wing of the Labour Party has never been explicitly Marxist, though many left-wingers acknowledge their debt to Marx in developing their ideas. When, in 1973, the German ambassador was trying to get Tony Benn to admit he was a Marxist, Benn replied:

> I don't know really; it is a foreign ideology. The British Labour movement is fundamentally based on Christianity, expressing itself through the trade unions, through the distrust of power, through social ideas of cooperation; and the only difference between me and Harold Wilson is that he boasts of the fact that he has got through three pages of *Das Kapital* whereas I am ashamed of the fact that I *only* got through three pages.[10]

It's a minor anecdote and it may say more about the British distrust of ideology than anything else, but it also suggests that, although the British are deeply imbued with class consciousness, class struggle has never caught on. We are more obsessed with the nuances of class and status than with fighting for the victory of one class over another. In the words of Patrick Joyce: 'The sense of a shared condition need not automatically issue in an understanding of social relations as tending inherently towards conflict.'[11]

Even though a left-wing socialist such as Tony Benn has not drunk deeply direct from the source, his angle on class is essentially Marxist. 'Class', he told me, 'means the hierarchy of a feudal society, which is still quite powerful. And the definition of class is, Do you live by selling your labour or by owning capital? Of course the notion of work has changed enormously. None the less the gap between rich and poor, nationally and internationally, is wider than it's been for a hundred years. And if that isn't about class, I don't know what it is about. As for Marx, he was the last of the Old Testament prophets, and what motivated him was a sense of justice. Anyone who obliterates Marx is doing the same thing as obliterating Galileo or Freud or Darwin. He threw light on the nature of society.'

I pointed out that those who unashamedly espoused the Marxist line, such as Arthur Scargill, received negligible support when they tested their ideas before the electorate.

'He got more votes in Hemsworth than Keir Hardie the first time he stood,' replied Benn, curiously thrusting Scargill back a hundred years. 'Arthur is a man who spoke the truth. I think he made a mistake. That's by the by. But the fact is he's now putting forward an argument at a time when all the political leaders in Britain agree entirely about everything. There is no debate in Britain, there is no representation. Everybody agrees with market forces, globalization, NATO, nuclear weapons, clobber the unions, liberate capital, Ireland and so on. They all agree.

'Now this is a really big crisis of representation. So you say class is all out of date because we've all got telly and a mortgage, we're all middle-class – this is a way of obliterating an analysis of what's happening in society. And look at the rest of the world, which is suffering from the evils of capitalism in a very class-explicable way.'

'If that were the case,' I responded, 'then somebody would be responding with a very radical agenda, and it hasn't happened.'

'With a hostile media? I'm having an easy time now, but almost everything I've ever said in my life has been denounced, mainly by the Labour Party. History just takes a bit of time to work its way through. In Chesterfield, for example, where they've closed all the pits, the arguments that are brought forward in my surgery make you weep. They don't talk about reshuffles and New Labour. They say: "They've closed the pits and we haven't got a job." Their daughter's married and can't get a house, their grandson can't get a grant to go to college, aunt can't get a hip operation, granddad can't live on the pension. That's what they say to me. And then people say, "Oh, class has disappeared."'

About fifty years after the publication of the *Communist Manifesto*, the German sociologist Max Weber refined the theories of Marx and Engels by distinguishing between class and status. The Marxist view held that class was destiny, a force from which none was exempt. There was no room for subjectivism. Weber maintained that, while it was undoubtedly true that economic forces largely determined class structure, subjective factors also came into play. Individuals could make choices which affected their status; and those choices could be validated by the community in which individuals dwelt. Status conferred social power and prestige. Class categories might be overriding, but status categories could hardly be ignored. Rather than accepting Marx's belief that class struggle would one day lead to the victory of the proletariat and thus the disappearance of class itself, Weber argued that the yearning for status would lead to increasing differentiation.

Weber's theory makes room, as Marx's did not, for commercial classes, and for intellectuals and down-and-outs, whom Marx consigned to the sidelines until the stage in the struggle when they would side with the winning team, the proletariat. Weber made room for them in a four-layered class system: from bottom to top it consisted of manual workers, the *petite bourgeoisie*, the intelligentsia and the propertied class. 'Status groups', which included special-interest groups such as political parties, were interwoven among this overall class structure. Related to such views is the argument propounded by Ralf Dahrendorf and others that 'class membership is derived from the incumbency of a social role'.[12]

The Marxist theory gives class a reason to live: participation in struggle. Weber's classes seem merely to jostle amiably. His four categories are descriptive, and spawned a profusion of different models as sociologists sought to devise structures that mirrored quite specifically the particular societies in which they were interested. The American sociologist Leonard Reissman has formulated the appeal of Weber's theories: 'The social philosophy of "status" does not jar a democratic value system but instead fits nicely into it at many points . . . To imply, as "status" does, an emphasis upon personal achievement rather than upon birth or historical process is to stress democratic qualities.'[13]

Despite the relative crudity of Marx's formulation, the concept of 'class consciousness' has proved useful. Historical works such as E. P. Thompson's *The Making of the English Working Class* are, in effect, exercises in the history of class consciousness. There have been English labourers since English soil was first tilled; but there has only been an English working class since the late eighteenth and early nineteenth centuries, a class forged into consciousness, argues Thompson, by the experience of industrialization and political awareness. 'Class happens', writes Thompson

> when some men, as a result of common experiences (inherited or shared), feel and articulate the identity of their interests as between

themselves, and as against other men whose interests are different from (and usually opposed to) theirs ... Class consciousness is the way in which these experiences are handled in cultural terms: embodied in traditions, value-systems, ideas, and institutional forms.[14]

Although historians such as Thompson and Eric Hobsbawm employ the Marxist concept of 'class consciousness' as the unlocking of a gate that makes it possible for groups to take action in their own defence, these historians also make room for a more Weberian notion that individuals and communities have a part to play in forging classes viewed more as social constructs than as mere economic forces.

Critics of this view have pointed to factors other than class that have nurtured solidarity among groups of workers. Some cite deference rather than militancy; others note the influence of religious education in teaching working-class children 'the values of self-discipline and respectability that would be required of them in the new urban-industrial world'; yet another critic, William Reddy, has asserted that it is 'quite possible to account for the whole of English social history down through 1850 without invoking class interest'.[15]

I do not wish to arbitrate between the late Professor Thompson and his critics, but the dispute is worth citing as an example of how difficult it is to navigate in these waters. Thompson was no doctrinaire Marxist, and his insistence that class is a relationship rather than a 'thing' allows for great flexibility in his narrative; even so, historians remain unconvinced by his magisterial work. It was bold on Thompson's part to conceive of some great binding force unifying a large band of individuals into a single group consciousness, but subsequent historians have tended to divide up the field, identifying numerous subgroups within 'the English working class'. With time the monoliths of Marxist and Weberian theory have crumbled. Whether that is a sign of progress in historical enquiry, it is not for me to say. But the dispute reinforces the huge disparity of views, even among trained historians, on the simple notion of class. There is still no agreement on the criteria that would determine at what point and by what means a group of individuals has become a cohesive class prepared to act in its own interests.

Whatever the deficiencies of Thompson's methods, I find myself in broad sympathy with his notion that class is a relationship, and also a 'social and cultural formation' and not merely an economically conditioned force. The character of a class can only be observed, and indeed can only be experienced, in relationship to other classes. An upper class, by definition, has to be perceived as socially superior to other classes.

P. N. Furbank plausibly writes: 'To use "class" terminology is a social *act* and (notionally anyway) is to enter into social relations with others. Further, in the case at least of the English "class" system, it is to engage in value-judgment.'[16] Perceived class relation can be value-free; but to employ the *language* of class can, in certain circumstances, be an act of snobbish self-assertion or of deference. The linguistic use of class concepts can, as Furbank notes elsewhere, be an exercise in 'prevarication, deviousness and the playing of social and political games'.[17]

Ultimately the idea of class as relationship is destructive of the notion of class itself. It is not only classes that relate to each other, but individuals within classes. Changing circumstances – sudden enrichment, say – can alter one's position within a class sector. Winning the lottery throws you into a spin in terms of your class identity, especially if it's working-class. Furthermore it is perfectly possible to occupy two classes simultaneously, even using 'class' in the sense derived from economic role and occupation. As William Reddy has observed, 'Smallholders in marginal areas spent many months each year migrating to engage in wage labour in cities or richer agricultural areas – were they workers or peasants?'[18] If I persist in finding the notion of class as relationship useful, it is because I interpret it in psychological terms, rather than in terms of occupation or economic role. If a miner rises through the ranks of his trade union to become a national organizer, then we can argue about whether, as an ex-miner, he is any longer a fully paid-up member of the working class. I don't greatly care what label is attached to this individual. What is interesting is how he perceives and acts towards others, and vice versa, as a consequence of his altered role.

As must now be apparent, defining class is a bog of misapprehension, partisanship and cross-purposes. Leonard Reissman, observing class in America, notes: 'Class, as a fact of social life, is interwoven throughout the institutional fabric of society. Each institutional sphere, whether the family, education, religion, or the economic and political orders, exerts some influence in setting the individual's class.'[19] If that were so, then class would be all but impossible to 'construct' in any individual or group case, since all the factors cited (and others not cited) would provide a permutation of overwhelming complexity.

Not surprisingly, the few people for whom class definition is a moneymaking enterprise – market researchers, pollsters, advertisers, political strategists – throw theory to one side and focus on one aspect alone: occupation of the head of household. This is the system adopted by the Institute of Practitioners in Advertising. Yet ascertaining class by occupation is deeply flawed. What, for example, are we to make of a plumber (annual income £60,000) married to a hospital administrator (annual income £35,000)? According to the so-called Standard Classification, the plumber is 'skilled manual' (Grade 5), the administr-ator is 'managerial and executive' (Grade 2). Do we assign class status to the family or to the individuals within it? The Census uses a class stratification which puts occupation ahead of background: in descend-ing order, Professional, Managerial and Technical Occupations, Skilled Occupations Nonmanual, Skilled Occupations Manual, Partly Skilled Occupations and Unskilled Occupations. Thus an aristocratic photographer such as Patrick Lichfield languishes in Class III, while my dentist lives it up in Class I. This kind of assessment may make some kind of sense in North America, but it seems way off the mark in Britain.

Another easy, but obviously flawed, method is simply to ask someone which class they belong to. To such a question there are numerous responses: the truth as perceived by the individual, which may be accurate or inaccurate; ignorance, as not everyone gives the matter much thought; a lie, by which an individual can promote himself to a more chic class bracket; puzzlement, as in the aforementioned case of the ex-miner. Thus, self-assessment is a highly questionable method of establishing class boundaries. Even lying in this area can be less straightforward than it appears. The socially ambitious shopkeeper's wife from a working-class background who responds that she is 'upper-middle-class' may act in ways that justify her response. If she accepts the value and material systems of the upper middle class – irons out her accent, spends much of her income on a trendy car, dresses well and so forth – it might be churlish to insist that she stay back where she belongs. British society accepts social, and therefore class, mobility. There is an element of choice in class designation. A contemporary of mine at Cambridge hung out with the hunting, fishing Etonians. I had a shrewd suspicion, despite his ludicrously pukka accent, that he was Jewish professional middle class in upbringing. He was so desperate to erase his origins, I surmised, that he was prepared to transform himself into a thing of horror – a loutish, drunken public-school toff – in order to scramble up the social ladder. Still, Americans are allowed to reinvent themselves; why deprive the British of the same pleasure?

In 1949 a Gallup poll asked respondents to identify their own class: 43 per cent said they were working-class, 52 per cent middle-class. Forty years later a similar poll discovered that 67 per cent of those asked considered themselves to be working-class, while the middle-class contingent had dropped to 30 per cent. Either pollsters are more than usually incompetent or there is something peculiar going on. By most objective criteria, the British working class has shrunk over recent decades, while the middle class has grown. Yet people's perceptions of their own class allegiance challenges this view. Is there a kind of bizarre pride at work here, by which the socially ascendant cling nostalgically to their class origins for fear of being accused of class betrayal? Or has working-class status become a fashion accessory? I don't have the answer and it doesn't greatly matter, but it is clear that self-assessment is often far removed from reality.

It is unavoidable that cultural and social factors must be taken into account when discussing class. It is bound to add to the confusion, but to assess class purely in terms of heredity, occupation or relation to the means of production is increasingly wide of the mark. If Kevin Kloggs is born into a working-class family in Glasgow, but by the age of forty owns a successful small business, drives a Mercedes, takes family holidays in the Seychelles and lives in an expensive suburb, it would be hard to insist that Kevin remains irredeemably working-class. If he adopts the trappings of middle-class life, then he is, to all intents and purposes, middle-class. Culture, in the broadest sense of the term, plays its part in class structure. When Richard Hoggart in *The Uses of Literacy* portrays in such loving detail the working-class community of his childhood, he is describing a culture, not an economic stratum. Drinking and eating habits, attitudes to women, gambling and money management, sporting allegiances, propensities towards cleanliness (or otherwise), church- or chapel-going and countless other factors all contribute. Combine culture with a sense, correct or not, of how you fit into the wider social world around you, and you have a sense of class.

I recognize that a predominantly cultural view of class comes close to rendering the concept meaningless. 'Enduring status differences', write two social historians, 'seem rooted not in lack of objective material ability to adopt superior life styles, but rather in a mass of intangible nuances of tastes affecting dress, furnishings, leisure pursuits etc. – a mass of preferences induced by tradition, supported by culture and transmitted in socialization.'[20]

It's hard to derive a useful class theory from 'a mass of intangible nuances'. But that's fine: there is no reason for British society to be wedded to class. Many of us recognize the liberating experience of visiting foreign countries where class distinctions are either minimal or illegible to outsiders. When you simply don't know where deference is due, you treat all men and women as equal, which in every fundamental respect they are. In Britain, however, social distinctions, whether derived from Marxist or cultural notions of class, reflect social inequality, which itself breeds resentment and can lead to conflict.

Recall that not everybody believes that social inequality is to be deplored. Many Conservatives of the old school based their entire political philosophy on the notion that people are innately unequal. Class, in their view, is preordained and the separation of the classes is desirable. Such a view may strike us as reactionary, but those who held it usually added that the classes, although distinct, owed each other mutual respect. Nor was there any political advantage to be gained from promoting class conflict. Indeed, the superior classes had a duty to look after those less fortunate (on the condition that they remained in their place). I suspect that today most Conservatives would disavow such views – as in Viscount Kilmour's assertion in *The New Conservatism* that social equality was 'intellectual and biological nonsense'[21] – but it was not that long ago that they were widely held. Angus Maude, writing in 1953, stated: 'No Conservative would ever frame a policy for education with a view to deliberately changing the class structure.'[22]

This concept of classes was akin to that of medieval orders, a romantic yearning for pre-industrial certainties. Duff Cooper, a former ambassador to France, now better known for having married the beautiful Lady Diana Manners, in 1953 defended class without equivocation:

Class is a word that in this age stirs passions and provokes people to talk nonsense. There are even those who would if they could, create a classless society. If such a society were possible it would be as useless as a tankless army and as dull as a wine-list that gave neither the names of the vineyards nor the dates of the vintages. Class is an inevitable adjunct of human nature. The aim of the lawgiver should be to render the relations between classes happy and to facilitate the passage from one class to another . . . The man who finds himself suddenly thrown into another class is ill at ease, whether he be a peasant in a palace, or a prince in a pot-house.[23]

The political journalist Simon Heffer, not normally given to sentimentality, appears to find positive beauty in class: 'The system is not a vehicle for snobbery or resentment: it is a means by which persons, of whatever class they may be, recognise the value and humanity of others, according to their place. It is a means of acknowledging differences without contempt for those differences. It is an acceptance of reality.'[24] Of course this is nonsense, since it implies that your value and humanity are strictly conditional, and it's the higher classes that set the conditions.

The element of *noblesse oblige* espoused by old-fashioned Conservatives is more or less extinct. Julian Critchley, one of the last survivors, mourns its passing. Once, he laments, 'gentlemen went into politics as an extension of their special obligation. Today, the Tory Party is overwhelmingly bourgeois.' No, the situation is even more grave: 'The *petit embourgeoisement* of the Conservative Party and its reversion to a form of 19th-century Liberalism have gone hand in hand.'[25] (I digress with a personal note. The blimpishness of the traditional Conservative Party drove me to the Labour Party in my teens; the thorough take-over of the Conservatives by the mean-minded *petite bourgeoisie* has kept me there. If my own attachment to the Labour Party is not class-driven, it is certainly class-sustained.)

If the dreadful old Tory theory of the inequality of the classes was essentially benign, its practice was not. I recall being on the receiving end of class hostility when canvassing for the Labour Party in 1983 in Kensington. I was admitted to a basement in Cornwall Gardens inhabited by a pack of young women, who, to judge from their accents and frocks, were from well-off county families. I was ushered in, but suspect they had assumed me to be a Conservative canvasser, because they could conceive of no other kind knocking on their door. As I briefly mentioned in the Introduction, the response of one of the women was to throw me out, calling me 'a nasty little oik' as she pushed me towards the door, her face writhing with distaste. It is true that 1983 was not one of the Labour Party's great years, and I had a tough time on many a doorstep. But even in high-toned Kensington I was greeted by the overwhelmingly Conservative electorate either with a firm but polite indication that my mission was doomed to failure or, in a few cases, with a commendation for my courage in even attempting to win them over to the Labour cause. However, to be called an 'oik' and manhandled was, quite simply, class warfare. I cannot think of any other European country where anything similar could occur.

Class may, then, be disintegrating as a coherent concept, but at a visceral level it has not faded into insignificance. We still relate to other people in terms of perceived class; often that is harmless enough, but not always.

TWO

The Aristocratic Ideal

What between the duties expected of one during one's lifetime, and
the duties exacted from one after one's death, land has ceased to be
either a profit or a pleasure. It gives one position, and prevents one
from keeping it up. That's all that can be said about land.

Oscar Wilde, *The Importance of Being Earnest*, 1895

The British upper classes have, as social beings, the unusual distinction of being very conspicuous and thoroughly insignificant. Their
most visible members, the peerage, are no longer the nation's movers
and shakers, despite their indefensible right to a parliamentary seat.
Once a tiny group of a few dozen families – supplemented by a
substantial number of knights and gentry occupying the foothills of
the peerage – they expanded into a formidable ruling class in the
eighteenth century and maintained their grip on public affairs until
late in the nineteenth.

One could easily tie oneself up in knots trying to define the upper
classes. To confine them to the ranks of the peerage will not do. The
almost automatic conferral of peerages on retiring Cabinet ministers
throughout much of the twentieth century, and the introduction of life
peerages in 1958, ensured that all manner of folk not remotely upper-
class were decked in ermine. The baronetage and much of the richer
country gentry certainly have closer affinities to the peerage than the
average life peer. Moreover, marriage has muddied the waters, as it
always has done in Britain. The Marquess of Milford Haven, who has
princely Battenberg blood in his veins, married the daughter of George
Walker, a working-class entrepreneur who started life as a Billingsgate
porter. None the less the pair (divorced) have children who will, more
likely than not, share the upper-class *mores* of their father. Indeed, it is

one of the striking features of the British upper classes that they can assimilate outside influences with ease and rapidity.

It can create marchionesses out of actresses. It can embrace a newcomer, but also cast off fringe members. Thanks to primogeniture, it is possible to drop out of the aristocracy. The youngest son of a titled friend of mine asked me what class he occupied. In his confidence, looks and considerable personal fortune, not to mention pedigree, I would have defined him as upper-class but slipping. In his case, and countless others, the aristocratic lustre is rubbing off, and his offspring will, no doubt, be indistinguishable from the scions of the upper middle classes.

However, we all recognize upper-class when we spot it, or hear it. The stooping, florid gentlemen stumbling down the steps of Boodle's or White's, the braying drawls of bescarfed women in the smarter enclosures at race meetings, the confident strut of the aspiring estate agent homeward bound to Kensington, the kilted Scots chieftain showing his castle to paying visitors – we have no doubt about their class identification.

In medieval times the nobility could be singled out because the monarch had conferred privileges, and usually land, upon them. Nobility also conferred obligations, usually in the form of providing armies in wartime. Nobles sublet some of their lands to lesser lords in exchange for a similar fulfilment of obligations; and so the chain of privilege and obligation spread down through the social structure. However, in early medieval times titles of nobility were not necessarily hereditary.

Medieval nobles were expected to conform to a code of behaviour, which one can loosely call chivalric, complete with tests of valour and a particular manner of speech. Their privileges set them apart from the rest of the population, which was ranked below them in a hierarchical system of orders. This kind of social structure survived up to 1789 in France and even longer elsewhere in Europe. The separation of the nobility into a caste was less pronounced in Britain, where the aristocracy's overwhelming political power did not include the same panoply of privileges as its French counterparts.

The nobility also enjoyed the privilege of perpetuating itself. In parts of eastern Europe this principle was carried to absurd lengths, where the breaking of the links between wealth, possession of land and nobility has left many families with noble titles and artisanal professions, and a hovel rather than a manor to call home. In Britain, until the late nineteenth century, nobility and wealth were virtually inseparable. The British system of primogeniture was rough on the younger children, but ensured that, for the most part, estates and fortunes could be left intact from generation to generation, maintaining the link between wealth and nobility. Knitting the two together was land ownership. The status of the gentry too was established by property qualifications, which were specified in the late seventeenth century as criteria for the right to serve in government at local or national level.[1]

In much of Europe, the aristocracy was essentially a caste. Its ranks were virtually impenetrable, and it fought to conserve its rights and privileges. Blood and breeding were the foundation of aristocratic values. Aristocracy became an ideal – perhaps a perverse one, since it could only feed on itself, but an ideal none the less. Exclusivity was treasured. Nora Wydenbruck recalls wryly: 'No one who has not known Austrian Court society before 1918 can quite understand what it meant to marry someone who did not have sixteen quarterings.'[2] In Spain noblemen could acquire dozens of additional titles over the generations by means of advantageous marriages, since Spanish women enjoyed rights of succession to titles. Those with particularly ancient titles could petition the sovereign for the status of grandee of Spain; the forebears of the current Duchess of Alba arranged their marital alliances in such a way that she is a grandee thirteen times over, and the Duchess of Medinaceli has forty titles of nobility stashed away, including nine other ducal titles.

Recruitment by advantageous marriages with the bourgeoisie was almost unthinkable and could lead to a nobleman's successors being barred from inheriting his title. The German nobility was firmly divided into a higher nobility (*Standesheeren*) and a lower, and marriage outside each caste, or between the two, was forbidden. The obituary of Duke Albrecht of Bavaria, who died in July 1996, echoes this tradition; both his wives were countesses when he married them.[3]

The German *Almanach de Gotha* divided the aristocracy into ranks, each with its privileges and rulebooks. Because, until well into the nineteenth century, Germany was divided into numerous tiny principalities, German princes and dukes enjoyed powers quite different from those of their British counterparts. In Franconia I have sometimes visited the little town of Castell, once the capital of a small princely domain. Although the princes of Castell were not of royal descent, they were *Standesheeren* who ruled over their domains as if they were monarchs. They maintained private armies and were answerable only to the Emperor. To this day Prince Albrecht zu Castell-Castell and his family own much of the town, as well as the castle, the bank and the vineyards and winery, just as they have done since the twelfth century.

Pride in noble status could be carried to extreme lengths. In the seventeenth and eighteenth centuries in Germany, 'a rope separated the aristocrat from the middle class at dances, operatic performances, and garden parties, and this separating rope was preserved in the small courts right into the 19th century – in Bavaria until just before the last [First World] war'.[4] Of course, not all German nobles clung so fanatically to their status. Nineteenth-century Germany had its fair share of educated and enlightened noblemen who contributed to art, politics, culture and even commerce. It was the Prussian Junkers who were the most stubborn in their self-belief as a caste. In Spain too the nobility adhered to their seigneurial rights, which allowed them to levy rents and feudal dues and, in some cases, to sell off municipal offices.

In 1833 De Tocqueville described the French nobility as 'an exclusive caste, which while monopolizing all privileges and hurting everybody's feelings, offers no hope of ever entering into its ranks'. Such attitudes, said De Tocqueville, provoked 'violent hatreds' which would have been felt only sporadically in contemporary England.[5]

A century later Louise-Marie Ferré surveyed the French aristocracy and found sixty thousand families with noble pretensions; she concluded that only eight hundred were rooted in the ancient nobility, and their characteristics were those

> of a caste fighting for survival, not clawing its way into power; these characteristics included the desire for isolation, an extreme hostility towards intrusion by strangers, an excessive concentration upon genealogy and precedence and the cult of ancestry, over-strict manners and extreme politeness within the family, the education of children by governesses and tutors and private schools, a preference for the peasantry and a hatred of the *bourgeoisie*, a love of riding and hunting and the chase, and a strict Catholicism.[6]

The diplomat David Kelly experienced Belgian high society in the late 1920s:

All the sons and daughters carried courtesy titles, and practically no one engaged in commerce or industry or even in high finance was admitted into the charmed circle . . . unless he happened to have been born in it . . . The rigid maintenance of the inseparable connection between land ownership, title and gentility had been the more easy to maintain because the great commercial families of Antwerp did not attempt to penetrate the Brussels society, and were on the contrary proud of and satisfied with their own local society.[7]

Sometimes, however, caste barriers were adjusted. Cecilia Sternberg, while engaged to Count Leopold Sternberg, recalls her first visit to his family in Bohemia: 'There was nothing really wrong with me, they thought, but my religion and my grandmother's being born a commoner. It was decided to change the former and forget the latter.'[8]

To the British such flexibility was nothing unusual. It was remarked upon by Hippolyte Taine, an acute observer of British society in the nineteenth century. In France, he pointed out, the aristocracy under Louis XV were 'simply privileged individuals, ornamental parasites, troublesome, unpopular, odious'. In contrast the British aristocracy was more fluid and receptive:

> They kept in touch with the people, opened their ranks to talent, recruited to their number the pick of the rising commoners; and they have remained the ruling class . . . They have made themselves into administrators, patrons, promoters of reform and good managers of the commonwealth; they have become well-informed and well-educated men, men who apply themselves to work and are capable and who, as citizens, are the most enlightened, the most independent and the mose useful, of the whole nation.[9]

This may be over-egging the pudding, although Taine later concedes that the British aristocracy inevitably includes 'a certain number of rascals, a few brutes, and a great many ordinary, mediocre people. But that is the price which must be paid to form an élite.'[10]

This was more than the extraordinary Anthony Ludovici was prepared to admit. In his *A Defence of Aristocracy* (1933) he presented a slavering vision of aristocratic perfection that is wholly decadent. The aristocrat, he believed, 'is the outcome of effort. He is the product of long, untiring endeavour. As a being in possession of highly developed instincts and virtues, he is essentially a work of human art, and as such he naturally prizes himself, and is naturally prized by others.'[11] This paragon also possesses physical perfection: 'The definition of the true superior man or aristocrat . . . precludes the very possibility of his being an ill-shaped or ugly man.'[12]

Even Anthony Ludovici may have stumbled across a misshapen viscount or a roguish earl, so he is compelled to admit 'that the aristocracies of Europe have on the whole wantonly blemished the sacred principle of aristocracy. It is also, however, a sign of the crassest and most unprecedented stupidity to repudiate the principle of aristocracy on that account.'[13] It is up to aristocracy itself to stop the rot: 'It is suicidal for any true aristocracy to allow its ranks to be filled by these forced plants, sprung from the artificial manure of modern conditions; it is even suicidal for them to allow their ranks to be filled at all at any time, save by their own choice and the exercise of their discrimination.'[14]

Such a heroically stupid defence can only be made after the cause has been well and truly lost. Ludovici cites the Venetian Republic as 'the most astounding example in Europe of a community governed by a well-disciplined and highly tasteful aristocracy', while neglecting to mention that this distinguished republic was terminated by Napoleon in 1797.[15]

No aristocracy could ever have lived up to the demands of a romantic enthusiast such as Ludovici. Yet, as Taine observed, the British upper classes, for all their occasional brutishness, had a sense of obligation towards the community around them. They were, in the overworked term, 'stewards' of their lands, their heritage, their county, their culture. Robert Lacey's elaboration of the notion of an aristocrat as a link between the past and the future is a trifle romanticized but has a core of truth: 'The true aristocrat, love him or hate him, is he who inherits and who passes on. His most cherished values lie in the past which has bestowed so many privileges upon him, and his ultimate priorities are concerned with the future to which he must pass on at least as much as he has inherited.'[16]

Sir Edward Cadogan described 'the code of squiredom' in his 1961 memoirs (by squiredom he meant the landed aristocracy):

It was founded on a narrow conception of human existence and a very cramped sense of values. The main ingredient of the code was the justification of our British landowning system. All the occupations and pastimes were definitely related to the system . . . Its faults were its exclusiveness, its self-sufficiency, its resourcelessness, its lack of inspiration, its incapacity to admit ideas from without as worthy of its consideration. Anything that it did not appreciate or understand – and that included a great deal – anything that served to conflict with its conventions was 'rot' – a bleak philosophy if philosophy it can be called, one to which never at any time did I for one moment subscribe.[17]

Aristocracy, certainly in Britain, is also a way of life. It is focused around traditional pursuits such as country living, horse racing, field sports, a fruity accent free of regional shadings, house parties, participation in the Season, an accepted standard of what constitutes good behaviour (however frequently ignored) and thus a code of manners, a horror of state education, respect for the past, indifference to religious enthusiasm and an acceptance of authority. It encompasses a stylish lack of stylishness for men, good grooming for women, a distinct but circumscribed lack of respect for mindless convention and a quiet belief in one's own superiority. An acquaintance of mine at Cambridge exemplified upper-class braggadocio when he flung open his wardrobe to show me a splendid array of morning coats and evening wear, and a pile of corduroy trousers and old sweaters – implying that a gentleman had no use for such middling items of clothing as a sports jacket or flannel trousers.

The male upper-class devotion to clothes that have seen better days – or, preferably, have been handed down – is, as Paul Fussell puts it, indication that archaism is the upper order's very own class principle. It has even been imported into America, where a variation on British style (or lack of it), as adapted by the outfitters Brooks Brothers, forms the wardrobe of the upper-class male.

The current irony of the Anglophilic class motif will not escape us. In the 19th century, with Britain commanding much of the world, it would seem natural for snobs to ape British usages. Snobs still do, but not because Britain is powerful but because Britain is feeble. To acquire and display British goods shows how archaic you are, and so validates upper- and upper-middle-class standing. Thus tartan skirts for women, Shetland sweaters, Harris tweeds, Burberrys, 'regimental' neckties. A general American male assumption among classes above high prole is that to be 'well dressed' you should look as much as possible like a British gentleman as depicted in movies about fifty years ago.[18]

Fortunately for British snobs, Americans can be trusted to get it slightly wrong, ruining the ensemble with button-down shirts, loafers with tassels, and tartan golfing trousers.

The British upper classes were not a closed circle, but their numbers were kept relatively small until the nineteenth century because so many creations within the peerage were promotions through the ranks rather than elevations from the commonalty. Although there was far less emphasis on blood and breeding within the British aristocracy, its members were few. This was in sharp contrast with the situation in Spain or Poland, where in the sixteenth and seventeenth centuries the nobility constituted between 8 and 12 per cent of the population. In the eighteenth century at least 750,000 individuals in both countries enjoyed noble status. In seventeenth-century Naples there were over one hundred princely families and over 150 dukes. The British aristocracy, in common with the nobility in Portugal, France and Austria, formed only about 1 per cent of the population, and the proportion was even smaller in Scandinavia and Bohemia.

The more sparing conferral of noble status in Britain naturally helped to maintain the prestige of the aristocracy. Whereas the British aristocrat or squire would, in social terms, dominate the area he inhabited, there were communities in Poland and Hungary which consisted entirely of nobles. In 1720 there were 1228 villages within Hungary populated exclusively by noble families. Entitlement to noble rank did not necessarily mean that the family was well-off. Indeed, in Hungary and Poland there were artisans, peasants and domestic servants with noble status, but without the means to sustain that status and maintain the supposed ideals associated with it. There were thousands of Russian noblemen in the mid-nineteenth century with estates smaller than the average peasant farm, a situation inconceivable in Britain.[19] Their nobility resided in the possession of juridical rights and a title, but that was all.

This occurred because of the varied ways in which noble rank was attained in different parts of Europe. Wealth helped greatly. Acquire an estate with a noble pedigree, and rank soon followed. Many states sold noble rank as a way of raising revenue. In 1772 the King of Savoy, Victor Amadeo II, sold titles for nearly four million lire to help pay for his wars.[20] To obtain a title from Emperor Joseph II of Austria in the late eighteenth century, you had to fulfil various stipulations: you needed enough wealth to maintain noble status and to acquire an estate, you had to guarantee that your offspring would only pursue acceptable careers, and you had to pay a fee which varied from six thousand gulden for a barony to twenty thousand for the rank of count.[21]

Many of those who purchased their titles needed to recoup their investment as rapidly as possible, which led to many abuses of seigneurial rights. Although there were French aristocrats who nurtured their estates and treated their tenants well, they were the exception rather than the rule. John Mitford, a British traveller visiting Paris in 1766, noted that the French nobility showed little interest in their country *châteaux*: 'They have no interest in [the country] to preserve, no voters in boroughs to treat, no inducement to display their riches to the peasantry, or to court the favour of a mob. The glare of a city residence is the only object of their ambition. Hence the magnificence of the Parisian *hôtels*.'[22] In Russia too, court and city were the primary focus of the nobility, whose rural estates simply provided the means to sustain a luxurious urban life and a pleasant spot to relax during the summer.

In France and Russia promotion to high military or civil rank carried automatic ennoblement. Tsar Peter the Great's Table of Ranks of 1722 was a codification of the nobility, specifying fourteen different ranks for public servants. In Germany a doctorate in law or theology was equivalent to a low-level noble rank. It was widely accepted in many countries that the adoption of a noble way of life, a course which required money as well as style, would within a couple of generations entitle the family to noble status. Indeed, in some places it was possible to assume noble status, usually on the grounds of wealth, military service or a distinguished ancestor, and simply wait for it to be confirmed.[23]

In Britain too there was a link between how you lived and the status you claimed. As Patrick Montague-Smith languidly observes, 'I suppose the usually accepted opinion of an aristocrat is he who lives and behaves like one.'[24] Richard Ollard, in his quaint book on education, puts it aptly: 'To live like an aristocrat for a couple of generations is to be one. This of course presupposes the existence of aristocrats for the aspirant to imitate. As in the making of whisky or sherry the new wines are added to a vat in whose depths lurk older liquors. Blending is the art of English society.'[25] There is a sting in the tail, however: 'Acceptance not pedigree is the test. And the openness, the fluidity of English society, preferable as we may think it to the hierarchical rigidity of the foreigners, does not make it any less snobbish.'[26]

Until the late nineteenth century the aristocracy was, automatically, wealthy. Low taxation permitted the transmission of estates to the next generation (though there was always the possibility that they could be gambled away or diminished by poor investments). Moreover, labour was cheap. Those days came to an end after World War I. Although many upper-class families remained very rich, vast estates under aristocratic ownership have become a rarity, and what remains is a network of shared values and assumptions.

Any discussion of the 'aristocratic way of life' is easily tainted with sentimentality. No doubt Clapham pubs and Leeds nightspots are filled with impeccably pedigreed young men and women scarcely distinguishable in dress, accent and body language from the mobile-phone salesmen and dippy television researchers crowding into the same space. 'Shared values' there may be, but they are fraying at the edges. It's understandable that not everyone of upper-class lineage wants, at least in their youth, to carry all that baggage of appropriate dress, rural pursuits and social obligation.

This makes the perpetuation of the aristocratic ideal even more bizarre. Ludovici's idealization of the aristocracy was eccentric, and contemporary chroniclers such as Mark Bence-Jones and Hugh Montgomery-Massingberd have their feet closer to the ground, while keeping their noses firmly within the pages of *Debrett's*. None the less their rhapsodic attempt to describe the aristocrat's 'basic qualities' seems hopelessly outdated, even though composed in 1979. 'Most British aristocrats', they write, 'have certain characteristics in common . . . They all stem from a few basic qualities which have always been part of the aristocratic make-up; notably toughness, self-confidence, love of the country, dislike of affectation and, of course, that 'gaiety' or 'easygoingness' which Castiglione calls *sprezzatura*.'[27]

Toughness makes them good travellers, easily adapting to extreme climates and primitive toilet facilities. It also leads to all manner of useful social graces denied to the hoi-polloi:

> This quality of toughness enables the aristocrat to stand for hours looking gracious and dignified on ceremonial occasions or while receiving guests. Aristocratic women do not collapse into chairs and throw off their shoes the moment the handshaking is over; and they pride themselves on the infrequency with which they are obliged to answer the call of nature.[28]

It's good to know that centuries of breeding and luxury have borne such rich fruit.

Our authors become wistful on the subject of the fairer sex. 'It is this aristocratic self-control', they fawn

> which enables the male aristocrat to observe the code of gentlemanly behaviour towards the opposite sex. The aristocrat may deliberately set out to seduce a woman whom he regards as fair game; but should he find himself in the company of a young and innocent virgin or of a friend's wife – both being, so to speak, protected by the gentleman's code – his self-control will prevent him from making advances, however much he may desire the girl or woman in question.[29]

If so, I imagine it is because he probably lusts after the lady's dishy younger brother.

Bence-Jones and Montgomery-Massingberd also admire what they see as an aristocratic tendency to make light of things.

> The aristocrat is inclined to play down anything really frightening. 'I had a slight spill,' he will say, after having had a motor accident in which he escaped death by the closest of shaves. A major calamity, mortal illness or financial ruin, is dismissed by the sufferer as 'rather a bore'. If he or anybody else has been in a towering rage, the aristocrat is likely to say that the person in question was 'a bit peeved'.[30]

Well, yes, this is certainly shaping up into the kind of character that built an empire. Our authors commend the aristocrat's 'dislike of affectation', though if describing a brush with death as 'a slight spill' (did anybody ever use such phrases?) is not affected, I don't know what is.

Sadly for our authors, the party's over. In bygone days the 'would-be fashionable' tried to acquire 'aristocratic values'. Now they are besotted by, horror of horrors, 'the fashions and manners of the proletariat . . . Gentlemanly behaviour suddenly ceased to count.' The 'unaristocratic new rich' no longer aspire to join the aristocracy. Instead our authors echo the snobbish lament of James Lees-Milne that the apogee of desires nowadays is 'a suburban villa with every "mod. con."', Jags and mink. (In 1979 fur was not yet regarded as a symbol of man's inhumanity to animal.)

I find it hard to recognize this rose-tinted gaze at the wondrous British aristocracy, although my acquaintance with the class is limited. They were certainly present *en masse* in Trinity Great Court, where I had rooms for a year in the late 1960s. My aristocratic neighbours, with a few exceptions, were stand-offish, acutely snobbish, incapable of holding their drink, occasionally violent, addicted to shooting and beagling, and fairly stupid. When in the course of college elections the ballot box was snatched from my hands by masked youths and the ballot papers subsequently destroyed (I am not making this up), I recognized my assailants as a bunch of Old Etonians in fascistic mode, giving middle-class lads such as myself a glimpse of the 'aristocratic way of life', lack of affectation, *sprezzatura* and self-confidence.

THREE

From Warlords to Grandees

The rich man in his castle
The poor man at his gate,
God made them, high or lowly,
And ordered their estate.

Mrs Alexander, 'All Things
Bright and Beautiful', 1848

The British aristocracy had its origins as a landed élite. The European distinction between a *noblesse de robe* and a martial and thus superior *noblesse d'épée* was always slight and had more or less disappeared by Tudor times. There was in England always a theoretical possibility that an immensely successful merchant or politician could join the ranks of the aristocracy, whereas the ranks of the European *noblesse d'épée* were closed. Families such as the Cecils, now regarded as quintessential British aristocrats, had their origins as office-holders under Queen Elizabeth I. In Tudor times the confiscation of monastic lands opened up possibilities of reward and enrichment for faithful servants of the Crown.

Yet there was no *noblesse de robe* as such. In Russia and France noble status was conferred automatically on men who rendered the sovereign service, whether as administrators or warriors, and in 1614 the French *noblesse de robe* was made hereditary. This did happen in Britain too – Russells and Marlboroughs, to cite two examples – but it was not an automatic preferment. Moreover, most of those promoted to knighthoods and the peerage in Tudor and Stuart times sprang from the landed gentry.

Indeed, the peerage as an institution is a latecomer to Britain. Until 1337, when the first duke was created, the earldom was the only title in existence, but held by only a few dozen individuals, many of whom were related to the sovereign. In 1385 Richard II introduced the rank of marquess, of which there are today thirty-six; most of them were created between 1780 and 1837, and they rank below dukes but above earls. This title became the traditional reward for viceroys of India. Earls are relatively plentiful; viscounts, less so, and the great majority were created in the later nineteenth and early twentieth centuries as consolation prizes for retiring Cabinet ministers. The rank was initially created in 1440 and today viscounts number about 130.

Barons came here with William the Conqueror but a barony was not a hereditary title. The first barony of the modern English peerage was created by Richard II as Baron Kidderminster in 1387. Knighthoods were plentifully distributed, and soon became dissociated from their military origins. Lawyers and landowners were frequently knighted, and in the later nineteenth and early twentieth centuries whole batches of orders were invented to reward service to the Crown. The title of 'esquire' may have had some meaning in medieval times – apprentice knights, sheriffs and heralds were entitled to it – but it soon became vacuous.

Although not peers, Highland chiefs, at least within Scotland, have aristocratic status, as do the chiefs of Ireland. Their ancestors were warlords, and thus more in tune with ancient aristocratic ideals than bankers or politicians elevated to the standard peerage. Some chiefs, such as Cameron of Lochiel, are major landowners; others have lost their estates. A few are peers as well as chiefs. Thus the Duke of Argyll is also – and more importantly, in the eyes of Scots – the chief of Clan Campbell. However, many clan chiefs were never elevated to the peerage, despite their status.

The Irish peerage is particularly complicated, being comprised of a handful of peers of Celtic descent, and a much greater number descended from English and Scottish settlers of the sixteenth and seventeenth centuries. Many Anglo-Irish peers were absentee landlords with few links, other than title deeds, to Ireland itself. A handful of peculiarly Irish titles, such as the Knight of Glin, are held by descendants of Anglo-Norman nobles. Irish peerages did not carry entitlement to a seat in the House of Lords, so such peerages were often given to men who, for political reasons, the government of the day did not want to admit to the Lords; many had no connection with Ireland. Robert Smith, the first banker to be elevated to the Lords, was first given a kind of trial period as an Irish peer before being promoted to the English peerage in 1797.[1] The Irish struggle for home rule and the subsequent civil war led to the destruction of about one-tenth of all Irish country houses; resentment against some Anglo-Irish magnates was probably well deserved. As long ago as 1838, De Tocqueville was reporting: 'I have met no man in Ireland, to whatever party he belonged, who did not acknowledge with a greater or less degree of bitterness that the aristocracy governed the country very badly. The English say it openly; the Orangemen do not deny it; the Catholics shout it out at the top of their voices.'[2] Many landowning families sold up and left the country, and to this day the Anglo-Irish are a dwindling band.

From the fourteenth century onwards the English aristocracy developed a tradition of service to the Crown as local government officials and magistrates. This sense of duty was exercised well into the nineteenth century and is by no means extinct. English peers (but not their families) enjoyed an assortment of rights and privileges, such as immunity from imprisonment for debt, freedom from arrest in civil causes and freedom from the requirement to swear an oath. The right to trial by their peers was only ended in 1949, and on the thirty-four occasions between 1499 and 1948 when it was used, it was not always to the advantage of the defendant. Until the late seventeenth century the English peerage enjoyed fiscal privileges of the kind that remained quite common among Continental nobilities until well into the nineteenth century.[3]

The juridical rights enjoyed by the English peerage were small fry in comparison with the rights and privileges of many of their European counterparts. The French aristocracy, for example, was exempt from most taxation and dominated the judiciary, so anyone taking legal action against an unjust or despotic landlord was unlikely to succeed. Moreover, landlords could impose a range of tyrannical tasks and punishments on their tenants, including death penalties for such offences as burning straw or stealing vines.[4] Russian nobles were exempt from personal taxation, military conscription and corporal punishment, and enjoyed the right to travel abroad and to appeal against a death sentence to the Senate and Tsar. Their wealth was sustained by the property right of owning estates to which serfs were attached.[5]

The ranks of the English peerage, fully formed by 1440, were swollen during the reigns of James I and Charles I, who realized that the dispensation of titles was a handy way to raise revenues. Even so their wheeling and dealing only doubled the peerage to 123. It was the gentry that benefited when James I doled out knighthoods and baronetcies like small change. By the time of his death there were 2600 new knights. Everyone did well out of it: James I pocketed £60 from each applicant, and heralds took a cut too. Because of their scarcity value peerages were much more expensive. A barony could cost up to £10,000, and in Lord Haughton's case a further payment of £5000 gained him an earldom.[6] For the most part the new peers created by the Stuart monarchs were magnates of wealth and influence. Families such as the Waldegraves, Cholmondeleys, Cavendishes and Stanhopes were among those ennobled. Many of them would later advance up the ladder of the peerage to marquessates and dukedoms.

Although one might have imagined that the generosity of King Charles II in creating four dukedoms for his bastard sons – Grafton, St Albans, Buccleuch and Richmond – would have devalued the currency, this does not appear to have been the case. Before the seventeenth century dukedoms, on the rare occasions that they were bestowed, were granted to the sovereign's relations. Of the older dukedoms, only Warwick and Somerset have survived. By 1726 the number of non-royal dukedoms had soared to forty. With the exception of the royal bastards, the royal favourite George Villiers (created Duke of Buckingham in 1623) and the great soldier Marlborough, dukedoms were in effect promotions offered to the mightiest landowners in the country. The last dukedom created was Fife in 1889. When Queen Victoria's granddaughter Louise became engaged to the Earl of Fife, the Queen bumped the earl up a couple of ranks to make him more worthy of his royal bride.

In the eighteenth century, with large estates providing financial security, the peerage consolidated its position as a nationwide network of magnates. Nevertheless, riches and title alone were rarely sufficient to entitle the possessor to high office; a modicum of talent was required too. This growing power on the part of the landed aristocracy had of course been aided by the English Revolution, which had weakened the powers of the monarchy. At the same time aristocratic power could not have been sustained without deference from the nation as a whole. Since power was exercised by a nationwide group, the kind of resentment and hostility that elsewhere in Europe was focused on autocratic monarchs was dispersed and dissipated. Moreover, despite the sinecures of the British system, there were no exemptions from tax liability such as prevailed in Europe.

Just as in Vienna grandees of the Habsburg Empire built town palaces within a stone's throw of the Emperor's palace, so palatial town houses rose in the fashionable quarters of London such as St James's and Mayfair. None the less the power base of the aristocracy remained rural, which was not necessarily the case elsewhere in Europe. Many of the great Florentine families, such as the Frescobaldi, began as merchants and bankers during medieval times, and only acquired their Tuscan estates (today numbering eight in all) subsequently. British aristocrats would visit such centres of commerce and culture as Florence during their Grand Tours of Europe; their leisurely pace and bulging wallets allowed them to furnish their houses with the finest paintings, porcelain, carpets, books and classical antiquities. Proximity to Court and Parliament increased their influence, while at home in the country they often controlled their county's parliamentary representation. As in Stuart times, the new peers of the Georgian era were already rural magnates. Families such as the Grosvenors and Herveys began their steady rise through the peerage at this time. Peerages could not be purchased in the eighteenth century; they were essentially a recognition of status and wealth.

It is often stated that the British aristocracy differed from its Continental counterpart by being more open to outsiders. This was emphatically not so in the eighteenth century. Until the end of the century, the English peerage remained a tiny group of the landed élite, whereas most European nobilities were stuffed with titles, often given to reward service to the state, or handed over in exchange for money. The aristocracy, it has been argued, survived largely by co-opting rising merchants or public servants, welcoming them into their ranks and thus neutralizing any potential threat. The evidence points the other way: it was exceedingly rare at this time for those not already well connected with the landed élite to be elevated.[7]

However, one or two businessmen did break into their ranks in the eighteenth century, such as Robert Smith, the banker and MP who was created Lord Carrington in 1797. Since land was always the basis for social prominence, the socially ambitious soon translated their assets into acreage. Great families such as the Chandoses and the Carringtons may have owed their worldly success to the law or to banking, and others to military prowess, but those were not sufficient conditions for advancement to the peerage.

You had to have land, and the sums required to obtain a substantial estate were immense. Ten thousand acres and an impressive house – that is, an estate appropriate to a peer of the realm – would cost about £100,000 in the mid-eighteenth century. This colossal sum was required to generate an income from rents of £10,000, which was the minimum needed to fund the lifestyle of the landed aristocracy. Only a handful of bankers or merchants or nabobs returning home from east India could come close to accumulating such a sum. Estates were more usually acquired and expanded over a number of generations. Social advancement in a single leap was also made difficult by the infrequency with which large estates were offered for sale. As much as two-thirds of English land was tied up in marriage settlements.[8]

What was more feasible for the successful London merchant or lawyer was the acquisition of a pleasant house with a few hundred acres, enough to elevate him into the gentry and allow him to rub shoulders with the aristocracy. Indeed, the game laws of 1671 had excluded those without estates from shooting and coursing, so entry into the ranks of those legally permitted to kill game singled one out as socially superior to countrymen forbidden such delights. These laws remained in force throughout the eighteenth century, despite attempts to repeal them, and only in 1831 did they finally disappear from the statute books.

If it was all but impossible for the merchant class to join the aristocracy, it was certainly possible to infiltrate the upper classes. The surest way was to endow a daughter with a substantial dowry that might snare a peer with heavily mortgaged estates or other financial difficulties. Such heiresses were usually accepted by the aristocracy and not required to wait three generations before being considered socially acceptable, as was the case in France.[9]

After all the effort and persistence required to acquire a title, there was no guarantee that your lustre would persist into future generations. In Britain, primogeniture proved a double-edged sword. It helped the peerage retain and expand its territorial possessions, but it also increased the possibility of extinction. A barren wife, an impotent husband, a batch of daughters – all of these posed a threat to the aristocratic line. M. L. Bush has shown how easily it could vanish:

The failure rate was spectacularly and constantly high . . . Of the 204 baronetcies created by James I only 97 survived after 140 years; and by 1800 667 of the 946 baronetcies created before 1701 were extinct. 33 percent of the peerages existent in 1485 had failed to produce male heirs by 1547, and of the 63 peerages existent in 1559 only 22 had survived by direct descent in 1641, 20 failing in the direct male line and passing by collateral descent and 21 failing completely in the male line.[10]

European nobilities were better protected. In Russia, the nobility had the right to adopt a relative in order to prevent extinction. Indeed, European nobilities were so good at perpetuating themselves that occasionally the state had to intervene to weed them out. In 1626 Gustavus Adolphus demoted about three-quarters of the Swedish nobility, and in eighteenth-century Spain the proportion of nobles fell from 12 to 4 per cent of the population. Commissions were set up to redefine the rules of the game, and those who failed to qualify were relegated to the commonalty.[11]

In eighteenth-century Britain, despite the vast wealth of the peerage, there was not a huge gap between the aristocracy and other men of influence. Peers, politicians and servants of the state spoke the same language, as it were, and many of those who rose to eminence in the law, the City or politics did not come from humble origins, but were already well connected with the aristocracy, either as younger sons or through a useful marriage. In the mid-eighteenth century between one-third and one-half of MPs were connected to the aristocracy.

It is often maintained that one reason for the social exclusiveness of the aristocracy was its disdain for commercial enterprise. It is true that there was earnest discussion about whether, in the case of a younger son going into business or the professions, he would thereby forfeit his upper-class status; certainly he might have been slithering into downward mobility. But many of the landed aristocracy – unlike, say, their proud Junker counterparts in Prussia – were very diligent at exploiting the resources at their disposal. Between 1540 and 1640 the aristocracy had no hesitation in owning ironworks as a sideline to collecting rents.[12]

In the eighteenth century the aristocracy bankrolled commercial enterprises, especially overseas, and leased out exploitable rights in their possession. They were backers rather than entrepreneurs. There was, to be sure, a snobbish prohibition against direct involvement in 'trade', but that did not preclude capitalist investment nor the immensely profitable development of urban properties. In the early nineteenth century, landowners became actively involved in enterprises such as coalmines, forges, woollen mills, docks and canals, especially if they sprang up on land that they owned. Such investments could be immensely profitable: the Lonsdales were receiving annual royalties of £30,000 in the early nineteenth century from their coalmines alone.[13] In Germany the Junker aristocracy maintained its grip on political, administrative and military power, while leaving economic development and trade to the bourgeoisie it disdained. The divisions between aristocracy and bourgeoisie were far less stark in Britain.

The landed élite also maintained a firm grip on local government and administration. Lords lieutenant, almost always drawn from the peerage, were immensely powerful figures, who enjoyed a monopoly over appointments to the Bench. The aristocracy and gentry also exercised much local control as justices of the peace, who in addition to judicial duties were responsible for issuing licences, administering the poor laws, collecting taxes and overseeing prisons and asylums.

It was William Pitt the Younger who expanded the peerage, famously declaring, 'Anyone worth £10,000 a year is worth a peerage.' His term as prime minister saw the creation and promotion of 119 peers. Pitt became Prime Minister in 1783. By 1800 the peerage had risen from 212 to over three hundred titles, without significant alteration to its social composition.[14]

Between 1802 and 1830, ninety-two new peers were created, many of them promotions to earldoms or marquessates for existing peers. For the first time the aristocracy was joined by men, such as Horatio Nelson, who lacked sizeable estates. Titles were becoming political rewards, and the connection between the possession of land and the aristocracy would gradually weaken. Inevitably, with the politicization of public life that began with Walpole earlier in the eighteenth century, corruption flourished. Sinecures were common, allowing men already privileged to shore up their fortunes. For example, the office of Hereditary Grand Falconer, occupied by the Duke of St Albans, carried a salary of £2000. None the less, the aristocracy was not solely motivated by self-interest and a defence of privilege. There were occasions, notably during the Napoleonic wars, when they agreed to taxes that would have to be borne in large measure by the upper classes.

In 1823, William Cobbett raged against one of the sinecure holders, the Marquis of Camden:

It is Bayham Abbey that this great and awful sinecure placeman owns in this part of the county. Another great estate he owns near Sevenoaks. But here alone he spreads his length and breadth over more, they say, than *ten or twelve thousand acres of land*, great part of which consists of oak-woods. But, indeed, what estates might he not purchase? Not much less than *thirty years* he held a place, a sinecure place, that yielded him about THIRTY THOUSAND POUNDS A-YEAR! At any rate, he, according to Parliamentary accounts, has received, of public money, LITTLE SHORT OF A MILLION OF GUINEAS.[15]

It is hard to gauge how widespread such sentiments were. Anti-aristocratic feeling was probably held in check by the fact that the upper classes were not perceived as a caste. As De Tocqueville observed in 1833:

What distinguishes it from all others is the ease with which it has opened its ranks. It is often said that in England men of all social ranks could rise to [important] positions. This was, I believe, much less true than was thought . . . But, with great riches, anybody could hope to enter into the ranks of the aristocracy. Furthermore since everybody could hope to become rich, especially in such a mercantile country as England, a peculiar position arose in that their privileges, which raised such feeling against the aristocrats of other countries, were the thing that most attached the English to theirs. As everybody had the hope of being among the privileged, the privileges made the aristocracy, not more hated, but more valued.[16]

The aristocracy never lacked self-esteem, and were aided by their convenient belief that heredity mattered more than competence. Whatever his political persuasion, a nineteenth-century aristocrat remained immovably convinced that he was, by right, a member of an immutable ruling class. The landed élite rested secure in its sense of social superiority to such an extent that the injustices and brutalities noted by radicals such as Cobbett were easily glossed over in a wave of self-approbation. Although there were doubtless many excellent and respons-ible landlords, others cared nothing for the welfare of their tenants.

The 1832 Reform Bill modified but did not essentially diminish the power of the aristocracy.

> Of 815 MPs btween 1841 and 1847, 8 were Irish peers, 172 were the sons of peers, 27 were grandsons and great-grandsons of peers (25 percent), while 82 were baronets and 53 were sons, grandsons and great-grandsons of baronets (16.6%). Add to this 240 MPs who were in direct line of male descent to families in Burke's *Landed Gentry*, and 71% of the House had close links with land, or nearly 80% if descent through wives and mothers is allowed.[17]

Cobbett, as usual, summarized the situation well: Britain was governed by 'one house filled wholly with landowners, and the other four-fifths filled with their relatives'.[18]

Later in the nineteenth century the ranks of the aristocracy were broadened; by 1900 four members of the Baring banking family, to give but one example, had been raised to the peerage. Many peers were avidly developing the commercial potential of their properties.

There were changes in upper-class *mores* too. The moral earnestness characteristic of the Victorian era inevitably infected some of the upper classes, and muscular Christianity took root in some families. Peers' wives and daughters would take a keener interest in the lives of their poorer tenants, while their husbands might spearhead campaigns of social reform. The Earl of Shaftesbury is the outstanding example of a peer who became a great Victorian reformer. The growth of public schools and the development of London clubs brought together the scions of the aristocracy and of the professional middle classes, lessening the gulf between the two.

A modicum of concern for the poor did not mean that the aristocracy developed a social conscience. Quentin Crewe, analysing the contents of *The Queen*, a house journal of the Victorian and Edwardian aristocracy, came to some stark conclusions:

> The attitude to servants raises the whole question of class conscious-ness, and the absolute certainty which upper-class women had of their

right to their position in society . . . A social conscience was a concept foreign to these Victorians – at least in the sense in which we understand it. There existed certainly the paternalism of a feudal society, a feeling of responsibility towards inferiors, untinged by guilt. The fact that some people were superior was an accepted and even a welcome fact. God, if anyone, was to blame for any seeming injustice and a proper awareness of God's impeccable judgement did not admit of any criticism of the system He had ordained . . .

The poor were there to be alternately bullied and watched over. No sentimentality was lavished upon them, the attitude towards them being governed by a strict practicality. The working class as a whole were regarded with gentle disapproval, coloured by a suspicion that they were extravagant and drunken. The poor were viewed with an active distaste except at Christmas time.[19]

The upper classes prospered in Victorian times. Rising rents, notably between 1850 and 1880, consolidated their fortunes. The definitive survey of the time, John Bateman's *Great Landowners of Great Britain and Ireland* (4th edition, 1883), calculated that over thirty peers owned estates of more than a hundred thousand acres, though only three (the Dukes of Devonshire, Cleveland and Northumberland) owned that much acreage in England. (Others, such as the Dukes of Sutherland and Buccleuch, owned vast tracts in Scotland, but their agricultural value was far lower.) In 1880 over half the area of counties such as Northumberland and Rutland were owned by magnates, and the entire county of Sutherland was the property of its duke. Over half the 331 landowners possessing more than ten thousand acres in 1880 were peers, with a further 15 per cent belonging to the baronetage or knighthood.[20] This landed élite included twenty of the twenty-one dukes, seventeen of the nineteen marquesses, seventy-four of the 115 earls and ten of the twenty-five viscounts. Yet 104 of the 331 were untitled, a reminder that the landed gentry included a number of exceedingly wealthy families.[21]

Bateman showed that about thirty-five thousand families owned over a hundred acres in England and Wales, accounting for almost 40 per cent of the land area. The most telling figure is that a mere 1500 landowners possessed three thousand acres or more, yet this amounted to 43 per cent of the land.[22]

Even though the strength of the landed aristocracy seemed undimin-
ished, new fortunes were being made in the cities through manufacturing, banking and trade. Historians Lawrence and Jeanne Stone are
struck by the absence of such businessmen from the landed élite:

> In the whole country in the 40 years between 1840 and 1879, less
> than 50 self-made men worth half a million pounds and upwards died
> owning 2000 acres of land or more. This represents only one-third of
> the new men who had acquired such gigantic riches, and these 50
> were virtually invisible – a mere 1.5 percent – among the 3200 other
> landowners with property of this size. One has to conclude that
> before 1879, the majority of the very wealthy business men in
> England were either landless or owners of very small estates
> indeed.[23]

However, a growing number of aristocrats, confronted by the
agricultural depression, turned their attention to business, so that by
1900 there was a partial fusion of the two worlds of landed aristocracy
and urban businessmen, thus creating a new plutocracy.

Meanwhile, the peerage continued to swell. A title became the
accepted reward for the occupants of certain offices. Between 1886 and
1914, 246 new titles were created, of which two hundred were bestowed
on commoners.

> More than a third of these new peers, some seventy, represented the
> new wealth of the industrial revolution; another third had risen in the
> professions, the law chiefly, and service to the state in diplomacy,
> colonies or the armed forces; and scarcely one-quarter are the heads
> of old-established landed families, the group which had formerly
> furnished the backbone of the peerage . . . In terms of their family
> backgrounds slightly more than half the new peers still came from
> landed circles . . . Two-thirds of the new peers had rendered political
> services.[24]

By the turn of the century the long-term prosperity of the landed
aristocracy was looking increasingly doubtful. Agricultural depression
struck from 1873 onwards, forcing landowners to lower rents in order
to retain their tenants. Revenues began to fall, dramatically in some
cases. By 1900 agriculture represented 6 per cent of the gross national

product, compared with 20 per cent fifty years earlier.[25] Investment in agricultural improvements took a low priority, levels of debt rose (in 1874 the debts of the 7th Duke of Devonshire were estimated at £1.2 million), and there were bankruptcies among families whose entire revenues were derived from agriculture. Those with sufficiently diversified investments were better equipped to weather this particular storm. Nevertheless by the 1880s the landed élite no longer dominated the House of Commons, and the creation of county councils in 1888 diminished its control over rural administration.

Some looked abroad for salvation. On the other side of the Atlantic roamed heiresses with impressively large fortunes, contemplated from this side of the ocean by aristocrats with dwindling ones. Publications such as *Titled Americans: A List of American Ladies Who Have Married Foreigners of Rank*, revised annually, laid open the prospects. English dukes such as Roxburghe, Marlborough and Manchester found American brides. There were some hiccups. Shortly before his wedding the Duke of Manchester was declared bankrupt and had to be rescued by his future father-in-law, Mr Eugene Zimmermann of Cincinnati. The French aristocracy was equally willing to revive its fortunes by marrying walking bank vaults such as the Singer heiress. In late nineteenth-century France, three princes, five dukes, three marquesses and numerous lesser aristocrats married American heiresses, whose average dowry was almost a million dollars.[26] Comte Boni de Castellane scooped the pool when he acquired $15 million and a bride, Anna Gould, the daughter of the financier Jay Gould.

Ruth Brandon points out that since, from the point of view of European nobility, 'all Americans were more or less equally unaccept-able, one might therefore pick the richest without compunction'.[27] Consolidating family fortunes by marrying an heiress was nothing new. Many aristocratic families lacking a male heir had to perpetuate the dynasty through the female line, which usually involved a merger between two great estates. This was how families such as the Norfolks, Grosvenors and Butes had become some of the largest landowners in Britain.[28]

FOUR

Gents and Gentry

Your reviewer of Miss Compton-Burnett's new novel describes its characters as 'upper-middle-class'. They are in fact large landowners, baronets, inhabiting the ancient seat that has been theirs for centuries. At this season when we are celebrating the quinquennial recrudescence of the class war, is it not desirable to be more accurate in drawing social distinctions?

Evelyn Waugh, letter to *The Times*, 17 September 1959

The titled aristocracy is a finite group, but the upper classes also include the landed gentry, some of whom have owned the same estates since medieval times without having ever bestirred themselves to petition for a title. None the less, they have a far greater claim to aristocratic status than, say, the descendants of an ennobled Victorian lawyer. Mark Bence-Jones and Hugh Montgomery-Massingberd have argued, indeed, that there is no distinction between aristocracy and gentry, that anyone who can claim to be a gentleman deserves to be counted among the aristocracy.

There is only one essential prerequisite for being counted among the British aristocracy: the right to be called a gentleman ... Anyone who has inherited the gentlemanly values, or, for that matter, has acquired those values for himself, can be regarded as noble; while the most illustrious noble of the realm values the name of gentleman above all his other titles. For this reason, the distinction between nobility and gentry is meaningless. Even when Victorian society was at its most rigid, a duke and an Indian Army subaltern, both being gentlemen, were equal in class, however different they may have been in rank or wealth.[1]

Because gentlemanly status was so vaguely defined in England, from medieval times onwards, the code of behaviour that corresponded to it was all the more strict:

> The foreign aristocrat, who belonged to a rigidly defined aristocracy, and had a title and 32 quarterings, did not need to worry so much about personal behaviour . . . as did the untitled English gentleman who might not even have possessed a coat of arms of his own . . . A gentleman may be selfish and entirely lacking in charity or philanthropy; but he will nevertheless do good works and serve the community for reasons of *noblesse oblige*.[2]

The code proved persistent, and in the early eighteenth century essayists such as Richard Steele affirmed: 'The appellation of gentleman is never to be affixed to a man's circumstances, but to the behaviour in them.'[3]

By this time, however, 'gentleman' was simply the name given to the lower fringes and tassels of the aristocracy, bumbling along beneath knights and esquires, although the greatest dukes in the land were equally entitled to consider themselves gentlemen. Birth alone was not the sole criterion for gentlemanly status, however. It was widely accepted that other factors such as education and wealth supported that status. The lack of exactitude proved a strength. As P. N. Furbank has pointed out: 'The social status of "gentleman" gains its suggestive force, and its enormous potential for rhetorical and ideological exploitation, from its vagueness and lack of semantic anchorage.'[4]

In Victorian times the term 'gentleman' was so widely used that it lost content. Mrs Swanscourt in Thomas Hardy's *A Pair of Blue Eyes* declares: 'My dear, you mustn't say "gentleman" nowadays . . . We have handed over "gentlemen" to the lower classes.' The handbook *Society Small Talk*, published in 1879, six years after Hardy's novel, insists that the term 'ladies and gentlemen' is essentially vulgar. The casual shortened form 'gent' was in use by the 1850s, when a typically unfunny *Punch* joke told of a railway guard asking passengers not to smoke: in 3rd class, 'the man that has been smoking', in 2nd class, 'Gents, smoking isn't allowed', and in 1st 'If you please, gentlemen . . .'[5]

Gentlemen became gentry when they possessed land. Anyone who made money in Tudor times could in theory buy a small estate. You couldn't purchase a title until James I opened up shop, but you could enjoy your country seat and your rental income and earn respect as the local squire. The dissolution of the monasteries released on to the market a colossal amount of land, some of which went to the great nobles of the day; other parcels were purchased by the burgeoning gentry, which by 1700 owned, it is estimated, almost half the land area of England, a proportion that remained constant until the early twentieth century.[6]

To be a member of the landed gentry was no guarantee of prosperity. Many freeholders of land, which unlike the gentry they farmed themselves, became far richer than their leisured neighbours. By the end of the eighteenth century traditional social distinctions had become blurred, especially since many gentry families made marital alliances with rich freeholders, often known as yeomen, in order to sustain their way of life. At this time there were about eight hundred families who could be classified as wealthy gentry, many of them knights or baronets and enjoying incomes of about £3000 a year. Beneath the wealthy gentry were the ranks of the 'squirearchy', a few thousand families with incomes of £1000 to £3000. The next rung down on the ladder was socially confused, with impoverished gentlemen, well-to-do yeomen and younger sons on small incomes all rubbing shoulders.[7]

William Cobbett had mixed feelings about the gentry he encountered in his travels, as this note written in 1821 in Burghclere confirms: a shallow fool, he wrote

> cannot duly estimate the difference between a resident *native* gentry, attached to the soil, known to every farmer and labourer from their childhood, frequently mixing with them in those pursuits where all artificial distinctions are lost, practising hospitality without ceremony, from habit and not on calculation; and a gentry, only now-and-then residing at all, having no relish for country-delights, foreign in their manners, distant and haughty in their behaviour, looking to the soil only for its rents, viewing it as a mere object of speculation, unacquainted with its cultivators, despising them and their pursuits, and relying, for influence, not upon the good will of the vicinage, but upon the dread of their power. The war and paper-system has brought in nabobs, lottery-dealers, bankers, stock-jobbers . . . You can see but few good houses not in possession of one or the other of these.[8]

As Cobbett suggests, the gentry was in an exceedingly fluid state in the early nineteenth century. In the twenty-five years that elapsed between the 1846 and 1871 editions of Burke's *Landed Gentry*, a quarter of the families listed in the earlier edition had vanished to be replaced by newcomers: mostly, one assumes, families that had purchased their estates over the preceding decades. This turnover persisted: half the families listed in 1863 were absent from the 1914 edition. As a rule of thumb, the transition from successful urban merchant or professional to fox-hunting landed gentry could be made within two, occasionally three, generations.[9] The number of families that could convincingly claim landed-gentry status in the mid-nineteenth century would appear to be between thirteen and fifteen thousand. A friend of mine recalled that his grandfather always maintained that their family was 'lower-class', which was a slightly perverse recognition that the landed gentry filled the lower ranks of the upper classes. Nobody else counted.

The gentry retained a tight grip on local government, notably as magistrates. Attempts to lower the property qualifications of those entitled to sit on the Bench failed, thus ensuring that men of probity such as farmers or lawyers were excluded from the administration of justice. The Earl of Albemarle, whose attempts to reform the system in 1875 met with failure, noted that the law as it stood was 'one of the last remnants of class legislation, vicious in principle and obstructive in operation, by which the administration of justice was subservient to the social elevation of a class'.[10] Even in 1887, 88 per cent of magistrates stemmed from the landed élite.[11] Despite the introduction of county councils in 1888, the land qualification for JPs remained in force until 1906. Jessica Mitford recalls her uncle Tommy:

> Uncle Tommy presided as magistrate at the local police court, and in this capacity doled out his own ideas of justice to the local citizenry. He was particularly proud of having given a three months' jail sentence to a woman driver who accidentally ran her car into a cow on a dark night. 'Clap 'em in the brig! That's one way of keeping these damn' women off the road.'[12]

(Since Nancy Mitford ticked off her sister by writing, 'We are all sorry you were horrid about Uncle Tommy,' this anecdote should perhaps be taken with a pinch of salt.)[13]

Although many of the gentry had suffered reversals of fortune in the

early nineteenth century, it was the agricultural depression of the late
Victorian era that brought the good times to an end for many families.
Many of the gentry were obliged either to farm their own lands (and thus
accept a loss of status) or to sell them outright. With aristocratic status
being so bound up with a particular way of rural life, the economic and
social demotion of the gentry was calamitous for many families.

There is a peculiar order standing midway between the landed gentry
and the peerage. Members of the baronetage take pride in the fact that,
belonging to a hereditary order, they are listed in the standard
genealogies alongside the peerage, but the majority of the original
creations stemmed from the landed gentry in the first place, whereas
creations made over the past century have usually been of middle-class
professionals.

James I conceived this wheeze in 1611. As approved by Parliament, it
required a sufficient payment from the aspiring baronet to finance the
upkeep of thirty infantrymen dispatched to Ireland for three years. In
this way, a colonizing army could be raised and financed at no expense
to the Crown. Charles I extended the principle by creating the
baronetage of Nova Scotia in 1625. In this case the money bought the
new baronets not only a title but land in the colony.

Since the initial qualification for a baronetcy was an annual income
from an estate of at least £1000, many of the beneficiaries were already
knights. However the financial qualification, together with a requirement that the family had been armigerous for three generations, limited
applicants to such an extent that it was later abolished. Even after the
King reduced the fee to £666 it still took him eleven years to find buyers
for the limited edition of two hundred baronetcies that he put on the
market. His son Charles I sold a further 458, some at the knockdown
price of £200.[14]

The new baronets were a discontented lot, often arguing about
precedence and increasingly bitter about their exclusion from the
privileges enjoyed by the peerage. However, the hereditary nature of
the order clearly elevated the baronetage above the knighthood, and
expanded the titled aristocracy without broadening its social basis. Of
the 417 baronets created between 1611 and 1649, only nine were
merchants, although about eighty others were either the sons of
merchants or married to merchants' daughters.[15]

In the eighteenth century baronetcies were distributed as rewards for political service, and George III bestowed no fewer than 525. During the following century, the ranks were expanded to include judges, physicians, lawyers, colonial governors and high-ranking military officers; most beneficiaries also had incomes from estates, so the baronetage never lost its connection with the landed élite. Lord Mayors of London also marked the completion of their stint in office by earning the right to the letters 'Bart.' after their name.

There was no let-up during the twentieth century. The baronetage proved a very useful form of political patronage. Between 1911 and 1965, 740 were created, most of them in the first third of the century. Lloyd George revived an ancient tradition by exchanging baronetcies for contributions to party funds. The going rate was said to be £40,000.[16] Labour governments discontinued the creation of baronetcies and none was bestowed between 1945 and 1951 nor between 1965 and 1970. However the intervening Conservative government resumed the practice and added another 105 to the rolls. Apart from the quirky decision to elevate the consort of Margaret Thatcher to the baronetage, one can assume that its ranks are now closed.

In 1995 I was invited to a dinner in Gloucestershire, and Londoners were lodged in the houses of other guests who lived closer by. Sir Toby and Teresa Clarke kindly took me into their home. The bedside reading included back numbers of *The Baronets Journal*, which Sir Toby edits. He also publishes the Roll of the Baronetage, which lists all current holders of the title in order of precedence, and records recent successions and extinctions. There are now about 1320 baronets in existence, of whom some 150 live outside Britain. They are becoming extinct at the rate of about three a year. Many keep a low profile, and when I mentioned a baronet I had known well at university, Sir Toby admitted even he, the world's authority on the order, had never heard of him.

I asked Sir Toby a stupid question, and got the answer I deserved: What do baronets have in common?

'The fact that they are baronets. Remember that quite a few baronets are also peers. The Grosvenors started out as baronets before being ennobled and ending up as dukes.

'We're baronets by an accident of birth, but our ancestors merited the honour. So having a baronetcy is an expression of family pride. It's been earned, and there's a sense that you're letting down the family if you take no pride in it. Being a baronet doesn't actually mean anything in today's classless society, and I'm sure there won't be any created in the future, but that doesn't mean it should be discarded. Baronets have never done anything dishonourable. No baronet that I've heard of has been stripped of a title or beheaded.

'It was traditional for Lord Mayors of London to be offered a baronetcy. They waited about twenty-five years to achieve the position, to which they are elected by their peers. Being Lord Mayor costs them a lot of their own money, so it's well deserved. As you know, for the past thirty years there haven't been any new baronetcies other than Thatcher, so knighthoods were substituted. But now the Lord Mayors have to wait six months or more for it. I find it rather insulting.'

What difference does being a baronet make to you?

'Being a baronet doesn't make the slightest difference to me. It's other people's perception that changes if you have a title.'

If people alter their perception of you because you have a title, doesn't it put an additional barrier between you and them?

'No. We're perfectly normal people. But an impoverished person with a title is still regarded as superior by the man in the street, rather than, as in America, the man with money. Having a title definitely does command a social premium. It also has monetary value, especially in the Middle East, where it's a big help in business dealings.'

Are baronets part of the aristocracy?

'Yes, I suppose we are. Baronets feature in all the statistical books. *Debrett's* appears every five years, and that defines what I call "title-itis" down to the rank of knight. We're listed in order of precedence. It may seem trivial that my wife takes precedence over a knight's wife, but there it is. The way I see it, precedence is the blueprint of the class structure, especially at such things as state dinners. And since we live under a monarchical system, titles are bound to be perpetuated.

'There are baronets I know who urged Thatcher and Major to reinstate the baronetcy. They were given a polite hearing, but nothing ever came of it, other than honouring Denis Thatcher. I would argue that Mrs Thatcher should have been made a life marchioness, an honour that was under discussion in the nineteenth century. A life peerage doesn't really seem sufficient recognition of her contribution.'

Why was her husband made a baronet?

'I don't think anyone knows.' (Sir Toby then advanced a theory that is probably true, but which I cannot risk printing.)

Would the titled aristocracy survive the monarchy, were it to disappear in the future?

'Probably not. If the monarchy goes, then the aristocracy rather loses its significance. I do think the monarchy needs more democratization. The Queen doesn't really need five palaces, and I see no reason why anyone outside her immediate family should be supported by the state. They live a life of privilege and luxury, and I would think Prince Charles and the others would be better regarded by the public if they drove around in old Fords rather than in huge cars with motorcycle escorts. But I do feel rather sad at the prospect that there won't be any more titles awarded.'

FIVE

The Survival of the Upper Classes

An aristocracy is proud. A pseudo-aristocracy is vain. The English upper classes are vain.

R. H. Tawney, *Commonplace Book*, 1913

Superficially, the arrival of the twentieth century made little difference to the upper classes. In 1900 the landed aristocracy remained very rich, but a new class of men had accumulated comparable riches without yearning to join the landed élite. Before World War I over a quarter of millionaires were self-made men, and very few came from landed families. Property no longer defined wealth. Apart from some casualties of the agricultural depression, the landed aristocracy was still very much in place, but was losing its dominant position within the social and political structure.[1] There was no clearer sign of the times than the willingness of the King himself, Edward VII, to consort not only with the landed aristocracy who provided him with so many golden partridge-assassination opportunities but with rich bankers, even bankers of, horrors, German-Jewish origin. The historian Harold Perkin estimates that London society in those days consisted not only of the titled, but of the almost five thousand other persons enjoying annual incomes of over £10,000, plus a professional élite of judges, doctors and so forth that probably numbered a further two thousand.[2]

By the time World War I broke out the peerage and baronetage consisted of some 1500 individuals – of whom about 570 were peers – supplemented by 1700 knights. Although many new knights and baronets had purchased their titles, the aristocracy remained a charmed circle. Lord Grantley recalled the aristocratic nonchalance of those Edwardian days:

> Birth in the small area of the upper classes was then a real capital asset, conferring powers of borrowing, begging and stealing without the accompanying penalty of appearing before a magistrate at a later date. Nobody ever thought of asking a Duke to repay a trifling loan, or a prominent clubman to redeem his card debts, if any disinclination was shown to do so. It was all very agreeable for the upper classes, and for them the times I record are dear departed days. But I would not defend them.[3]

Although for many aristocrats the war ended or curtailed their privileged way of life, this was by no means universal. World War I, Grantley wrote, 'never really made much difference to the general way we lived. By the end of it, I was paying my chauffeur £4 a week instead of £3.10s., but that was about all. My father had four footmen before the war, and he still had four footmen after the war.'[4]

However, not all the new peers were rich. When the Prime Minister wished to honour Field Marshal Haig, the soldier responded that he could not accept a peerage 'unless an adequate grant was made to enable a suitable position to be maintained'. A grant was duly forthcoming to the tune of £100,000, and Haig accepted his earldom with a clear conscience.[5] However, that was exceptionally fastidious on his part, and other new peers cared little if they lacked a country seat to go with their new handle.

Meanwhile, many established families were struggling to maintain their position, all the while expressing outrage that anyone should dare to question their God-given right to rule. In Edwardian times the pages of *The Queen* were filled with self-righteousness:

> The idle rich has become a byword of the moment, but to those who know, this term seems a rank injustice. In real truth, people in a high position are often the most hard-worked class in the community. This bitter abuse of the upper classes is cruel and unjust, and bids fair to become a danger to the nation. Centuries of power and wealth have given us the chance to perfect our social system. The English aristocrat has a just sense of his responsibilities, and has always been willing to give service in return for privilege. Let the Socialists rail as

they will, our upper classes are the finest body of thinkers and livers in the world.[6]

The post-war panic among the landed aristocracy was often attributed by the upper classes themselves to punitive death duties, which were introduced in 1894. However, the maximum rate was 8 per cent and that only applied to estates worth at least £1 million. Overall, death duties scarcely diminished the resources of the large landowners. The agricultural depression undoubtedly prompted sales of agricultural land before World War I; but such sales tended to be of outlying or less valuable parcels disposed of as a way of rationalizing estates. The acreage that changed hands was considerable – 104,000 in 1910, 174,000 in 1911 and even greater areas in 1912 and 1913 – and, although such volatility was in stark contrast with the stability of the eighteenth century, the figures hardly amounted to a crisis.

It was immediately after the war that major changes took place. Much land was offered for sale before the 1919 budget, which was certain to raise death duties on the capital value of large estates, and indeed did so. Duties rose from 20 to 40 per cent on the few estates valued at over £2 million. By March 1919 over five hundred thousand acres were for sale, and within months the figure had risen to two million, of which perhaps one million were actually sold during the course of 1919. It was estimated by the *Estates Gazette* that between 1918 and 1922 one-quarter of the land area of England and Wales changed hands. However, by 1925 the process had ground to a halt. Many of the new owners were former tenants, so there was a measure of continuity. None the less the centuries during which the landed élite had sat securely on their estates, enjoying a leisured life, were definitely moving to a close.[7]

Other peers found different ways to economize. The palatial London mansions established by the leading families in the eighteenth century passed out of aristocratic hands. The Duke of Sutherland, who had entertained thousands at his mansion near the Mall (Lancaster House), did not renew his lease. Devonshire House was sold for £750,000. Country houses were demolished if considered surplus to requirements. The whole process was spurred on by the economic crises of the late 1920s.

More significantly, the enormous political power of the aristocracy had at last passed into other hands. The grandees who had occupied ministerial posts in the eighteenth and early nineteenth centuries were now largely absent from Cabinets. By 1935 the only magnate in the Cabinet was the Marquess of Londonderry. Already by 1911, under Asquith, the powers of an arrogant and obstructionist House of Lords had been curtailed, and the traditional association of land and wealth was no longer axiomatic. By 1956 only one-third of peers possessed estates.[8]

The woes of the landed aristocracy did not mean that the traditional élite faded away. Until 1895 aristocrats had formed a majority in every Cabinet, and as late as 1935–1955 the ratio of aristocrats to commoners in Cabinets was twenty-one to seventy-eight. The first landless prime minister did not assume office until 1908. Of course the aristocracy, even in political office, was not an ideological monolith, and by the twentieth century aristocrats usually acted as motivated individuals rather than as representatives of a magnate class.[9]

In terms of social energy, the upper classes were still strong. Many of their members were no longer rich but they had limitless self-confidence. The letters of Nancy Mitford recording her giddy youth in the 1920s and 1930s make it very clear that she mixed overwhelmingly in aristocratic circles (to which of course she herself belonged), and that her aristocratic friends tended to marry within those same circles. Some fun-loving members of the middle class, such as Evelyn Waugh and John Betjeman, were admitted, but they were avid social climbers. Yet it is equally clear from the Mitford letters that many of these titled Bright Young Things were living very modestly indeed, either on small allowances from Papa or eking out a living from journalism or other forms of employment not considered too taxing or demeaning. The correspondence between Lord Esher and his bohemian daughter Dorothy Brett reflects her wish to be supported by her family, and her family's increasing reluctance to do so.[10]

At the same time some grandees looked back nostalgically to a better world of undiluted privilege. 'Would it be hopelessly reactionary', purred the Duke of Manchester in 1932

to speak a word in praise of the old, corrupt electoral system, with its 'pocket boroughs', the preserves of the great families? That system did at least give us statesmen; today the mob-electorate gives us only politicians. Say what we will about the justice of government 'by the people for the people', it cannot be denied that the old-established families, with 'a stake in the country', as the phrase goes, and even the 'captains of industry' of more recent rise, more truly reflect the real needs of the British nation than a pension-bribed, dole-ridden democracy.[11]

A few grandees didn't need nostalgia. Their aristocratic way of life continued unabated throughout the 1920s and 1930s. The present Duke of Bedford recalls his grandfather Herbrand, the 11th Duke, whose annual income of £200,000 allowed him to maintain Woburn Abbey and two houses in Belgrave Square:

> He kept four cars and, I think, eight chauffeurs in town, eating their heads off. They were responsible for the first part of the journey down to the country of any guests. The town car used to take you as far as Hendon, where you had to get out and join the car which had been sent up from Woburn. You never travelled with your suitcase, that was not considered the thing to do. It had to come in another car, so you had a chauffeur and a footman with yourself, and a chauffeur and a footman with the suitcase, with another four to meet you . . . This regime went right on until my grandfather died in 1940.[12]

At the house

> you were allotted your own personal footman, who stood behind your chair at meals, while a small army of another fifty or sixty indoor servants kept the archaic household going. My grandfather had refused to install central heating at Woburn except for the corridors, so that there were always seventy or eighty wood fires crackling throughout the Abbey in the winter, even in the bathrooms.[13]

Life at Woburn may have been extravagant, but it certainly doesn't sound much fun:

> In the midst of all this magnificence my grandfather lived a completely lonely and austere life. He had no contemporaries or friends of his own and most of the people who came to stay were cousins or other relatives. He had very little time for human beings and rarely spoke. My grandmother, being deaf, used to say that as he

never started a conversation and she never heard anything, there was no sense in anybody coming to the place. Hardly anybody ever did.[14]

The 11th Duke's nephew, Conrad Russell, clearly didn't relish his visits to Woburn in the 1930s:

> Dinner was a choice of fish and a whole partridge each. No drink except inferior claret and not much of it. Nothing else. The second that I had swallowed my peach Herbrand sprang up and we all trooped out . . .
> Dinner a repetition of last night. Rough claret. And Herbrand puts a lot of ice in his. Miss Green's stinking dog sits on a tray on a high chair next to me . . . I enclose a card stolen from my bedroom: 'You are particularly requested to refrain from giving a gratuity to any servant.'[15]

In the post-war era the British aristocracy has staggered on. The modern landed estate is no longer simply a rural paradise supported by rents; it is more likely to be a sophisticated business, often combining farming, exploitation of mineral rights, forestry, sports and tourism. In the next chapter we will see how the 'heritage industry' has helped the remaining upper-class families to survive and, in many cases, prosper.

Some European nobilities have not done too badly either. Many aristocratic families, in Florence, Rome and elsewhere, retain their *palazzi*, are active in banking and other industries, and make high-quality wine and oil from their extensive estates and vineyards. However, the romantic shabbiness of the ancient but bedraggled southern Italian nobility has all but vanished. Harold Acton recalled the faded Sicilian nobility earlier described by Lampedusa:

> The Princess of Trabia held a formal court of abbés who still took snuff, pallid ladies dressed in black, jaded gentlemen with pointed beards, a rubicund private chaplain, a learned librarian, an antiquated English governess of Jane Austenish gentility, and retainers who wore their liveries with a Catalan air. Social changes had been superficial: the same polysyllabic titles resounded.[16]

Such exotic households of retainers are surely extinct.

Modern Italy is still cluttered with titles, some of them bogus. Aristocratic titles were formally abolished in 1948, but you wouldn't know it. As in Germany, the profusion of small states and courts before the *risorgimento* and reunification led to competing networks of aristocrats. The nobles of Piedmont were, and to some extent still are, involved in military affairs, while those from Genoa were often merchants and bankers. The Venetian patricians under the Republic never bore titles, but were compensated by the Habsburgs for the loss of their independence with titles on a wholesale basis, which some of the *patrizzi* spurned. Florentine families such as the Frescobaldi and the Antinori give every appearance of flourishing, with diversified business and farming interests. Many large estates remain in aristocratic hands.

Shortly before the fall of the monarchy in 1946, King Umberto II was persuaded to issue a large number of patents of nobility. The recipients are collectively derided as 'Counts of Ciampino', after the Rome airport from which Umberto left the country. Others simply invented a lineage and titles. The papal nobility, on the other hand, was abolished in 1968.

For the east European nobility, the war brought disaster in the form of Russian occupation. Prussian Junkers fled west, if they could, but lost their estates. Many of those who stayed put were massacred by Russian forces out for revenge after the destruction wrought by Germany on their own country. Surviving German aristocratic families have abandoned their disdain for middle-class pursuits and now blend smoothly into the essentially meritocratic structures of modern Germany.

Other east European aristocracies were only slightly more fortunate. Land reforms in 1919 greatly reduced the holdings of the mighty Bohemian and Hungarian families in the former Habsburg Empire, but some of them were tenacious until anti-German sentiment (in some cases) and Russian troops drove them out. Their estates were colossal. The holdings of British dukes seem negligible compared to those of, say, the Liechtensteins and Schwarzenbergs. The Esterhazy family owned 735,000 acres in Hungary, and some twenty-five families each governed at least 250,000 acres. The Liechtensteins owned twenty-four castles in Austria and Bohemia, plus their principality tucked between Austria and Switzerland. Their Bohemian estates, once populated by a million people, were lost.

The collapse of Communism has meant that some of these family domains have been returned to the pre-war owners or their descendants. The Liechtenstein principality was originally acquired in 1719 as an estate worthy of the princely status of the family. Over a century went by before any members of the family could find the time to visit the mountain domain. Ejected from their estates in eastern Europe, they settled in Liechtenstein itself after the war. The now ultra-rich principality offers a tax shelter to foreign companies and manufactures false teeth. As an example of snatching victory from the jaws of defeat the Liechtensteins' story is hard to match among the annals of the modern European nobility.

Other Austro-Hungarian aristocrats live on in Vienna, where nobility originating in the nineteenth century are looked down on by those with more ancient titles, who are themselves caricatured by Austrian humourists. A typical aristocrat is sometimes portrayed under the name Graf Bobby, endowed with a rather nasal voice, considerable stupidity and affectations such as the use of adapted French words (e.g. *retourniert*). Graf Bobby only consorts with the upper middle classes at school and dancing classes.

The French aristocracy also have their affectations, such as an addiction to English nannies and Scottish tweeds. The two hundred *grandes familles* prefer intermarriage as the best means of preserving family fortunes and traditions, although they won't turn down a middle-class heiress if the dowry is sufficiently impressive.[17] Some titled families have emerged into the open and begun to organize dances modelled on British débutante balls, with a distinctly French note being sounded by the participation of the great Parisian houses of *haute couture*. All this offers some consolation for the fact that most French aristocrats have no privileges, no land and no influence. In place of these they cling to notions of blood and correct behaviour. Power passed long ago into the hands of the meritocratic middle-class élite educated at France's professional colleges such as the École Normale d'Administration. So there is a distinct air of unreality about the pretender to the French throne, the Comte de Paris, proudly tracing his lineage back to Hugues Capet, reaffirming the royalist principle and urging immigrants to adapt to French ways.[18]

In Spain the nobility fared well under Franco, retaining large estates and controlling many of the country's banks. But after the fall of Fascism their fortunes were eclipsed. King Juan Carlos, well aware of the anti-democratic tendencies of many Spanish aristocrats, distanced himself from the nobility until 1991, when he finally consented to meet the grandees. Since inheriting a title in Spain also rendered the holder liable to tax, many titles were unclaimed over past decades. However, the burgeoning of the Spanish economy has enabled some ex-nobles to reclaim their titles. Despite the political as well as social prominence of a number of Spanish aristocrats, titles are hardly a burning issue, and many nobles, especially those with active political careers, have chosen not to use them.

Meanwhile, in Britain, the political clout of the aristocracy remains scarcely diminished.

I spoke to a member of a once-rich aristocratic family, no longer quite so rich but not exactly suffering. From the terrace of his country home in southern England, he enjoys an uninterrupted view over fields and woodland much of which, until a few years ago, belonged to his family. He was raised in a vast country house a few miles from his present home. I wondered whether he was aware as a child of his privileged position.

'There was a time when I would consciously walk through the corridors with my nose in the air. But this was bravado, not a reflection of my feelings towards our staff. I wasn't aware of social differences when I was at school. But during the war the boy who lived at the lodge gates went to a different school, and my brother and I were very conscious of the difference between his world and ours. But he taught my brother how to snare rabbits, and my brother taught me, so we didn't look down on him. On the contrary, we valued the transmission of skills. During the war our house was inhabited by East End evacuees and their mothers. They lived apart from us, mainly because the house was so enormous. They mocked us, and we found this excruciating. We were greatly relieved when we found a boy among them with whom we had a shared interest: watching birds.'

He and his brother went to Eton. 'My father was very keen that we go to Eton because he hadn't been. I loathed the élitist dress we had to wear, making us the butt of jibes when we strayed outside the areas where Etonian garb was taken for granted. The way my brother dealt with the social disparities was with humour; he was very good at making them seem unimportant. There were snobberies within Eton too. Because we were Home Counties aristocracy, we were seen as inferior to other grand families, especially those with grouse moors and Scottish titles. I had a brief socialist phase. I squirm to think of it, but I remember once asking a bus conductor, "Do you like your job?" I felt I needed to get to know the working class.'

After school and the obligatory spell in the Guards, he got to know the working class rather better by working abroad as a miner. Was it deliberate?

'It was a deliberate attempt to broaden my experience of life. And in those days you could only take a small amount of sterling abroad, so you had to work to earn additional money. After Cambridge I took up a different career, as you know. My family always assumed that I would work, even though I could afford not to. To have lived off my private income would have meant that I was a playboy, and my family would not have approved.'

Did people kowtow to him because he was titled and rich?

'Oh yes, there was always a fair amount of forelock-tugging. We used to enjoy parodying such behaviour, especially middle-class ingratiation. We would invent middle-class circumlocutions such as "Have you imbibed a sufficiency?" when offering a second cup of tea. There was a shared view among our social stratum that aristos were adored by the working class, and we were united with them in our loathing of the middle class.'

And that was a myth?

'Absolutely, and a snobbish one.'

By 1945, with very few exceptions, the way of life enjoyed by a majority of the landed élite before World War I had vanished. Rising taxation eliminated the armies of servants. Some aristocrats cut and ran: a few dukes fled to the Caribbean or to Kenya, where they could maintain large estates and brigades of servants without having to endure British levels of taxation.

But after the austere post-war years, when everything looked bleak for the aristocracy, there were the boom years of the 1960s. Land prices rose consistently. Although taxation also rose steeply, wily lawyers devised ways of reducing estate taxes. Trusts and roll-over tax relief enabled landowners capable of forward planning to keep their estates together.[19] However, successive governments have been equally diligent in pursuing their goals, and measures such as the 1975 capital transfer tax, which replaced estate duties, plugged many of the loopholes formerly offered by discretionary trusts. None the less, reductions in the top bands of taxation introduced by the Thatcher governments, as well as rising land values, have given a boost to the landed élite. Large agricultural estates have by no means disappeared, and many remain under aristocratic ownership. Some of the dukes have prospered. The Duke of Buccleuch owns 275,000 acres, and the Dukes of Northumberland (ninety thousand), Roxburghe (sixty-five thousand), Devonshire (still with seventy thousand acres despite Harold Nicolson's observation of an earlier duke in 1939 that 'all his grandeur is gone for ever'[20]) and Beaufort (fifty thousand) are also in the major league. But even these magnates are outshone by the Duke of Westminster, present head of the Grosvenor family, with three hundred acres of Mayfair and Belgravia under his belt, as well as enormous estates in Scotland.

Others have fared less well. Three dukes, Newcastle, Manchester and Montrose, settled in Africa. Montrose became a minister in the Rhodesian government and died in 1992; the present Duke of Manchester appears to have returned to England, but remains obscure; Newcastle died in 1988, leaving no heir. The Duke of St Albans practises chartered accountancy, like his father before him. The Duke of Leinster, who died in 1976, was bankrupt and lived very modestly with a succession of wives, including Mary Etheridge (described by *Debrett's* as 'the stage soubrette') and the housekeeper at the block of flats where he once lived. The dukedom of Portland became extinct in 1990.

The Duke of Bedford had little pleasure from his inheritance. When he proposed marrying a woman of whom his father disapproved, his allowance was cut off and the Bedford estate passed not to him, but to trustees. The duke became the tenant, not the owner, of his family home. Furthermore, his father died owing enormous estate duties. The opening of Woburn Abbey to the public was the duke's escape from financial nightmare. In 1974 he turned over Woburn Abbey to his son, Lord Tavistock, and retired to Monaco.

There is a question mark over the future of the dukedom of Atholl. The owner of a fine Perthshire estate and the sole man in Britain with the right to maintain a private army, the 10th Duke died a bachelor in 1996. His heir was a South African kinsman whom he did not care for, so he bequeathed Blair Castle and its vast acreage to a charitable trust. The new duke does not seem greatly perturbed, and has no wish to exchange his pleasant life in South Africa for a chilly Scottish dukedom.

Vast tracts of London, including many Georgian squares and

terraces, are still owned by the aristocracy. The Portmans have owned property between Oxford Street and Regent's Park since the reign of Henry VIII. Lord Howard de Walden owns most of Marylebone, the Cadogan estate rules over ninety acres of Chelsea and the most celebrated of all London property owners, the Grosvenors, own much of Mayfair and all of Belgravia. The Bedfords were less fortunate, and had to sell much of Bloomsbury, although they still own parts of Bedford and Russell Squares.

Mark Bence-Jones and Hugh Montgomery-Massingberd estimated in 1979 that there were throughout England some 1600 estates of at least a thousand acres and supporting a country seat, that had been in the hands of the same family for a few generations, plus a further 150 in Wales and five hundred in Scotland.[21] It is not a bad tally after almost a century of hand-wringing. Thus the true gentry lives on: families such as the Swintons of Berwickshire, owners of the same land for a thousand years; the Giffards, proprietors in Staffordshire since the twelfth century; and the comparably pedigreed Dymokes of Scrivelsby, Lincolnshire, and the Berkeleys of Berkeley Castle in Gloucestershire. There are also a handful of relics of the squirearchy who own entire villages, men such as William Bulwer-Long of Heydon in Norfolk.[22]

The landed élite has been gradually withdrawing from its involvement in local administration. As recently as 1960, the members of English county councils included four dukes, nine earls, nine viscounts and viscountesses, and innumerable lesser aristocracy and gentry. That is no longer the case.[23] Many magistrates' benches were also filled by aristocrats, and for many years miscreants appearing before one of London's magistrates' courts would have been surprised to learn that their cycling-without-lights cases were being judged by a duke's sister. Many livings of the Church of England remain in the gift of the landed élite, and even in the 1960s, it has been estimated, 'roughly a fifth of the lords were marrying the daughters of other lords. Of the remainder most were choosing wives who were either related to the peerage or who came from landed gentry or upper-class families.'[24]

Politically, the aristocracy has fared remarkably well. The Duke of Devonshire was a Conservative minister in the early 1960s, though in the 1980s he forsook the Conservatives for the short-lived Social Democratic Party. Margaret Thatcher may have despised the

Conservative grandees, but both her government and that of her successor John ('Classless') Major were stuffed with ministers of impeccable aristocratic lineage: William Waldegrave and Nicholas Ridley (siblings of peers), Lord Carrington, the Earls of Gowrie and Caithness, two earls (Ancram and Kilmorey) permitted under the rules of the Irish peerage to sit in the Commons, Viscount Cranborne, Sir George Young (the cycling baronet) and Lord James Douglas-Hamilton, the son of the Duke of Hamilton. However, few of these upper-class ministers, with the exceptions of some of the dimmer lights from the Lords, owe their political success to social standing alone.

The members of the upper classes obliged to earn a living often seek out professions where their contacts and/or inherited knowledge may come in useful. That is why auction houses, public-relations firms, the wine trade and the smarter end of the antiques business are stuffed with those of aristocratic lineage. And a title of itself can be regarded as of commercial value. A title bewitches the untitled, as businesses and charities are only too keenly aware, although this is a consequence of snobbery rather than genuine aristocratic influence. Viscount Norwich has observed: 'The moment I succeeded to the title twelve years ago I was absolutely overwhelmed with requests to become chairman, patron or president of this or that charity or organisation. They never even bothered to ask whether I had any qualifications for the job. Extraordinary, isn't it?'[25] For about a century there has been a kind of reciprocal insemination by business and aristocracy, with aristocrats maximizing the potential of their properties and other resources, while businessmen profit from the reflected glory of association with the titled.

The future does not look particularly bright for the peerage. The remaining large estates may not survive intact beyond the next generation or two, and hereditary peerages are in constant danger of extinction. The proportion of the extant peerage that can claim descent from medieval or Tudor forebears is very small, and by 1956, shortly before the creation of life peerages, over half the titles had been created since 1900; peerages had lost all connection with landed wealth and had become medals dished out to retiring servants of the state.

Despite Margaret Thatcher's bizarre revival of the hereditary peerage in a few special circumstances, it is highly unlikely that new creations will be announced in years to come, unless, of course, England wins the World Cup.

SIX

A Life in the Country

'We haven't got a home,' said Gavin. 'This home is Grandpa's. It is
because we are poor.'
    'You are not,' said Mullet, in a sharper tone.
    'Mother said we were.'
    'That sort of poorness in our kind of family is different.'
    'It is better, isn't it?' said Nevill, in a consoling tone.
    'It is considered superior to the money of ordinary people.'
                        Ivy Compton-Burnett, *Parents and Children*, 1941

With the aristocracy's ancestral dependency on its income-generating
estates, it is not surprising that a complex social life, rooted in rural
pursuits, should have evolved. The country house served a number of
purposes: it was the administrative heart of any estate, a centre of
political influence in the district, a museum and art gallery, and a base
for entertainment. Whereas in France the social life of the nobility was
focused around the court and capital, most entertaining by the British
aristocracy took place at country seats. London mansions on a palatial
scale, suitable for great balls and dinners, only came into existence in
the eighteenth century. The *hôtels* of provincial French cities such as
Montpellier or Aix have few counterparts in provincial England.

The countryside famously provided sport. Hawking and then fox-
hunting became tremendously popular in the sixteenth and
seventeenth centuries. To be horseless was to be at a severe dis-
advantage. When Fanny Price comes to live at Mansfield Park, in
Jane Austen's novel of that name, the first deprivation to be rectified
by her kind cousin Edmund is her lack of a horse. Without a horse,
Fanny was in effect housebound. To this day, the British aristocracy
remains enthralled by the horse, both as a means to pursue the chase
and as the object of breeding and betting. The immense stable blocks

attached to great country houses confirm the important role that horses have played.

Although the British upper classes were never renowned for intellectual vigour, many grandees were not without taste or cultivated interests. Especially when the Grand Tour came into vogue, art collections were formed and great libraries established. Not all the surviving collections are of great interest, but there are wonderful treasures tucked away in country seats, though in recent years many of them, such as Warwick Castle's famous Roman vase, have been sold to help pay estate duties. Other aristocrats patronized antiquarian societies and embellished their churches, usually with funerary chapels. But there were few of the private theatres and opera houses quite commonly encountered in, say, the country houses and castles of Bohemia and Moravia.

Inevitably the owners of country seats vied with their neighbours. This competitiveness is already apparent in Elizabethan times, where rooms such as the Great Gallery in Hardwick Hall, with its acreage of windows, were created as much for display as for illumination. Enormous houses such as Burleigh and Knole were deliberately palatial; their function as a family home seems secondary. If a certain modesty and decorum returned to country-house design in the seventeenth century, the Palladian movement provided another excuse for construction on the most opulent scale, as though there were a national contest for the broadest bays and the most sweeping staircases and the tallest pediment. By this time, the early eighteenth century, the wealthiest aristocrats wintered in London, so it hardly mattered that the vast ballrooms and marble halls of the grandest Georgian mansions were frigid and unheatable in winter. The agricultural depression of the late nineteenth century put the brakes on country-house-building, and since the turn of the century more energy has been put into demolition than construction.

The aristocracy marked its superiority to the rest of the populace by emphasizing its role as a leisured class. The larger the house, the greater the consumption, the more lavish the entertainments, the more clear water between the indolence of the élite and the energy of the commercial classes. To some extent that indolence could be justified as the reward for the supposedly selfless consecration of the landed élite to public service. Local administration and other tasks that fell to the aristocracy were unpaid, though there were ample sinecures for those with political connections in the eighteenth century. Aristocratic patronage of charitable causes and devotion to public service was real but patchy, and did not preclude the defence of privileges and the accumulation of wealth. Such attitudes persisted until the late nineteenth century, when businessmen who did not hanker after counties and palaces were, overall, even richer than the landed aristocracy.

The Habsburg aristocracy had a habit of collecting castles and estates, and it was not unusual for the grandest families such as the Esterhazys to own a couple of dozen very large houses. In England, even the richest aristocrats usually restricted themselves to two or three. A nineteenth-century Lord Grantley, however

> inherited five houses when my grandfather died, of which Grantley was the largest. On one occasion, going up there by train, he was looking out of the window when he saw an uncommonly attractive house standing on a little hillside. He was so taken by it that he got out at the next station, and went to the largest estate agent in the town. He described the house in detail, and said 'I want to buy it. I want it as a hunting box . . . Find out the name of the house, the owner, and what he wants for it' . . . After a while the agent came up deferentially. 'We are making some progress, Sir,' he said. 'The house is called Elton Manor. The owner is Lord Grantley.'
>
> The final upshot was that my father had not only never lived in Elton Manor, but sold it soon afterwards. Having been reminded that he owned it, he promptly became bored with it.[1]

Television and film adaptations of Jane Austen novels have given the impression that social life among the gentry was a constant round of dinners and dances, and to some extent that was true. At the great houses, the true power centres of provincial England, a far greater formality prevailed. The larger the house, the more stifling the atmosphere.

Consuelo Vanderbilt married the 9th Duke of Marlborough in 1895 when she was nineteen, and was immediately plunged into the inflexible routines of Blenheim Palace. After the relative informality of American life, even among the ultra-rich, dining alone most nights with her dull husband must have become increasingly hard to endure:

How I learned to dread and hate these dinners, how ominous and wearisome they loomed at the end of a long day. They were served with all the accustomed ceremony, but once a course had been passed the servants retired to the hall; the door was closed and only a ring of the bell placed before Marlborough summoned them . . . As a rule neither of us spoke a word. I took to knitting in desperation and the butler read detective stories in the hall.[2]

The rules of correct behaviour were thickets of social confusion and potential embarrassment. Those bred within the system might understand the niceties of good form; for outsiders they were nightmarish restrictions on spontaneity. When in 1921 Lord Curzon, as Chancellor of Oxford University, was sent a specimen menu for a Balliol dinner at which he would be presiding, he returned it with the single comment: 'Gentlemen do not take soup at luncheon.'[3] So now you know.

Duchess Consuelo came to dread the pomp of late-Victorian entertaining:

I remember a dinner in honour of the Prince and Princess of Wales at which I wore a diamond crescent instead of the prescribed tiara. The Prince with a severe glance at my crescent observed, 'The Princess has taken the trouble to wear a tiara. Why have you not done so?' Luckily I could truthfully answer that I had been delayed by some charitable function in the country and that I had found the bank in which I kept my tiara closed on my arrival in London. But such an incident illustrates the over-importance attached to the fastidious observance of ritual.[4]

The world's worst dinner parties were probably those hosted by Emperor Franz Josef in Vienna. Court etiquette dictated that no one should continue eating after the Emperor had put down his knife and fork. But the distances between kitchen and dining room were so great that the Emperor had usually cleaned his plate before some of his guests had even been served. Knowledgeable courtiers took the precaution of booking a late-evening table at a restaurant when dining at the Hofburg. The situation was little better at Blenheim:

There it was a rule that dinner must not take longer than one hour. As the kitchen was at least 300 yards from the dining room, and the meal consisted of eight courses, the difficulties were considerable. Two soups, one hot and one cold, were served simultaneously: these were followed by two fish courses. After that, an entrée that was succeeded by a meat dish. Usually the meat consisted of game in season, otherwise quails were imported from Egypt and ortolans from France. An elaborate pudding followed, then a hot savoury which accompanied the port. Dinner ended with peaches, plums, apricots, nectarines, strawberries, pears and grapes.[5]

For children, country-house existence could be a chill and lonely experience. The 6th Earl of Carnarvon recalled:

On Christmas Eve, presents would be delivered to our Nanny for inclusion in our stockings. They were obviously chosen with little care or regard for our personal tastes. We would see nobody but our Nanny and the servants on Christmas Eve or on Christmas morning until after luncheon when we might be sent for to be shown off to the house guests. After about a quarter of an hour my father would say, 'I think you should go out now for a brisk walk before dark and perhaps we shall see you tomorrow.'[6]

Lord Grantley, writing in the 1950s, looked back on visits to his mother with some astonishment:

The pomp kept up in those days, even by modest families like ours, seems unbelievable now. I can remember being summoned to tea with my mother as a mite of four years, and a procedure of almost Germanic complexity ensued. My nurse 'Old Brown' would lead me as far as the picture gallery, a cosy little apartment 150 feet long. At the end of this interminable walk I was taken over by a footman-in-waiting and handed to the senior footman, two rooms on. Then, one room from my dear Mother's boudoir, I was passed to the butler, and finally announced by the Steward . . . He would throw open the door of the boudoir and trumpet: 'Mr Norton.'[7]

It gets worse. 'Once, after [my father] had reluctantly been persuaded to attend a family wedding, he suddenly nudged me and demanded, confidentially but not inaudibly, "Richard, who is this extremely intelligent and charming lady sitting the other side of me?" "Father," I replied as quietly as I could, "that is your daughter Joan."'[8]

The aristocracy's treatment of its servants, meanwhile, was often appalling. The sentimentalization of the aristocracy has led to a myth of 'faithful retainers'. No doubt there were contented upper-class households, and Lord Carnarvon in 1980 paid tribute to Robert Taylor who was with him for forty-four years and 'the greatest living example of the perfect butler', his chauffeur of twenty years and his 'beloved cook'. 'They are the lynchpin of this establishment which is probably one of the last links of the feudal system. We are all part of one big family and share in each other's joys and sorrows.'[9] But most of the literature suggests that the upper classes were hard-nosed about their servants. As Quentin Crewe, surveying the contents of *The Queen*, notes: 'There was really nothing good ever said about servants in the magazine.'[10]

Part of the problem may have been the difficulty of remembering who they all were. In 1923 Lord Carnarvon felt compelled to economize, and trimmed his staff at Highclere Castle

> to what I believed then to be the minimum necessary for the running of the house. We ended up with my butler and valet, a first footman, second footman, a hall boy, an usher, a head chauffeur and a second chauffeur, a chef, a first kitchen maid, a second kitchen maid, a scullery maid and a still-room maid, a housekeeper, five housemaids, an electrician, a nightwatchman, a head groom and two other grooms.[11]

At Blenheim, Duchess Consuelo, born in a land where central heating was not regarded as an effeminate indulgence, was shocked by what she found: 'The housemaids lived in the Housemaids' Height up in a tower where there was no running water, but since housemaids had so lived for nearly two centuries, I was not allowed to improve their lot.'[12]

Lord Carnarvon was also familiar with Blenheim, where as a young man he stayed with the 9th Duke:

> He was a pompous little man and I remember one Boxing Day, just as we were finishing breakfast and looking forward to a day's shooting, the butler came in and said, somewhat nervously, 'Your Grace, I have a message from your head keeper to say that he is ill and will not be able to come out shooting today. He wishes to assure Your Grace that he has delegated all his responsibilities to the keeper on the beat and he hopes you will have a good day.'
>
> Sonny listened in chilly silence which communicated itself to all the guests.

'My compliments to my head keeper; will you please inform him that the lower orders are *never* ill.'[13]

The servants' hall mirrored the etiquette that prevailed above stairs. James Lees-Milne chatted up the housekeeper at Blenheim in April 1943:

Miss James the housekeeper told me over a cup of tea that at Blenheim up to 1939 precedence in the servants' hall was rigidly observed. The visiting valets and maids were, as I already knew, called after their masters and mistresses, viz. Mr Marlborough and Mrs Bibesco; and, which I did not know, the valet of the eldest son of the house always sat on the housekeeper's right, taking precedence even over the valet of the most distinguished guest, whether Archbishop, Prime Minister or Prince of Wales.[14]

Not all the aristocracy lived in such grandeur. Lord Sackville at Knole, also visited by Lees-Milne in 1943, had a rather smaller staff: 'I went to Knole for luncheon. Just Lord Sackville and me. We ate in the large oak-panelled dining-room. He has a butler, a cook, and one housemaid who has 250 bedrooms to keep clean.'[15]

Lady Diana Cooper recalled the regime at her father's seat, Belvoir Castle, as it was in the days of her grandfather, the 7th Duke:

The gong man was an old retainer, one of those numberless ranks of domestic servants which have completely disappeared and today seem fabulous. He was admittedly very old. He wore a white beard to his waist. Three times a day he rang the gong – for luncheon, for dressing-time, for dinner. He would walk down the interminable passages, his livery hanging a little loosely on his bent old bones, clutching his gong with one hand and with the other feebly brandishing the padded-knobbed stick with which he struck it . . . I suppose he banged on and off for ten minutes, thrice daily. Then there were the lamp-and-candle men, at least three of them, for there was no other form of lighting.[16]

Perhaps the regime at Belvoir was relatively benign. It's hard to tell from this account. But a gardener's memories quoted in *Akenfield*, Ronald Blythe's superlative oral history of a Suffolk village, are chilling:

I went to Lordship's when I was fourteen and stayed for fourteen years. There were seven gardeners and goodness knows how many servants in the house. It was a frightening experience for a boy. Lord and Ladyship were very, very Victorian and very domineering ... We wore green baize aprons and collars and ties, no matter how hot it was, and whatever we had to do had to be done on the dot. Nobody was allowed to smoke. A gardener was immediately sacked if he was caught smoking, no matter how long he had worked there.

We must never be seen from the house; it was forbidden. And if people were sitting on the terrace or on the lawn, and you had a great barrow-load of weeds, you might have to push it as much as a mile to keep out of view ...

Ladyship drove about the grounds in the motor-chair and would have run us over rather than have to say, 'get out the way'. We must never look at her and she never looked at us. It was the same in the house. If a maid was in a passage and Lordship or Ladyship happened to come along, she would have to face the wall and stand perfectly still until they had passed.[17]

This account dates not from 1850, but from 1942. The chairman of the Akenfield Women's Institute saw things differently: 'People *loved* being servants. There was so much fun in the servants' hall. Such laughter. If you got into a bad place it was usually your fault. You had probably lost your character, or perhaps your mother had ... The ladies maids had a lovely time and they could watch how things were done and become educated. It was lovely.'[18]

As for the fine old tradition of looking after one's poorest tenants (begging the question as to why poverty was considered acceptable on an aristocratic estate), it was not always undertaken with the greatest tenderness, as Duchess Consuelo recalls:

It was the custom at Blenheim to place a basket of tins on the side table in the dining room and here the butler left the remains of our luncheon. It was my duty to cram this food into the tins, which we then carried down to the poorest in the various villages where Marlborough owned property. With a complete lack of fastidious-ness, it had been the habit to mix meat and vegetables and sweets in a horrible jumble in the same tin. In spite of being considered impertinent for not conforming to precedent, I sorted the various viands into different tins, to the surprise and delight of the recipients.[19]

The classic trio of hunting, shooting and fishing continue to give particular delight to the upper classes. Weekends at my Cambridge college could be tranquil times, as the more aristocratic undergraduates would don their tweeds and set off to woodland and moor. On Sunday evenings in autumn there were always a few windows from which pheasants would be speckling the flagstones of Trinity Great Court with droplets of blood.

Field sports and related activities have not, since the repeal of the game laws in the nineteenth century, been the exclusive preserve of the aristocracy and landed gentry. Despite the severity of those laws, they were somewhat less draconian than some of the measures adopted in Europe to prevent poaching. The Duke of Manchester recalled in his memoirs of 1932 that Count Larisch had told him that in his native Hungary poachers were shot: 'The ladies of the party were shocked at such a drastic penalty, and the men agreed that it seemed slightly severe in proportion to the offence; but Count Larisch disagreed with us and expressed the opinion that it was no more than such people deserved.'[20]

Part of the reason why fox-hunting has remained fairly popular is that it was never subject to the game laws; countrymen of all classes regarded foxes as vermin rather than game. Nor was possession of a horse essential, as large crowds could follow the chase on foot. None the less the packs of hounds were mostly kept by the landed élite. In the 1830s the typical cost of maintaining a pack in the Midlands was at least £4000.[21]

Shooting, as an organized group activity, was a relative newcomer to the English countryside. Those permitted by the game laws to shoot had done so as a fairly casual activity, but in the latter half of the nineteenth century beaters were used to drive the birds towards the men with the guns. This supplied an abundance of flapping birds, and a reasonable chance that anyone with a good rifle could bring one down. Shooting developed its own rituals, its potations and refreshments, its game bags and game books. It rapidly developed into the most coveted way for the landed élite to pass the winter months.

For some it became an obsession. Lord Walsingham and Maharajah Duleep Singh bankrupted themselves by organizing shoots, in which dozens or hundreds of gamekeepers and labourers could be involved.

To appease the expectations of the gun-toting aristocrats, a vast number of birds had to be raised, again a very costly activity. At Sandringham in 1900, twelve thousand pheasants were being raised annually.[22] The most prodigious (or bloodthirsty) shot of all time was the Marquess of Ripon, who between 1867 and 1900 disposed of 370,728 head of game.[23]

You didn't need to be out on the grouse moors to adopt the mentality of the adept shot. Alec Douglas-Home, the former 14th Earl of Home, reminisced: 'Even in the Foreign Office I could set my watch by the evening flight of the ducks from St James's Park – over the Horse Guards Parade to the Thames estuary – and select a right and left with my imaginary gun.'[24] Whereas hunting in Britain is the preserve of farmers and the upper classes, in North America it is a working-class pastime, as those who have seen the film *The Deer Hunter* will recall.

British sporting activities with a much broader social base included horse racing which, as Frith's famous painting of 'Derby Day' (1858) confirms, was appreciated at all levels of society. Again, the upper reaches of the sport, such as the maintenance of studs at Newmarket, were almost exclusively aristocratic preserves, and certain race meetings – Ascot, the Derby, Goodwood – attracted the landed élite in droves, even though they might only frequent the most fashionable enclosures.

Rugger has always been played at public schools, so there is a clear upper-middle-class identification with the sport. Cricket, while played by a broad cross-section of the population, has since the early nineteenth century enjoyed aristocratic patronage at county-club level. In 1877 the Middlesex County Cricket Club had 2291 members, of whom 337 – 14.7 per cent – were titled, although later in the century the proportion dropped by half.[25] None the less it represented an extraordinary aristocratic endorsement of the sport. To this day the MCC membership prides itself on its powers to exclude. Women are not permitted to be members, so the MCC is limited to a bunch of dozy men in striped ties.

Those with no interest in field sports or quadrupeds do best to avoid the 'county sets'. Such sets are not clubs; they are open to families who move into the area, so long as they have enough money to compete and share the general preoccupations of the set. Orbiting around the gentry or aristocracy, they provide an agreeable social life for the like-minded.

The survival of the country house is remarkable, even though very few estates can still fund traditional country-house life, with its servants, gardens and entertainments. Some landed families derive incomes from other sources – investments, stockbroking, whatever – but others have clearly struggled to maintain their houses and way of life.

The obvious way to do so was to open the house and grounds as a tourist attraction. The Marquess of Bath led the way with Longleat in 1949. It was a great success, and within a couple of decades the heritage industry had been born. Zoos, amusement parks and motor museums offered added attractions to lure those visitors with a less than fanatical interest in, say, Jacobean architecture and furnishings. Yet only a small minority of the aristocracy found it necessary to admit the paying public.[26] Writing in 1959, the Duke of Bedford, who was regarded as something of a showman, noted:

> Although we had a gross income from Woburn of some £80,000 in 1958, it should not be supposed that this shows a penny of profit. The place tumbles down much more quickly than you can possibly keep it going . . . The best that can be said is that we are nearly breaking even, and that for the moment, at any rate, there is no danger of Woburn falling down from sheer neglect.[27]

Under threat from the new taxes of the 1970s and high inflation, country-house proprietors banded together in 1973 to form the Historical Houses Association (HHA) as a kind of lobby group. It appears to have been quite effective in fending off further changes that might force current proprietors to sell or demolish. In the early 1980s the historian Heather Clemenson selected five hundred country houses existing in 1880, and found that 78 per cent were still standing, but only 120 were still in private hands. Others had been given to the National Trust or sold to institutions.[28] Some proprietors, such as the entrepreneurial Earl of Bradford, have looked at their houses and estates as a business asset, and turned them into conference centres, while moving their families into the former stable block or dower house.

The HHA represents many owners who have never admitted the public, but their houses too will benefit from whatever tax exemptions or modifications that pressure group can persuade the government to adopt. Others cling on to their country seats in the face of large tax bills, leaking roofs, wings sealed off to save on heating bills, and ragged gardens.

However, there has been a price to pay, as homes make the slow transformation into museums. No longer, in so many instances, viable economic units, country houses have been transformed into 'heritage', implying that they somehow belong to us all, and we are performing some kind of national duty by visiting them, contributing to their upkeep and helping what remains of the landed élite in their struggle to retain ownership and occupation. This has been achieved by a fairly cynical appeal to sentimentality, snobbishness and nostalgia.

I have always enjoyed visiting country houses and am a life member of the National Trust. I am as absorbed as any visitor by the great architecture of Longleat or Hardwick, the furnishings of Knole, the park at Stourhead, the turrets of Burleigh, the grandeur of Chatsworth. However, visitors are increasingly invited to view the country house not aesthetically or historically so much as nostalgically.

There is now a widely held belief that country-house living represented some kind of apotheosis of civilized life. Of course certain houses must have been a delight to inhabit and visit: luxurious accommodation, perfect facilities for recreation, a good cellar, sparkling company. Others were vast tombs, cold and inhospitable, inhabited by montrous people enriched by the labour of their tenants and servants, which they took for granted. Many aristocrats, such as Lord Curzon, devoted themselves to public service. Others led lives of indolence and selfishness, their principal entertainment being the shooting or hunting of small animals.

The descendants of these fine people are the current occupants of the surviving houses, people described by the historian David Cannadine as 'the self-appointed, live-in guardians of the "national heritage"'. They are no doubt as varied in their personalities as their ancestors. It is not self-evident, however, that as a class they need to be treated as an endangered species that the general public is obliged to save from extinction. Novelists such as Evelyn Waugh in *Brideshead Revisited* have sentimentalized the country house, as though a building were capable of emanating moral virtue. Television adaptations, by understandably seeking out the visually spectacular, have given further weight to the sentimentalists. Then propagandists such as Mark Bence-Jones and Hugh Montgomery-Massingberd have weighed in with their rosy idealizations of the aristocracy.

The most inflated piffle of this nature that I have encountered was penned by James Lees-Milne in his contribution to an exhibition

catalogue entitled *The Destruction of the Country House*, which chron-
icled the hundreds of burnings and razings of country houses during
this century. Lees-Milne mourned: 'Countless country houses, great
and small, were throughout the centuries until the Second World
War the inspiration of genius, just as they themselves were the creations
of genius. Is it purely fortuitous that the decline of our civilization and
the collapse of the country house way of life are coincidental?'[29]

Most country houses open to the public no longer represent a living
culture. No wonder the artful proprietors usually permit access to one
room 'still used by the family'. They never look as though they're used,
but they are invariably furnished with a few family photographs, copies
of *Country Life* on the coffee tables, monographs on racehorses or other
country houses on the sideboards, a fireplace with a smearing of ash
around the grate, a desk laid out with headed notepaper and a fountain
pen. The kinds of country house where the children's toys clutter up the
place are usually not the kinds of country house worth paying a few
pounds to visit.

In Victorian times, Cannadine reminds us, these houses were
bought, sold, demolished, expanded, redecorated. 'They were not then
regarded as shrines to be venerated, as relics of a vanished golden age
which must be preserved untouched and unchanged, at all cost.'[30] If the
cult of the English country house were simply a means of preserving
some masterpieces of architecture and landscape gardening, there
could be no objection to it, and country houses would become
museums. But when that cult is used to preserve the occupation of great
estates and houses by their bankrupt owners, then it seems like a
peculiar prolongation of the class system, conferring privilege on an
already fortunate élite. Default on your mortgage through no fault of
your own, and your home will eventually be repossessed. But the
aristocracy is presumed to have some right to perpetual possession that
is denied the rest of us.

This nation indulges its upper classes to the most extraordinary
degree, and even the feared mass media come over all deferential and
mumbly when they try to portray them. In January 1997 the BBC
presented a series of television programmes about the aristocracy that
consisted of little more than a series of anecdotes and dips into family
albums to see what Great-Uncle Horace was wearing at Lady
Barnacle's ball. Genial old buffers were wheeled out to reminisce. The

Duke and Duchess of Devonshire were shown doing their *noblesse oblige* number at a party for the estate workers' children, and later the duke shook his jowls and repeated that the aristocracy was a spent force, though both he and his Derbyshire palace and acreage looked anything but. One programme focused on the Lygon family: two sisters reminisced about parties at Madresfield before the war, and the programme's final voiceover intoned that the family titles of Beauchamp and several others were now extinct, as though this were cause for national mourning.

A year before, the journalist Tony Parsons had presented a slightly more ambitious series on class. As representatives of the upper classes he picked a family of northern gentry, the Gordon-Duff-Penningtons of Muncaster Castle, whose forebears have lived in those parts for eight centuries. They seemed a nice enough family, but they inspired in the dour Mr Parsons an attack of obsequiousness: 'There is much to admire about the upper classes,' he intoned; 'with their limitless self-confidence and lightness of touch, they always seem at ease with the world.'

Certainly Mrs G-D-P seemed a prize specimen, with wonderful upper-class vowels ('Orf' for 'off') and a vocabulary preserved in aspic from a more frivolous age ('giddy-making'). But all is not well at Muncaster. Repair bills run into the millions, and the family can only stay put by selling its heirlooms and praying for a more generous grant from English Heritage. A former gamekeeper offered consolation: 'Tradition', he mourned, 'has gone to the dogs.'

Mr Parsons was close to tears by this point, reminding his viewers of 'the enormous sacrifices made by the aristocracy for their country. In World War I one in five of all peers and their sons never came back from the trenches.' True enough, but it's not as though the privates fared much better. 'What they are fighting to preserve belongs to us all,' declared Parsons. (Oh yeah? Just try moving into Houghton.) His conclusion was predictably pat: 'The barbarians are at the gates and some time soon they may not be leaving on their coach at the end of the day.' Barbarians? Are these middle-class coach parties he's referring to? Of course one feels sorry for the G-D-Ps, but with an unbroken run of eight centuries as part of the landed élite, undisturbed by guillotines and Bolsheviks and plundering armies, they haven't been too harshly treated.

SEVEN

The Middling People

The higher and lower classes, there's some good in them, but the middle
classes are all affectation and conceit and pretense and concealment.
Lord Melbourne, quoted in David Cecil, *Lord M.*, c.1827

A modern Briton must show very good cause to establish that he or she
is *not* middle-class. The working class, for the most part, aspires
upwards, and with considerable success. The upper class is shrinking,
its ranks no longer refreshed with infusions of new, rich blood. Who
would claim that a life peerage confers upper-class status on the
recipient?

Of course the middle class is no more monolithic than any other
class; indeed, it is infinitely stratified. The term 'middling class' or
'middle class', as the historian John Seed has pointed out, originally
described one eighteenth-century stratum that was 'merely positional':
'not something that exists in its own right but a grouping that fails, or
refuses, to fit the dominant social division between upper and lower,
rich and poor, land and labour'.[1] Whereas the upper class lived off rents
and the lower classes sold their labour, the middle classes exploited
material resources and hired labour or earned an income from
professional expertise. Far from wallowing in their wealth, the rising
middle classes often took the lead in establishing hospitals, charities,
learned societies and cultural outlets that greatly enhanced their
communities. If the middle classes are often overlooked, by class
analysts, at least in comparison with the upper and working classes, it
may be because their existence is marginal in Marxist analysis, and
because they have always been diffuse, ranging from shopkeepers to
entrepreneurs, teachers, clerks and engineers.

We middle-class folk lack clear identity, and we're all over the place, so much so that we can't get any perspective on ourselves. The class's fluidity is constant, as its constituents float from lower middle to middle middle, from occupation to occupation. The working class have their culture and their pride, their cheek-to-cheek kinship; the upper classes have their status, their small certainties, their countryside, their tribalism.

The middle classes have anxiety. Lift yourself by education and hard work from an industrial working-class background to a managerial job; then buy a saloon car, take the family to Majorca for the usual two weeks, encumber your bank account with standing orders for insurance, pension, school fees, club subscriptions; then lose your job, and with it your house, grindingly repossessed; and, nearly homeless, you are back where you started.

To be middle-class is to be obsessed with qualifications, those diplomas that testify to your competence, those tickets to a career that work like a dream in good times and prove useless in bad. Because only at the top end do the middle classes enjoy status; the rest of us crave it, scheme for it, cling to it. Presumably someone is gratified by brochures such as one put out in 1996 by the Great Western Railway. Entitled *Business First*, it contains such margin headings, designed to flatter and reassure, as 'Reflecting Your Status – Meeting Your Needs'. And buttering up your insecure little ego.

In the modern jargon, the middle classes need to 'make statements', sending out signals that will help the world to place us in the appropriate niche. Hence the clothes we wear, the cars we drive, the suburbs we inhabit, the schools our children attend, the foods we eat, these are all indicators of status. They matter to the middle classes. The working and upper classes don't worry, because the choices have already been made by their respective cultures and incomes. The middle classes have no manual called 'Tradition'. They, we, have to make it up as we go along. It's Chilean Cabernet one year, sun-dried tomatoes the next; a Cabriolet this season, a GTi for the year after. Absurd Sunday-newspaper supplements chart the ins and the outs, relieving anxiety for some and stirring it up for others. Two journalists writing a book on class went to the trouble of compiling a list of the kinds of people who buy certain cars. Thus secretaries and typists buy small Peugeots, which, one deduces, are to be avoided by those with higher aspirations. It is the authors' contention that large purchases 'work rather like a voucher system: you hand over your cash and in return you are immediately hoisted up the class ladder'.[2] That, of course, is misleading. The most you can achieve is to enhance your status.

The American term for what I, borrowing from Lawrence Stone,[3] have called status anxiety is, predictably, more extreme. It was the sociologist C. Wright Mills who coined the phrase 'status panic', and the American literary critic Paul Fussell who described in rather flamboyant terms what it means within an American context:

> The middle class is distinguishable more by its earnestness and psychic insecurity than by its middle income. I have known some very rich people who remain stubbornly middle-class, which is to say they remain terrified at what others think of them, and to avoid criticism are obsessed with doing everything right. The middle class is the place where table manners assume an awful importance . . . The middle class, always anxious about offending, is the main market for 'mouthwashes', and if it disappeared the whole 'deodorant' business would fall to the ground.[4]

Despite Fussell's decidedly snobbish tone, one understands what he means.

Considering how numerous the middle classes are, they have precious little history behind them. With their origins in commerce and the guilds, they were statistically insignificant until Tudor times. Even then the power of the landed interest was so great that whilst some merchants prospered in the cities, they enjoyed little status. It was comparatively late in the seventeenth century that the 'middling sort' began to make some impression. Amateurism made room for professionalism. The growing wealth of the country demanded a kind of professional service economy to keep it housed, clothed, administered and entertained. In 1741 Horace Walpole wrote that 'there was nowhere but in England the distinction of the middling people'.[5]

Although the social distance between the rising middle class and the aristocracy was great, there was little antagonism directed by the former at the latter. The upper classes may have been misguided, self-interested and sometimes corrupt, but they were active participants in the administration of the nation at all levels. For many in the middle classes the aristocracy offered role models: of gracious living, polite behaviour, education. In the nineteenth century, when the running of an industrialized and colonial power required a large and skilled class of administrators and professional people, the middle class adopted the values of their social superiors. The rise of public schools, in particular, instilled values of service and fair play and all the other fitfully observed tenets of the British aristocratic code.

De Tocqueville gives a clear-sighted view of the burgeoning middle classes in 1833:

> If you speak to a member of the middle classes, you will find he hates some aristocrats but not the aristocracy. On the contrary he himself is full of aristocratic prejudices. He deeply distrusts the people; he loves noise, territorial possessions, carriages: he lives in the hope of attaining all this by means of the democratic varnish with which he covers himself, and meanwhile gives a livery to his one servant whom he calls a footman, talks of his dealings with the Duke of—, and his very distant family links with the house of another noble Lord . . .
>
> The English are still imbued with that doctrine, which is at least debatable, that great properties are necessary for the improvement of agriculture, and they seem still convinced that extreme inequality of wealth is the natural order of things. Notice that it is not of the rich I am speaking here at all, but of the middle classes and a great part of the poor.[6]

Unlike their counterparts in, say, France, the British aristocracy did not keep the upper middle classes at bay. At schools, at clubs, in politics, the two strata intermingled. As we have seen, it was possible, if rare, for merchants and bankers from the late eighteenth century onwards to penetrate first the gentry and then the landed aristocracy. However, many successful middle-class figures had no interest in aping the aristocracy and were perfectly content in the bourgeois splendour of their capacious town houses; their idea of pleasure was more easily met in the theatre or museum than on the grouse moor. It was equally inevitable that the middle classes should slowly resent their lack of political power, and that reform of the parliamentary system should gradually broaden its base.

Movements for reform provoked bitter debates but did not tear the country apart, despite the vigorous resistance of the aristocracy. By the mid-nineteenth century it was no longer feasible for the country to be run as though it were no more than a collection of large estates; the economic balance was swerving towards manufacturing industry, and those who generated wealth away from the land were not content to remain unrepresented. Trade may have been unfashionable, but what was the point of an empire without it?

The ruling élite did not comprehend until very late in the day the necessity for commerce on an international scale. It failed to perceive how colonial expansion could be of any interest to it, and some expressed resentment of the need to finance distant campaigns that could benefit the 'commercial interest'.[7] It was the very strength of what in the eighteenth century could be dismissed as the 'middling sort', but which a century later had become a numerous and decidedly prosperous segment of the population, that provoked tension between a complacent landed élite and the vigorous entrepreneurial class seething below it. Yet if some businessmen resented the strong grip on power exercised by the aristocracy, others, content to leave the business of ruling in the hands of the upper classes, were free to get on with more important matters, such as making money and enjoying urban life. Furthermore, the infusion of aristocratic values into the scions of the middle class by means of public-school education meant that the middle classes were slow to develop ideological positions with which to confront their aristocratic masters.

Egalitarianism had never endeared itself to the class-conscious British, but there was throughout the nineteenth century a chipping-away at privilege. The franchise was extended, the disabilities of Nonconformists and Roman Catholics were done away with, sinecures abolished, army commissions could no longer be purchased, and competitive examinations determined recruitment into the civil ser-vice. It was only common sense that professional and administrative posts should be filled from the largest pool possible, giving ability the edge over accidents of birth. Nor was this any threat to the supremacy of the landed élite. As R. H. Tawney wrote: 'The middle classes acquiesced in sharp distinctions of wealth and power, provided that, as individuals, they were free to scale the heights. The upper classes were glad to be reinforced by individuals of means and influence, who sprang from below, provided that, as a class, they remained on their eminence.'[8]

By the end of the century Britain had changed beyond recognition. There was firmly in place an establishment of upper-middle-class professionals – lawyers, businessmen, bankers, academics, doctors, scientists, administrators, officers, engineers, architects – with their own codes and institutions. By founding professional associations, they could both regulate their practice and confer dignity upon it. The Royal College of Surgeons was founded in 1800, the Law Society twenty-five years later, followed in 1834 by architects, in 1841 by pharmacists, and by physicians in 1856. These associations were inclusive in that they defined, sometimes by examinations, the qualifications required by practitioners of a particular profession; at the same time they excluded amateurs and charlatans. Doctors and builders had always been required, even in medieval times, but by the Victorian era they claimed a professional dignity they had not previously enjoyed.

Careers were as vertically structured as the class system itself, and within each profession there were tiers of seniority and competence. Professional associations awarded associate or fellowship status to their members; the civil service was meticulously graded; the growing managerial class also found itself functioning within a hierarchy. This would consolidate the middle class but also impose on its members a stratification every bit as complex as the tiers of the peerage. However, the system was never as stifling as it was, say, in Austria, where it was obligatory to address people by their professional title, and that also went for their wives. So it was '*Herr Doktor*' to your physician and '*Frau Doktor*' to his wife.

The middle classes also benefited from vastly improved communications from the mid-nineteenth century onwards. No longer was the choice between rural and urban living so stark. The development of the railways opened up the possibility of suburban living, where space, fresh air and social stability could be acquired without cutting off families from workplace and cultural activities. Manufacturing cities such as Manchester developed a richness of urban life that rivalled that of the capital. Its theatres, its orchestra, its municipal self-importance and, of course, its wealth allowed an opulent way of life to develop quite independently of the more isolated rural grandeur of the aristocracy. Katharine Chorley's *Manchester Made Them* gives a detailed and affectionate portrait of Alderley Edge in Edwardian times, where the professional middle classes mingled with mostly benign, patriarchal businessmen and artistically inclined German-Jewish families. Overall the portrait is one of security and stability, of quiet female domesticity revolving around tea parties and charitable works, and, of course, the same petty but essentially harmless snobberies that fictional accounts of nineteenth-century life – from Jane Austen to Mrs Gaskell to George Eliot and Thackeray – chronicle so exactly.

Such families existed throughout the land, enjoying steady incomes and keeping a couple of servants. Even the *petite bourgeoisie* – shopkeepers, teachers and clerks – were often able to maintain a servant to deal with the tasks common to every Victorian and Edwardian household: lighting fires, cooking, laundry and so forth. The most prosperous and influential members of the upper middle class may have sought to mingle socially with the aristocracy with whom they were sure to be thrown into occasional contact; and at the other end of the scale, there was already a blurring between the prosperous working class and the modestly paid white-collar workers.

Yet within the great mass of the middle class, firm distinctions remained, as described by Harold Perkin:

Its various layers and segments were mutually and plurally exclusive, with minutely refined gradations of status, expressed not only in dress, style and location of house, number of servants, and possession of personal transport in the form of a riding horse, carriage and pair or pony and trap, and other visible possessions, but in the intangible rules about who spoke or bowed to, called on, dined with or intermarried with whom . . .

From top to bottom the middle class was riddled with such divisions and petty snobberies, not only of income and geography but also of religion: Church of England (in some country villages the Roman Catholic squire) at the top, the Quakers and Unitarians next, followed by the Congregationalists and Baptists, the Methodists and finally, by a curious inversion, the Anglicans and the Catholics again at the bottom, mostly in the working class; of education: boarding schools at the top, followed by private day schools, and only amongst the lowest white-collar worker the non-fee-paying church or local board school; and of leisure: exclusive West End or provincial city clubs (men only) and country tennis and old clubs at the top, Sunday-school teaching, men's Christian societies and mother's unions at the bottom.[9]

What the middle classes did share with the working class, at least until the introduction of the welfare state, was insecurity. Unemployment, illness and death of a breadwinner could all be crippling blows to families at a time when there were few safety nets. Existing charities could not begin to satisfy such needs. Hence the intense jockeying for position within the middle class, the emphasis on competing with one's neighbours, or at least in not falling below their standards, the identification of possessions with status. None of this has changed. Although the welfare state has largely banished abject poverty, expectations have also risen, and children can no longer be satisfied with a rattle and a penny whistle. We remain as preoccupied by status as ever.

Moreover the security enjoyed by the middle classes over recent decades has been whittled away. The ravages of recession and growing unemployment among the managerial classes and the growing use of short-term contracts are among the many causes of middle-class disquiet. In the 1960s and 1970s it was possible to make long-term financial commitments, such as mortgages, that most people in employment had no difficulty in fulfilling. Now middle-class people are much more wary.

Tony Benn MP, who sees a disillusioned middle class as the seedbed of Fascism, is uneasy about the situation as he perceives it: 'People are really terrified now. The one thing about the middle class is that they were secure. If you define middle class in terms of security and insecurity, there isn't a middle class, except for the handful so rich they don't go to work. Security and insecurity may be quite a good definition of what class is about. Insecurity is about class, it's about your relationship with the economic system. In the nineteenth century the middle classes were secure and the working class weren't. Now nobody's secure.'

Earlier in the century the divisions between manual labourers and the lower middle class were much sharper than they are today, which is why those who elevated themselves into the ranks of the middle class were often so eager to set down markers that would definitively establish their social progress. The simplest way to do this was to live among your peers. If you were able to exchange a grimy terraced house in Southwark for a semi-detached with garden in north-east London or

Essex, you had made a clear statement that you had left the urban working class.

I grew up in a flat within a modest Edwardian house close to Kilburn underground station in north-west London. From our living room I could see the broad streets, lined with large houses (mostly subdivided into flats), that led towards Willesden. This was clearly middle-class territory, boringly suburban, but solid, comfortable and safe. But by walking south a mere hundred yards into Kilburn, I was in a very different world: strongly Irish, as it still is, and essentially working-class. Here there were terraced houses, late-Victorian or Edwardian, probably built originally for lower-middle-class families but now run-down and converted into flats. Our Irish cleaning lady lived in one of these unappetizing side streets off Kilburn High Road, and sometimes I would visit her and her husband, a saxophonist. There was a powerful contrast between their crowded flat with its bruised furnishings and the more solid bourgeois comforts of my own home.

Little has changed. Kilburn remains fairly rough, while the streets where I grew up now feature in estate agents' listings as high-priced Brondesbury. The class division between the two remains marked. Housing has always been a powerful class denominator in Britain. Whereas in an Italian or Austrian city a *palazzo* or large urban block would house an aristocratic family (often the owners of the building) on the *piano nobile*, other floors would be occupied by artisans or professional families. In Britain we prefer to dwell in individual units, in which class emblems are bound to be more visible. We may live on council estates, in an Edinburgh tenement, in a mock-Tudor house in the stockbroker belt or a gentrified inner-London Georgian house; where we live sends out a powerful signal about how we perceive our place in the class structure.

Because of the perpetual status anxiety of the middle class, a great deal of value is placed on education. Education is not only seen as worthy in itself, but as the best path to qualifications that will facilitate advancement to a higher-status career. Two journalists, the authors of a glib manual on self-promotion published under the misleading title *Class*, write boldly:

It is a crucial distinction: the middle classes invest in the future of their children, while the working classes spoil them in the here and now. Middle-class couples pay up to £3000 a year to ensure that children as young as two get the 'solid grounding' they need to secure a place at the best independent schools. They recognise the importance of nurturing the potential of their offspring rather than satisfying their immediate needs. The working classes, by contrast, can be seen every weekend traipsing round Toys R Us.[10]

Apart from the patronizing last sentence, there is evident truth in this.

A friend of mine who teaches in eastern England observes of his pupils: 'My students are mostly rural lower-middle-class with aspirations. They consider themselves "normal", and are aware of "common" people beneath them and "posh" people above them. What they want is two cars per family rather than one and not to live in a council house. But they don't aspire to increase their social standing as a goal in itself; rather they want to increase their wealth within their "normal" group.' Thus education is perceived as a useful tool for improving status and gaining wealth, but not primarily as a means of climbing the social ladder.

There are few other class-wide attributes, which is hardly surprising given the breadth of the middle class. Mark Bence-Jones and Hugh Montgomery-Massingberd, experts on the upper class, become very exercised over this slack definition of 'middle-class': '"Middle"', they write, 'implies equally distant from top and bottom; but now everyone, with the possible exception of a mere thousand peers and their immediate families, is described as middle-class; so that in a nation of 60 million people, the middle is deemed to be situated only a couple of thousand down from the top.'[11] Vexing, I dare say, for the upper class and upper middle class to be separated by such a wafer, but that's the way it is.

The upper-class unease expressed by these two authors reflects the undeniable fact that there is no longer an aristocratic ruling class in Britain. The landed élite in Britain has been replaced in this function by what has become known as the Establishment. This ruling class may include members of the aristocracy, but they are merely part of a large, informal politburo drawing on various spheres of influence, from politics to the Church, from journalism to big business. There is nothing mysterious or sinister about it, and a similar élite dominates other sophisticated Western societies such as Germany and the United States. Thus the middle class has long been co-opted into the ruling class. A distinctive feature of a middle class of this size and breadth is that it precludes any possibility of class conflict. Encompassing as it does the lowliest of white-collar workers on the one hand and nuclear physicists on the other, there is no possible shared agenda, no unified sense of relation to the other classes.

That is why there is no such thing as the middle-class vote. A few years ago some friends came to dinner: they were all well-off professionals with high-powered jobs, and large houses in fashionable parts of London. They all revealed themselves to be Labour Party supporters. Since at that time Labour was being branded as the party of high taxation, my friends were, in a way, acting against their class interest. At that time the *petite bourgeoisie* were still fairly solid in their support for the Conservative government, expressing a mixture of greed and deference, both of which were eagerly encouraged by Margaret Thatcher and quietly tolerated by John Major. I'm not sure why I should have been so surprised, since I too have been a Labour Party member for decades, on the grounds that I couldn't possibly support a party ideologically fuelled by the mean-mindedness of the *petite bourgeoisie*.

In the late 1950s, my parents moved to the London suburbs. Suddenly, after living all my life in the agreeably raw, socially varied ambience of Kilburn – with its Irish labourers, Jewish refugees, Fijian garage mechanics, Polish delicatessen owners and plain London middle-class folk – I was transported to Wembley, the dull heart of the middle middle class. There was no shortage of interesting neighbours. A celebrated Canadian tenor lived three houses away; across the street lived a demure orchestral violinist and through her uncurtained windows I could see but not hear her weekly string quartet sessions. I also recall a married woman with a complex sideline in other men, and a Greek-Cypriot family who invited us to their daughter's whisky-soaked wedding.

But these were other people's lives, mostly inaccessible though interesting to observe. The awfulness of Wembley was that there was nothing to do. Everyone seemed confined to their houses and gardens. All around were streets and houses, some larger than others, some detached, some terraced, and here and there a row of shops. Whereas in

Kilburn I had been able to trawl the length of the seedily exotic Edgware Road to Marble Arch itself, in Wembley the sole excursion was walking the dog through the monotonous streets. Suburbs disperse. My school was six miles away, and my nearest friends almost as distant. Visiting them was time-consuming and costly.

Worse still was the fact that the house was the sole unit of differentiation. The domestic virtues took on an absurd importance. My essentially urban parents suddenly began doing things I had never seen them doing before: washing the car, mowing the lawn, tending the compost. To add insult to injury, I was expected to join in the fun. Inevitably households competed with each other. Every facet of everyone's life was up for comment, comparison and, usually, disparagement: no. 12 had painted their front door a hideous colour; no. 14 never picked up fallen leaves from their lawn; no. 16 didn't wash their car often enough; no. 18's daughter was a tart; no. 20 rarely returned a polite greeting in the streets. The ambience defeated my family too, but only after I had been confined for my entire adolescence to this arid suburban boredom. Once I had left home my family headed back to a cosmopolitan inner suburb packed with Victorian villas, spacious parks, cosy restaurants and canal walks.

Richer friends in richer suburbs were, essentially, no better off. One of them, outwardly upper-middle-class with all the trappings of country cottage and children in posh schools, warmed to my theme: 'People romanticize the working class but overlook how ghastly middle-class life can be. I grew up in the stockbroker belt and have spent the rest of my life running away from it.'

My decade in the wastes of Wembley had taught me one indelible lesson: to live in the barely beating heart of the middle class is to replace your anxieties about class with anxieties about status.

EIGHT

The Great and the Good

It's very middle-class to be in a hurry.
Nancy Mitford, quoted in Jessica Mitford, *A Fine Old Conflict*

Since wars, taxes and the decline of empire had trimmed down the aristocracy's wealth and influence, it was inevitable, especially with the extensions of the franchise, that power would have to be shared with the upper middle class. Because of the vagueness of the British constitution, it has never been easy to define exactly how the new ruling class was formed, and what its powers were. That senior politicians, the Court, the judiciary, the Church of England's bishops, the governors of the Bank of England, university vice-chancellors, leading industrialists, powerful landowners, rich philanthropists and many others constituted a network of influence was impossible to contest. What was more difficult was to pin it down.

Henry Fairlie made a famous attempt in the *Spectator* in 1955 when he wrote:

> By the 'Establishment' I do not mean only the centres of official power – though they are certainly part of it – but rather the whole matrix of official and social relations with which power is exercised. The exercise of power in Britain (more specifically in England) cannot be understood unless it is recognized that it is exercised socially. Anyone who has at any point been close to the exercise of power will know what I mean when I say that the 'Establishment' can be seen at work in the activities of, not only the Prime Minister, the Archbishop of Canterbury and the Earl Marshal, but of such lesser mortals as the chairman of the Arts Council, the Director-General of the BBC, and even the editor of the *Times Literary Supplement*.[1]

Although Fairlie has been credited with the coining of the word, 'Establishment' was already current, as expounded by a more radical figure, the historian A. J. P. Taylor, writing in the *New Statesman*:

> Trotsky tells how, when he first visited England, Lenin took him round London, and, pointing out the sights, exclaimed: 'That's *their* Westminster Abbey! That's *their* Houses of Parliament!' Lenin was making a class, not a national emphasis. By *them* he meant not the English, but the governing classes, the Establishment. And indeed in no other European country is the Establishment so clearly defined and so completely secure. The Victorians spoke of the classes and the masses; and we will understand exactly what they meant. The Establishment talks with its own branded accents; eats different meals at different times; has its privileged system of education; its own religion, even, to a large extent, its own form of football. Nowhere else in Europe can you discover a man's social position by exchanging a few words or breaking bread with him. The Establishment is enlightened, tolerant, even well-meaning. It has never been exclusive, rather drawing in recruits from outside, as soon as they are ready to conform to its standards and become respectable. There is nothing more agreeable in life than to make peace with the Establishment – and nothing more corrupting.[2]

Taylor perceived the Establishment as slightly sinister, hugger-mugger, a law unto itself. Fairlie took a more benign view, as Jeremy Paxman has pointed out:

> Fairlie, who claimed that the existence of an Establishment was 'desirable' because it kept out unspecified worse influences, conceded that membership was not closed. But the central feature of the Establishment, ignored by many then and now, is not who's in or out. Its essence was not individuals, it was shared opinion, a way of viewing the world, a consensus, agreement on the right way of doing things.[3]

This was quite close to a nineteenth-century view of the same phenomenon, as perceived by the Frenchman Hippolyte Taine:

> On the whole, whereas we *suffer* our government, the English *support* theirs. An establishment which is so firm in the saddle can stand

assaults on it: speeches, meetings and leagues cannot overthrow it. It follows that criticism has the right to be incessant, energetic, and even violent. The stability of the constitution makes it possible to allow the citizens complete freedom to check, verify and supervise its workings.[4]

Only the final sentence no longer rings true.

Unsurprisingly, the modern Establishment tends to be upper-middle-class and male. These men are also known as 'the Great and the Good', worthy, reliable, conservative. They are the men, and occasionally women, who are appointed to royal commissions, a handy way for governments to subject contentious issues to a snail's-pace inquiry for a couple of years, giving eventual birth to a report that no one reads and no one heeds. They are the people appointed to run quangos, to head up Oxford colleges. They are the people who remain behind the scenes and have no public voice – civil servants, senior army officers, industrialists and BBC governors. These individuals may not always agree with each other, but they work from the same assumptions. Each one is part of the glue that holds together the upper reaches of British society; they often come from the same backgrounds, attended the same schools and universities, join the same clubs, and hence speak the same language. They are unlikely to be bookmakers or butchers, or actors or artists; they *are* likely to be white.

They are protective of each other; when a corner of the social fabric is torn, they come running with a needle and thread: the reassuring radio interview, the trenchant opinion piece in a newspaper, the refusal to comment. Within government they protect themselves with a preposterous web of secrecy, invoking the Official Secrets Act to prevent light being shed on the way we are ruled. There is a presumption, profoundly undemocratic, that everything is secret unless a minister or civil servant deems otherwise. They are, in Enoch Powell's words, 'the power that need not speak its name'.[5] They are our governing class.

None the less the Establishment that Fairlie described has changed greatly, if only as a consequence of upward mobility. The men holding the powerful jobs in Britain are not necessarily patrician figures. Press barons are no longer barons, but businessmen from Australia and Canada who are aware of their power and eager to exploit it. The Establishment is very much London-based, since the capital radiates national and financial power, and it may be a very different grouping that holds sway in Birmingham or Newcastle. If their background has changed, their powers have not; and their evasion of democratic control is every bit as successful as it was in, say, 1962, when Kingsley Martin wrote:

> Probably the best definition of the Establishment is that it is that part of our government that has not been subjected to democratic control. It is the combined influence of persons who play a part in public life, though they have not been appointed on any public test of merit or election. More important still, they are not subject to dismissal by democratic process. They uphold a tradition and form a core of continuity in our institutions.[6]

Take the case of William Rees-Mogg, the antiquarian bookseller and former editor of *The Times*. Rees-Mogg is still a power in the land, contributes turgidly argumentative opinion pieces to his former newspaper and has a fine gift for wrong-headedness. With a life peerage under his belt, he can give further utterance to his views in the House of Lords. He was also appointed chairman of the Broadcasting Standards Council, an organization which allowed Rees-Mogg and his colleagues to wag their fingers at any programmes they disliked or disapproved of. If William Rees-Mogg is not the very model of an Establishment figure, then it is hard to know who would be.

The social and professional mix of the British Establishment is in marked contrast to, for instance, the French ruling class of technocrats, meritocratic but very powerful given the centralization of French government and bureaucracy. It is comprised principally of the *énarques*, graduates from France's top professional training colleges, notably the École Nationale d'Administration. The ENA has produced France's crack corps of administrators, bankers and politicians. Jacques Chirac and his three immediate predecessors as president attended ENA, as did the present French Prime Minister Alain Juppé. Juppé is also an *inspecteur des finances*, one of a curiously named group linking those who scored the highest marks of their year at ENA. It is rather as if those graduating with starred firsts from British universities formed a club entitled to various privileges, notably trouble-free movement between top jobs in the private and state sectors. For some time the *énarques* have been accused of arrogance and élitism, and no doubt the security of their high-powered lives within the centralized French bureaucracy isolates some of them from the rigours of daily life. Once it became apparent that some leading *énarques* were also self-serving and incompetent, French society shuddered under the impact as an entire ruling class became tainted. Institutions such as the Crédit Foncier bank, which collapsed in early 1997, were run, like most leading French banks, by *énarques*, which didn't prevent both it and the equally prestigious Crédit Lyonnais from losing vast sums of money in recent years. It is certainly arguable that the influence of the *énarques* has been exaggerated, but their cohorts still represent an establishment to which entry is gained by competitive examination, in stark contrast to the more amorphous British ruling class.

The British Establishment has undoubtedly altered in composition over recent years, but not in its nature. Ironically, the greatest assault on its influence came not from the radical left but from the radical right, in the ferocious form of Margaret Thatcher. The left-wing Labour bovver-boy Brian Sedgemore MP correctly perceived the Establishment as favouring a Britain that should be 'élitist, oligarchic, bureaucratic and secretive',[7] but it took a Tory to undermine it. Margaret Thatcher had little time for the sages of Whitehall, St James's or the City. She had none of the ingrained conservatism of right-wing Labour politicians such as James Callaghan. She was, to her credit, not deferential, and the Establishment depends on deference to maintain its quiet mystique.

She had no greater tolerance for the grandees in her own party, and clearly despised men such as Sir Ian Gilmour and Francis Pym. The Establishment she resented was cosy, safe, uncompetitive, self-perpetuating. It lacked dynamism, it distrusted change. Mrs Thatcher wanted to change Britain, and was not going to allow a bunch of clubmen, academics, lawyers and civil servants to stand in her way. Thatcher wanted a Britain that was dynamic, ruthless, competitive and assertive.

Curiously, despite her determination, not that much has changed. The Establishment has been shaken and stirred, but not stripped of its influence. She could not even rid her Cabinet of the patrician classes, and we have already seen how strongly the aristocracy remained entrenched in the Cabinets of both Thatcher and John Major.

Since the whole rationale behind a power-wielding Establishment is that it is secretive, a discreet network of nudges and winks, it is to be expected that its members should deny its very existence. Just because the Great and the Good tend to enjoy certain shared characteristics does not mean that they operate as a united front, pursuing sinister goals. None the less, those shared values, which can reasonably be interpreted as class solidarity, can cover up a multitude of sins. In 1979 the distinguished art historian Sir Anthony Blunt was revealed to have been a Russian spy. As Surveyor of the Queen's Pictures, Blunt was an archetypal Establishment figure. It is inconceivable that no one in his circle of acquaintance ever suspected what he had been up to. His fellow-spies, almost as patrician and even more disreputable, weren't rumbled either, until Philby, Maclean and Burgess fled to premature retirement in Moscow. Is it fanciful to suppose that their class, their education, their sophistication utterly blinded their colleagues and contemporaries? After all, Guy Burgess, stupendously drunk, stupendously homosexual, was not exactly known for his discretion. But they were all gentlemen, and gentlemen, by definition, couldn't be spying for Stalin.

The former editor of *The Times*, Simon Jenkins, has argued that the term is outmoded:

> The idea of an Establishment is simply not a helpful concept any more. It is an outsider's term. These days, it's the career path, not the access that counts. As chief whip of the governing party, you're a member of the Establishment; as soon as you're fired, you're not. It's the same with the prime minister. Birth, school, university, army service, residence in the southeast of England: it's all immaterial now.[8]

Well, not entirely. When you leave a position of influence, you do not necessarily hand in your cards at the gate, as Jenkins suggests. The former Labour minister and historian, Roy Jenkins, became President of the European Commission, Chancellor of Oxford University and a life peer, though few would dispute that he was well qualified for these dignities. Or take Norman St John Stevas, an agreeable dilettante whose budding ministerial career was torpedoed by his puckish sense of humour and reluctance to take himself (or the Prime Minister) too seriously. After his dismissal his career was by no means in ruins. In the decade or so since he left office, the honours, the quangos, the prestigious rewards have been piled on lavishly: a life peerage, the mastership of a Cambridge college, recognition as an expert on the monarchy and constitution, the chairmanship of a cosy quango. Indeed, an ex-minister would have to be very dim or unambitious to fail to capitalize on his experience: most of them, such as Norman Lamont and Douglas Hurd, drift on to the boards of banks at salaries three times their ministerial ones; there they are prized, one assumes, as much for their political contacts as for their managerial skills.

There is, it is true, a handful of individuals who wield enormous power who could not conceivably be described as members of any Establishment. Rupert Murdoch of News International is an obvious example. As an Australian he has no allegiance to the subtleties of British culture or to the British class system. Indeed, it is clear that the whole thing strikes him as slightly repugnant, if not downright stupid.

A member of the House of Lords shares Simon Jenkins's scepticism, and believes the Establishment is a thing of the past: 'Those who think of the Establishment as a kind of Kafkaesque inner ring, subtly disposing of immense power, are the victims of an illusion. True, in the Lords the other day the new Duke of Northumberland was being sworn in and asked to sign the book. And there was a general murmur of approval from dozens of people who all knew him, probably because they'd been at school with him. So there is this interconnection within the ruling classes, and perhaps I was witnessing the last echoes of it, but that is not the same as demonstrating that it wields any influence.'

However, as long as there is political patronage there will be an Establishment, a pool of potential appointees. The unelected sphere of governance is widening, not narrowing. There are burgeoning quangos and commissions to be staffed. Since the ability to offer patronage is one of the most powerful weapons at a prime minister's disposal, it is hardly surprising that prime ministers, of whatever political party, are reluctant to introduce any idea of accountability. Tony Benn gives a revealing account of an attempt to water down patronage during James Callaghan's government in 1978:

To GEN 119, a committee set up to consider a paper on public appointments written by Sir Douglas Allen before he left. Allen suggested that we issue nomination papers so that the appointments list could be broadened, but I wanted a system which included proper applications and selection boards. I recommended to Jim [Callaghan] that where an appointment has been made – say, Chairman of the Coal Board – there ought to be a confirmation procedure, as in the American Congress, where the relevant committee could hear evidence. I said there was a much broader question to consider here and that was patronage.

Jim said, 'I just sign every name put through to me.'

'Well, that's not surprising,' I told him. 'As Prime Minister, you must be flattened by the burden of your patronage. Harold Wilson appointed 103 Cabinet Ministers, 403 Ministers of State and junior Ministers, 243 peers, 26 chairmen of nationalised industries, 16 Chairmen of Royal Commissions and all the bishops and judges.'

'I don't find it a burden at all,' Jim replied.

I said, 'That's not the point. There is too much patronage. Why shouldn't people be able to apply for jobs in the public service? It's honourable work.'

In the end, proposals for a new system were turned down – even Allen's limited proposal for nominations.[9]

The civil service, especially the Foreign Office, was, until fairly recently, an enclave within the upper strata of British society. Senior civil servants were customarily elevated to the peerage, beginning with Lord Blachford in 1871. The nobility, it was assumed, had a particular gift for diplomacy, since they were accustomed from birth to mingling with the powerful and thus unlikely to be fazed in the presence of foreign potentates. These high-born first secretaries and ambassadors came with all the usual baggage: an Eton education, often; an Oxbridge degree, usually; the male sex and white skin, always. Moreover, until 1918 it was impossible to get by without a private income, since attachés deployed abroad were unpaid for two years and had to guarantee that they were receiving an annual income of at least £400.[10]

This is no longer the case, to be sure. The only one of my Cambridge friends to go into the Foreign Office was the product of a grammar school and the possessor of a fine Yorkshire accent. He has done well. I, who also wished to apply, did less well. Indeed, I was told I was ineligible to apply, on the grounds that my parents were foreign-born. That my father had fought in the British Army and that I was London-born cut no ice. Given the doubtful record, in terms of loyalty, of some of the Foreign Office's British-to-the-core recruits in the 1930s, I found all this quite rich, especially as this was only a few years before the appalling Henry Kissinger became US Secretary of State, even though he was German-born and sounded it.

Excluded from diplomatic service, I turned my sights on the administrative grades of the civil service. This organization raised no objections to my insufficient Britishness. I performed exceptionally well in the preliminary examinations, and was duly summoned to the two-day selection-board sessions in Savile Row, where we high-fliers would be subjected to further tests. I had a pleasant time composing papers on where a new prison should be sited, and I enjoyed the discussion groups we had with our examiners. The final session consisted of an interview with the former governor of an African colony. We had a jolly time, chatting away about opera and other mutual interests. If I had had my wits about me, I would have realized I was in trouble. When the results were published, I was not even listed. I had simply failed the whole procedure. I know precisely why: in a discussion group on the arms trade, I opposed selling weaponry to South Africa on moral grounds. It is not the job of a civil servant to express views on moral grounds. I was crossed off the list. In their own terms they were right to do so. I would have made an appalling civil servant.

My middle-class background and education equipped me perfectly for a career in the civil service. But it simply hadn't occurred to me that being a civil servant meant being a servant of the state, not a philosopher. Such positions call for virtues with which the upper middle class is heavily imbued: discretion, intelligence, subtlety, self-confidence, self-effacement.

Doctors, also middle-class figures, find themselves, often to their surprise, regarded as members of a controlling Establishment. The north London general practitioner Dr Ron Singer observed: 'The GP's role as a power broker is essential. Sometimes we're referred to as gatekeepers, but I'm not keen on that word as it implies that everybody has a place to which we can give them access, and that simply isn't so. But it is true that GPs know all the options available. We are required to interpret the world. I don't think there is any other professional group that, as a collective body, comes into contact with everybody.'

Another doctor pointed out: 'Middle-class patients see me as one of them. That makes our discourse collusive, as we have shared assumptions. With working-class and ethnic patients, especially blacks, their assumption tends to be that I am a representative of the Establishment. More and more the role of the GP is to provide access to a whole range of services and benefits, such as disability and mortage payments, prescriptions, pensions and housing. This involves putting questions and assessing qualifications. For many working-class patients this line of questioning is automatically seen as intrusive, and the more deprived people are the more defensive they are in responding to questions. It's not surprising, as I know they see me as a voice of the Establishment, of the bosses. It's a problem of trust. Many working-class or impoverished people assume there must be strings attached to such questions. A paternalistic role for the GP is somehow built into the system.'

Clubs, however, are emblems of class because that is what they are intended to be. They are by definition self-selecting, so that the membership resembles an extended family. Much of the satisfaction in belonging to a club stems from the fact that a group with the power to include or exclude has deliberated and opted for the former. Some clubs remain aristocratic and slightly raffish – White's, the Turf – while others, such as the Reform or the Athenaeum, attract academics, bishops, civil servants and intellectuals. The Garrick, famously, is the haunt of actors, writers and journalists; the Carlton, a gathering place for Conservative shock troops. In Scotland, where the upper classes form a more compact group, their interests and values are watched over by the Royal Company of Archers. The company's ceremonial role is to act as the sovereign's honorary bodyguard in Scotland, but in practice it forms an élite club composed of chiefs and lairds, and prominent members of respectable professions such as the law, banking and brewing.

Clubs don't inform one about class, because of their predictability. Aristocratic clubs elect new members in the image of the old; but it's no different at a Durham working men's club. All clubs have an element of snobbery, devising rules that heighten the sense of superiority enjoyed by their members. Dress codes, enforced with particular glee against non-members, who by definition have not subscribed to the club ethos, are an obvious example. The pleasures of exclusion are considerable but essentially pathetic.

One would imagine that the City of London, enlivened by the cut and thrust of high finance, would offer a complete contrast to the sedate certainties of the legal profession or the civil service. Yet central institutions such as the Bank of England are still a law unto themselves. Its governing body, the Court with its eighteen members – governor, deputy governor, four bank employees and twelve directors – is not so much appointed as summoned. Its structure does not appear to have changed very much since it was set up in 1694. Some years ago a token trade unionist supplemented the industrialists and merchant bankers who make up the bulk of the Court, but at the time of writing this is no longer the case. You can't apply to join the Court, and no interviews are conducted. Its membership is officially at the disposal of 10 Downing Street, but in practice the governor of the Bank has the greatest say in who is invited to join. The top echelons of the Bank have their own dining room – hardly unusual, except that they can eat for free, whereas more lowly employees have to pay up at a less luxurious canteen. The facilities for the directors were known scornfully as the Golden Trough, but I am assured it no longer exists, although there remain separate dining facilities. Until the 1970s junior employees of the Bank did not speak until spoken to.[11]

Yet the Bank of England, like much of the City, is not a traditional grazing ground for Oxbridge graduates. A public-school education was considered appropriate, but not necessarily a university degree. The atmosphere has long been formal and stiff, from the elaborate costumed gatekeepers in their eighteenth-century dress to the hierarchical structure of the Bank itself. The intense competitiveness of the City, especially since the late 1980s, has modified this formality and replaced it with a greater emphasis on professionalism and ability.

The City is one of the few places in Britain where a class-dominated structure seems to be crumbling. Even the merchant banks are no longer the domains of rich, upper-middle-class banking families. Some old families survive, such as the Hambros and the Rothschilds, although their banks have been fissured by internal disputes. Barings went down the plughole in a blaze of publicity thanks to the delinquency of one of its traders, Nick Leeson, and the presumed incompetence of the Barings directors. Other once distinguished names – Samuel Montagu, Morgan Grenfell, Hill Samuel – survive as letterheads only, since they are now owned by larger institutions. There is no longer much room in an increasingly international financial world for small, comfortable, intimate family banks. The view of Victor Sandelson in the late 1950s is now certainly outmoded: 'The very few, the *elite*, are not so much members of the Establishment because they have succeeded in the City; they have succeeded in the City because they are members of the Establishment.'[12]

The élite is being replaced by a more meritocratic structure. The ranks of stockbrokers are not closed to outsiders. In its heyday even syndicates at Lloyd's, for all their cachet, would take capital from any source. Outside the City company directors are a mixed bag. It was in 1974 that Philip Stanworth and Anthony Giddens wrote:

> Only a tiny minority [of company directors] are from a working class background, and some two thirds have been educated at a public school; of those who are graduates, about the same proportion as this attended Oxford and Cambridge. Moreover, there is a definite hierarchy according to size of firm: the larger the firm, normally the more marked the proportion of directors with public school and/or Oxbridge backgrounds ... Of our total population (460 chairmanships), there are no more than 5 cases in which chairmen can be definitely identified as working class by social origin.[13]

That would emphatically not be the case now. The Thatcher years in particular saw a broadening of the social base of the business world. The swift changes in retailing, the opening-up of new areas of business activity, such as computing and software development, that called for entrepreneurial verve, brought all manner of people into the business orbit. By 1993 half the chairmen of Britain's top companies were the products of the state educational system.[14] The annual list of Britain's five hundred richest individuals, published by the *Sunday Times*, contains growing numbers of self-made millionaires from the most modest backgrounds, who have made immense fortunes in such unfashionable industries as packaging, electronics, car parks, recording, bus companies, sportswear and carpets. This trend is likely to continue. There are, no doubt, companies where snobbishness and exclusiveness still count, but they are now a distinct minority.

In the City the livery companies remain a vestige of traditionalism, bastions of middle-class self-importance and, to be fair, charitable endeavour. Of course they were always dominated by the middle class, as a way of protecting and developing trades in medieval times. The companies are funded by legacies or, more recently, by property developments on some of the choice sites they own. Not all the companies are ancient; four were created as recently as 1977. A few retain some of their original functions: the Goldsmiths still monitor the quality of gold and silver, as they have done since the fourteenth century, and the Gunmakers still proof firearms.[15]

The seventeen thousand liverymen belonging to the ninety or so companies tend to be recognized movers and shakers in some corner of the City. Today you do not need to be a haberdasher to join the Haberdashers; the most likely entry point is through a family connection. There are different ways in which one can join a livery company: apprentices can be 'bound' to a master until the age of twenty-five and then adopted as freemen; children born after their father or mother was a freeman may apply; and sponsors may nominate those who have given service in some way to the company. The Haberdashers are trustees of seven schools, so long-serving teachers might be recruited in this way. The Haberdashers Company has 430 freemen. To progress to the next tier, that of liveryman, of which there are 320, you must pass an interview stage. Then you may progress by the same means to become an assistant, of which there are forty-four, and then master.

Naturally the whole set-up is immensely hierarchical. Twelve of the livery companies are grander than the others, and within each company there is a master, a few wardens, a clerk and a beadle. The school I attended was founded by the Haberdashers, and there was still a connection with the livery company, as every prize-giving day a bunch of elderly men would turn up swathed in heavy robes. Some wore big fur hats; another carried what looked like a mace. We pupils hadn't the remotest idea who these old buffers were, and their solemnity invariably provoked giggles.

Outlandish costume is also, astonishingly, a feature of the dispensation of justice. I remember watching the circuit judges parade through Trinity Great Court to their lodgings adjoining the Master's Lodge. It was both impressive and risible. The solemn procession of bewigged and berobed impersonators of Samuel Johnson led me to believe, rightly or wrongly, that the law was dominated by conservative, tradition-bound, pompous men who had all made the same progress through public school, ancient university and the Inns of Court. I dare say the legal profession is considerably less stuffy today than it was thirty years ago, but it is still far from user-friendly.

Until a few years ago, the judiciary was appointed from a small pool of barristers. Americans, in contrast, have a number of ways of appointing judges, including election. There is traffic between university law departments and the Bench, which is not the case in Britain. No one would claim that the American or European system is ideal, and there is no shortage of stupid and occasionally corrupt judges in America. But the net is cast more widely than in Britain, where the system of appointing judges has, until very recently, been arcane. In most European countries there are career judges, who have the merit of being precisely trained for the task.

In Britain barristers maintained their iron grip on the judiciary until 1994, successfully excluding solicitors from consideration. Barristers may pursue various routes as they gain experience and courtroom victories. They may apply to 'take silk' and join the select band of Queen's Counsels (about five hundred practising lawyers, representing approximately 10 per cent of the Bar), which signals that they are of outstanding ability and integrity, and thus entitled to the very high fees they charge.

Class can be a factor in the success of a barrister. Well over half of all QCs are Oxbridge graduates, which may be a tribute to their intellectual qualities more than a class indicator, but the structure of the Bar can favour the well-connected. Earnings are low while a barrister is beginning his or her career, and those with minimal resources may be deterred from pursuing a career at the Bar. One judge told me: 'The law isn't class-ridden, but the Bar can be. If you've been to a good school and a good university, it can help you get into good chambers, which you can define as chambers where there are people who can help advance your career and give you opportunities to shine. The drawback with this class element in the Bar is that some mediocrities do rather better than they should. But the best people will always rise to the top, whatever their background.'

A barrister who prefers glory and a quiet life to very hard work and very high fees may seek to become a circuit judge or high-court judge. Senior members of the legal profession scrutinize the names of applicants and deliver an oral report to the Lord Chancellor's department. If appointed, a judge can hope to rise to the dizzier heights of the Appeal Court (presently thirty-five lord justices, each automatic-ally entitled to a knighthood) and the eleven law lords, who sit in the House of Lords as a court of final appeal. Until a liberalization of the rules in 1994, judges were drawn from a small pool of successful barristers, so they tended to perpetuate shared values. Judges, in effect, chose other judges. In this respect the Lord Chancellor's department resembled a smoke-filled room in which deals were struck. The conservatism inherent in the system is reinforced by the late retirement age of seventy-five. It is almost impossible to remove a judge from the Bench once he has been appointed; misbehaviour on a quite staggering scale would be required.

At the lower level of the magistrates' courts, however, no legal qualifications are required in order to become a justice of the peace, and legally trained clerks are always on hand to advise JPs on points of law. The thirty thousand justices of the peace, also appointed by the Lord Chancellor, tend to be pillars of the community. In rural areas JPs were formerly appointed from the ranks of the local aristocracy and gentry, giving a patrician air to the administration of justice. The Lord Chancellor's department's booklet on becoming a magistrate stresses that although there was a time when 'JPs came from the higher social classes, this is far from the case today and magistrates are drawn from a broad cross-section of society'. Individuals are welcome to put their own names forward as potential JPs. JPs are unpaid, which has the benefit of limiting magistrates to the civic-minded, and the defect of limiting magistrates to the kinds of people with sufficient time or money to give up a certain number of hours a week for no pay. However, allowances are paid to cover travelling expenses and some of the financial loss incurred in the course of duty.

Under Lord Mackay as Lord Chancellor the door to the smoke-filled room has been cranked open. High-court judges are still appointed in mysterious ways, but the Lord Chancellor's department now advertises openings for district and circuit judges, and both solicitors and barristers with the requisite legal experience may apply. (Before 1994 the only path from the solicitor's office to the Bench was via a recordership, which is a part-time position.) Stipendiary magistrates can also apply to become circuit judges. A recorder in northern England told me: 'The judiciary does tend to be self-perpetuating. But that doesn't mean you can become a circuit judge because of class or influence alone, especially now that plenty of solicitors are joining the pool of potential judges. The whole system is becoming far more meritocratic.'

A senior QC doubts that the changes will make a great difference to the character of the judiciary. 'Top solicitors are more business managers than practising lawyers these days. They organize their offices and solicit clients and let the juniors get on with the actual work. Solicitors are expected to look after the interests of their clients, not to disappear for stints on the Bench. Everyone knows that the money's in the Bar, and high-fliers will always be drawn there. When I was a young lawyer I didn't begin my career as a barrister. There was a class element to it. I had no connections, so I became an academic lawyer and only later became a barrister. Today, though, the Bar is entirely merito-cratic. I belong to one of the top commercial chambers in the country. Young lawyers needn't even think of joining us if they haven't got a double first. We're not remotely interested in their social background.'

It cannot be denied that the judiciary has had an unrepresentative character. Most judges are over fifty and upper-middle-class, and the overwhelming majority are white and male. (Magistrates are drawn from a wider social circle and there is a much larger proportion of women on magistrates' benches.) That they share a similar social background and education does not necessarily mean that they are doggedly conservative in their social values; but it does mean that the judiciary is not typical of the community over which it passes judgement. Even if the judiciary is far more open-minded and rooted in the modern world than its passion for costumes and Latin phrases would suggest, it presents to witnesses, defendants and juries the impression that it represents a comfortable, conservative élite that is remote from the lives of those passing through the courtroom. A populace, if it is to retain respect for the law, should feel that it is being judged by its peers.

The stereotype of judges as remote and isolated figures is reinforced by judges' lodgings, which can be very grand indeed. A recorder justified the system to me, while acknowledging its defects: 'The assumption used to be that all circuit judges lived in London, so they had to be looked after when travelling around the country. Not all judges' lodgings are luxurious, but they are pretty comfortable. Judges are provided with butlers, cooks and a chauffeur. But that doesn't mean that judges live permanently in some ivory tower. When they're not actually on circuit, they're taking the Tube to work in London. On circuit they have to use lodgings even if they live near by. It's largely a problem of security, or avoiding staying in the same hotel as defendants, which can easily happen in a town with only one decent hotel. You can justify the system, but it's undeniably expensive to run.'

It is hard to imagine any justification for the finery and wiggery in which judges attire themselves. If the might and impartiality of the law has to be symbolized by wigs (£1600 each), pantaloons, silk tights and buckled shoes, then there is something wrong. Even in Victorian times, visitors to courtrooms were struck by the fancy-dress element. Alexander Herzen in 1853 noted 'the comicality of the medieval mise-en-scène' and described the judge as 'wearing a fur coat and something like a woman's dressing-gown'.[16] Twenty years earlier De Tocqueville was equally perplexed:

> Why are wigs retained in his assembly and on the Judge's Bench? I could just believe that one must appear in the House of Lords in medieval costume in order to show the unchanging continuity of the English constitution. But why from all our ancestors' clothes have they chosen the *wig* which brings no age of heroes to mind and which is neither ancient nor modern, dating only from the 18th century?[17]

If foreign visitors were baffled 150 years ago, they would be simply amazed, were they to be reincarnated and ushered into a modern courtroom, to find that little had changed.

The reliance on fancy dress and on arcane legal language impenetrable to laymen – circumlocutions such as 'pray it in aid' and '*per incuriam*' and the bowing and scraping before 'my lord' and 'Your Worship' – are mystifications, letting laymen know that they can never fully understand the complexities and subtleties of the law, nor rival the learning of those who practise it. David Pannick QC observes that

> lawyers do not dress up when dispensing justice in tribunals, or in magistrates' courts, or in High Court cases heard in private. The Law Lords, sitting in the highest court in the land, do not wear wigs and gowns, merely ordinary suits. Such proceedings presumably attain the requisite degree of dignity and majesty . . . without the presence of legal costume.[18]

It does appear, however, that the use of extensive Latin phraseology and arcane legal jargon is declining, at least in the courtroom.

This separation of the judiciary from those over whom it has power, and the monotony of its social composition, turns judges into a kind of caste. It may be mistaken to deduce that because many, perhaps most, judges share a similar background and values they are necessarily reactionary or even Conservative. Simon Lee, in a book about judges, rejects the assumption that

> because judges are old, white, rich, upper-middle-class, educated at public school and Oxbridge . . . they therefore all think in the same, Conservative and conservative way . . . The thesis does seem to assume, mistakenly, that judges have homogeneous views. It does seem to assume, mistakenly, that judges always agree with one another. It does seem to assume, mistakenly, that they always decide for the Conservative government.[19]

Point taken. But then he goes on to say: 'It does seem to assume, mistakenly, that the interests of the State, its moral welfare, the preservation of law and order and the protection of property rights are all dangerous values to be associated solely with the Conservatives.'[20]

Interests of the state? As opposed, perhaps, to the interests of the individual? Moral welfare? As defined by whom, using which standards of moral rectitude? This kind of list does seem to give the game away. In this sense, the judiciary does indeed represent the Establishment at its most protective. Nor is justice served by growing restrictions on eligibility for legal aid and the sharp increase in basic legal fees announced by the Lord Chancellor's department in January 1997, both of which make legal action more costly. Increasingly, the law is accessible only to the very poor and the reasonably well-off.

A recorder of my acquaintance insists: 'In twenty years I haven't encountered class prejudice on the Bench. In fact, I suspect that judges come down particularly hard on those, like Darius Guppy and Lord Blandford, who come from privileged backgrounds and thus have less excuse for their misdeeds. The problem is not so much unequal treatment by the courts on a supposed class basis as access to the law, which is increasingly restricted.'

In general, this may be true. But it was hard not to be stirred by an account of a trial that took place in May 1996:

A millionaire auctioneer had to be led to safety from an Old Bailey dock amid uproar yesterday after being cleared of causing the death of a charity worker by dangerous driving. Nicholas Bonham, a friend of the Prince of Wales, appeared stunned as the son and daughter of Eric Franklin, 59, hurled themselves at the dock, screaming 'You killed our Dad.'

Police were called to quell the disturbance as Mr Franklin's daughter ran from her seat in the public gallery, shouting, 'Scum, upper class scum. Bastards like him don't get justice.'

Bonham . . . was fined £500 and disqualified for 12 months for careless driving, which he had admitted . . . Before he was escorted from court, Steve Franklin added: 'We are the lower classes. The likes of us would be locked up.'[21]

The Church of England is formally linked to the state, yet seems ill at ease with its role as the Established Church. The sovereign is head of the Church of England and is therefore required to espouse Christian moral values. Since the Church has never been militant in drawing up, let alone enforcing, a moral code, this has rarely presented much of a problem – until recently, when Prince Charles's confession to adultery troubled clergymen who would, in the course of time, have to acknowledge him as head of their Church. In the eighteenth and nineteenth centuries the clergy were recruited in large part from the lesser echelons of the aristocracy and gentry, so links between the civil and the religious sectors were evident at local as well as symbolic levels. To this day patronage in the form of livings remains partially in the hands of what is left of the landed élite.

The automatic membership of the House of Lords enjoyed by bishops also blends secular and religious authority. There are no firm rules about which issues are open to comment from bishops, although they tend not to become embroiled in party political matters. But there is nothing to stop them doing so, and in January 1997 the Bishop of Edinburgh declared his support for the Labour Party.

The government of the day tends to be very sensitive to interventions by bishops, as was demonstrated by the frosty reception given to views expressed at various times by Robert Runcie while Archbishop of Canterbury and David Jenkins while Bishop of Durham. There's a fine line between moral judgement and political opinion, and government ministers are apt to stamp hard when they feel it has been crossed. Clearly some issues – homelessness, abortion, capital punishment – are inextricably moral and political. The Establishment of the Church of England makes this an especially sensitive issue.

Sensitive, but not, perhaps, of great importance. The authority of the Church of England is obviously diminishing. Britain is increasingly multi-cultural, and other religions proliferate; vast numbers of people are utterly unmoved by organized religions. Some still believe that the Church does, or should, speak as the moral voice of a Christian nation; others that such views carry less and less conviction. However, the civic role of the Church has arguably contributed to its moderation. Its need to be all things to all men has deterred its leaders from adopting extreme or authoritarian positions. This has been the strength as well as the weakness of the Church.

The Roman Catholics have had fewer qualms about speaking out forcefully on such matters as abortion. Cardinal Basil Hume, the perfect representative of the upper-middle-class brand of British Catholicism, does so with discreet fervour; his colleague Cardinal Thomas Winning of Glasgow, descended from the working-class stratum within Catholicism, has not been afraid to take his gloves off and give the Labour Party a bruising on the subject. British Catholicism has always been an odd marriage between aristocratic assurance – from the Duke of Norfolk downwards – and working-class loyalty.

The Establishment of the Church of England would appear to be an anomaly. It gives the Church, some argue, a voice and an authority it no longer earns. It also compels the Church to speak timidly for fear of disrupting the consensus it believes it should represent. At the same time it puts the Church at the mercy of political masters. Prime ministers such as Balfour, Lloyd George, Neville Chamberlain and Harold Wilson, none of whom adhered to the Church of England, none the less had the power to appoint bishops. Were Michael Howard to realize his ambition to become prime minister one day, then the Established Church would be in the bizarre, and indeed rather amusing, position of having its bishops chosen by a Jew. Naturally prime ministers take advice on such matters and do not exercise their power on a whim, but there is little to stop a prime minister opting for the candidate he or she finds politically congenial. It was only in 1976, under James Callaghan, that the procedure was adopted by which the

Crown Appointments Commission was invited to draw up a shortlist of two names.

One bishop was adamant that control over senior Church appointments remained in ecclesiastical hands. 'It's rubbish that the Prime Minister has powers of patronage over Church appointments. The shortlist is prepared by an ecclesiastical appointments commission stuffed with the clergy plus two secretaries. Of course its precise composition is a state secret, so don't ask me to reveal more, but this is the body that composes the shortlist, and it represents all factions of the Church.'

The Church is probably not greatly at ease with the political legacy of decades of Tory dogma. Given its moral duty to comfort the poor and the afflicted, it was in tune with the ideals of the welfare state. It seems inevitable, even under a Labour government, that the notion of the state's obligation to look after its weaker brethren will be seen as increasingly outmoded and financially burdensome. Hard-working priests, sometimes risking or losing their lives in inner-city areas virtually abandoned by the social services and educational authorities, may feel somewhat betrayed by the retreat of the state, but they are, in effect, resuming their traditional role. The Church of England could not possibly be described any longer as 'the Tory Party at prayer', as used to be the case. Many senior clerics have not hesitated to voice, albeit in guarded terms, their disquiet at policies that might, for example, increase unemployment.

The clergy certainly used to recruit heavily from the upper classes, but that is clearly no longer the case. From 1791 to 1830 nearly 60 per cent of all bishops were from landed backgrounds: 'The see of Durham was occupied successively by relatives of the Duke of Bridgewater, Lord Thurlow, and Lord Barrington.'[22] Jane Austen in *Mansfield Park* permitted her characters to voice dismay at the indolence of the clergy: 'A clergyman has nothing to do but be slovenly and selfish; read the newspaper, watch the weather, and quarrel with his wife. His curate does all the work, and the business of his own life is to dine.'[23]

Well into the present century, the Church was a career option for the more impoverished members of the élite. The overwhelming majority of bishops, until quite recently, were the products of public schools and Oxford and Cambridge colleges. In the late 1960s an acquaintance of mine consulted his Cambridge tutor about his uncertain career prospects. 'Have you', his tutor wondered, 'considered taking holy orders?' My friend replied that he did not actually believe in God. To which his tutor slowly responded: 'I do not see that as an insuperable obstacle.' It was not, I dare say, a response made with complete seriousness, but it was hard to tell. Today, I suspect, a career as a clergyman only attracts those with a firm religious vocation. The pay is lousy, the accommodation less and less tempting (even bishops are being discouraged from occupying their palaces), the status minimal.

If the Church of England has ceased to be the mouthpiece of Conservative values, it still seems rooted in middle-class England. The Church is as much a cultural as a religious institution. Thousands of people, myself included, take great pleasure from visiting country churches. They are not only repositories of architectural harmony and inspired craftsmanship; their engraved monuments and ancient cemeteries, their sidesmen's rosters and parish council notices, all tell a story about a particular community. Chanted psalms at Evensong or the wheezing of the organ accompanying the hymns are as quintessentially English as cricket or scones. Whereas Baptist chapels or Quaker meeting houses are fringe buildings, the parish church often occupies the heart of the village or the country town.

The bishop I interviewed conceded that the Church was often a repository of middle-class values: 'I suppose there is a sense in which the Church of England is middle-class. Certainly in rural areas it attracts the middle classes and the deferential, especially in places like Lincolnshire, which are still immersed in the fourteenth century. But it's not true in London, which is much more volatile.

'I recently confirmed a large number of people. They weren't attracted to the Church because we are middle-class or established. They come for spiritual reasons. For millions of people we are once again the church on the corner. We are free of fads and dogma, we embrace charismatics as well as traditionalists.'

None the less the connections, especially in the countryside, between the gentry and the Church of England are perpetuated through patronage. In 1831 well over half of all livings – 7268 out of 11,342 – in England were in the gift of the aristocracy and gentry.[24] Even today about one-sixth of all livings remain in the hands of the peerage, the gentry, Oxbridge and other colleges, and livery companies. Some individuals dispose of fifteen or more appointments. Some vacancies may be advertised; others offered as gifts to family members or acquaintances. Roy Perrott, writing in the 1960s, recalls the Yorkshire landowner Lord Middleton, who appointed fifty-two vicars in forty years. 'He once had to appoint five in one year. "I once advertised for a vicar in *Horse and Hound*," he told me. "The Archbishop found it a trifle unorthodox but I satisfied him it got me the right man." . . . On a religious level, noble patrons show a strong unanimity in what they are looking for – and that is, not too much "religion".[25]

Quentin Crewe recalls that he and his brother had the right to nominate six livings including the substantial parish of Nantwich in Cheshire.[26] Jessica Mitford's father, Lord Redesdale, shamelessly dictated terms to the clergy he controlled:

> We heard Farve explaining that he would personally choose the hymns to be sung at Sunday service. 'None of those damn' complicated foreign tunes. I'll give you a list of what's wanted . . .' He went on to say that the sermon must never take longer than ten minutes. There was little danger of running over time, as Farve made a practice of setting his stop-watch and signalling two minutes before the allotted time was up.[27]

One vicar I spoke to found the system of patronage defensible on the grounds that it avoids what he called 'a monochrome clergy': 'Appointment through the Crown tends to favour a safe pair of hands, as a vicar, once appointed, can't easily be dismissed. Patronage opens up the possibility of a more eccentric or individual choice.'

The bishop pointed out that patronage was far less extensive than it had once been despite the statistics: 'Many patrons have handed over their livings to the bishops. Others have retained their patronage in parishes close to their seat, while dispensing with those in more distant parts of the country. Oxbridge colleges are very formal about disposing of livings. Your old college, Trinity, advertises them, and there's no nepotism or granting of favours, I regret to say. Of course in the nineteenth century livings could be sold, just as lordships of the manor are put up for sale today. Nowadays most livings are at the disposal of colleges, special trusts and livery companies. A local patron may seek to choose a priest who will suit a particular locality, but most patrons will be more interested in seeing a task undertaken than a particular individual chosen. Patronage also imposes responsibilities, since pat-rons are responsible for the upkeep of the chancels of their churches.'

Although it seems to me there is a strong case for disestablishment, as a benefit to Church as well as state, it is not a burning issue. Perhaps the lessening relevance of the Church of England as a moral and cultural arbiter has made the argument arcane. The bishop, who concedes his views are conservative, was adamantly opposed:

'I have little patience with arguments for disestablishing the Church. The Church of England is not established in the sense that the Scandinavian church is established, making every priest a civil servant employed by the state. You have to remember that the Church of England predates the state, and its establishment is a recognition of that ancient historical role. By remaining established, the Church functions as an intermediate body between secular and spiritual, a body that has its own ancient memories.

'Because the Church is established doesn't mean that it can be used as an instrument of state oppression. Its very links to the secular world have helped to ensure that there has been no anti-clerical tradition in Britain. There has always been room for a Christian opposition that could assault the *status quo*. You will doubtless recall that not very long ago an Archbishop of Canterbury made the thoroughly Christian suggestion that we should remember in our prayers the Argentinian dead and bereaved as well as our own. This caused political embarrassment, but that did not deter the Archbishop from performing what he saw as his Christian duty.

'It's too simplistic to see the Church as a creature of political fashion. The Church has always recognized that its relationship to secular power is not supposed to be conflict-free. The Established Church has its own credentials and doesn't need to be validated by the government of the day. The Church is in many respects primitive and ancient, and its quirks and peculiarities serve the nation well by ensuring that no individual within it can run riot or impose faddishness upon the faithful.

'Disestablishment would not, as some maintain, free the Church, since the Church is already free. I would actually argue, therefore, that establishment is good for the health of our society. It enables spirituality to interconnect with all the facets of the life of our nation. It would be dangerous to dispense with this integrating role. A disestab-lished Church would soon dwindle into a ghetto of privatized pieties. Reflect on the fate of the Methodists.'

NINE

Officers and Gentlemen

He learned the arts of riding, fencing, gunnery,
And how to scale a fortress – or nunnery.
Lord Byron, *Don Juan*

Aristocracies originate on the battlefield. The possession of land, the provision of military services and troops in exchange for privileges, the glory that comes with victory, the royal conferral of titles and honours on great generals – all of these are bound up together. There are, quite simply, knights on the one hand and foot soldiers on the other; those who command and those who follow. So it is not surprising that the officer corps in most countries was drawn from the ruling class until professional armies developed in the late eighteenth and early nineteenth centuries.

In Britain it took a long time before anything like a professional army was formed. In Elizabethan times military companies were essentially mercenary organizations, run by commanders who operated as contractors. Much the same was true of most European armies in Renaissance times. There was no necessary connection between command and competence. In a system harking back to feudal times, the nobility were expected to provide regiments in times of war. Oliver Cromwell tried to organize military affairs on a more professional basis, creating major-generals with responsibilities for specific districts. But this affronted the local grandees, as professionalism will always offend the amateur. After the Restoration, military matters were returned to a more informal basis, with no single ministry responsible for the armed forces. Promotion, and thus the composition of the officer corps, was in the hands of the sovereign. To officers without private fortunes, the only way to secure promotion was by stepping into the shoes of a fellow-officer slain in battle.

The simplest way to become an officer in the late seventeenth century, as in Elizabethan times, was to purchase a commission. The price tag of a colonelcy in the Foot Guards in 1681 was £5100, a considerable sum, but less senior ranks were available for much less.[1] It was a ramshackle system, but it proved so lucrative to the state that it became entrenched. The complex organization of a regiment offered its officers ample opportunities for corruption, which generated the major part of their income.

Even in the early eighteenth century there was no professional army as such. Officers were racketeers or young men of independent wealth; their soldiers, whom they ruthlessly exploited, were little more than an ill-paid rabble. In 1769, one-third of all colonels of regiments were either peers or the sons of peers. In the Navy, where purchase did not operate, the proportion of aristocratic serving officers in 1800 was even higher than in the Army.[2] It was perhaps a heroic British trait to distrust the professional armies associated with autocratic European states such as Prussia and France, but the British armed forces were far from impressive. As the century progressed, however, the Army did acquire a more institutionalized basis while remaining under parliamentary control.

In Europe, there was an even closer relationship between the aristocracy and the Army. Prussia is the classic case; there the king himself often selected cadets from the ranks of the nobility. In eighteenth-century France proofs of nobility were required in order to qualify for officer status. Purchase was rife, but after 1758 conditions were laid down stipulating seven years' service before an officer could command a regiment, and promotion was based on recommendation by a commission of senior officers.[3]

In England purchase remained in force, offering a glamorous occupation to the upper classes, though it proved a counterproductive way to organize an efficient fighting force, as a graphic letter from the Duke of York's adjutant-general written during the Flemish campaigns of the 1790s makes clear:

That we have plundered the whole country is unquestionable; that we are the most undisciplined, the most ignorant, the worst provided army that ever took the field is equally certain: but we are not to blame for it . . . there is not a young man in the Army that cares one farthing whether his commanding officer, the brigadier or the commander-in-chief approves his conduct or not. His promotion depends not on their smiles or frowns. His friends [i.e. family] can give him a thousand pounds with which to go to the auction rooms in Charles Street and in a fortnight he becomes a captain. Out of fifteen regiments of cavalry and twenty-six of infantry which we have here, twenty-one are commanded literally by boys or idiots.[4]

All this was in marked contrast to the post-revolutionary French armies, whose officer corps was no longer drawn exclusively from the nobility. Napoleon's initial successes were not unrelated to the fact that military prowess and strategic skill determined rank in his armies. Yet after Napoleon's defeat at Waterloo, little changed in the British Army. There were piecemeal reforms, such as the ending of the purchase of commissions for boys as young as twelve. But well into the nineteenth century the Army remained as diffuse as before, shrinking to a band of fifty thousand in 1830, scattered about the country in relatively small groups. The gap between the rich, dedicated but inadequately trained officer corps and their underpaid, underfed, ill-housed troops remained as wide as ever. In 1830, 27 per cent of all officers were titled.[5] The foundation of a military college at Sandhurst in 1802 at least laid the basis for more professional training, despite the continuing narrowness of the social class from which officers were drawn.

By mid-century it became evident that the ramshackle organization masquerading as a modern army was inadequate to contemporary needs, which now included the servicing of an expanding empire. None the less purchase as a system lingered on, reflecting the continuing British reluctance to set up a standing army that would, or might, impinge upon or challenge the civil authorities.

It was the royal commission of 1856 that declared explicitly that purchase was 'vicious in principle, repugnant to the public sentiment of the present day . . . and irreconcilable with justice'. Its abolition was the crucial reform: with wealth rather than competence determining who occupied the higher ranks of the Army, and regiments functioning as private fiefdoms rather than as components of a national army, no structural reorganization was possible.

Gladstone's administration, and notably Edward Cardwell of the War Office, determined to get rid of purchase, which still offered the sole access into the officer corps of Guards and cavalry regiments. As there was no recruitment by purchase in the Navy, marines, artillery or engineers, its persistence elsewhere became increasingly anomalous. Cardwell's reforms were costly, as those who had purchased commissions had to be bought out, often at inflated prices. A colonel running a cavalry regiment could expect to receive £14,000, and the total bill was £7 million.[6] Despite fierce opposition from the House of Lords, Cardwell had his way and his Army Bill became law in 1871. Now army reorganization was at last possible, and military policy was brought under centralized political control. Twenty thousand men were added to the British Army, a decision which, together with the costs of re-equipment, set the nation back some £3 million.

Competitive examination replaced purchase, and promotion became based on competence and seniority alone. Sandhurst remained the principal training ground for infantry and cavalry officers, although engineers and gunners were trained at Woolwich until the two colleges were amalgamated in 1947. In the late nineteenth century the fees at Sandhurst were £150 a year, which enabled many middle-class professionals to launch their sons on military careers. For the most part commissions were sought by men from military families. In contrast, in Russia in 1912, nobles constituted 55 per cent of all commissioned officers.[7]

Although the tuition fees were far from exorbitant, an officer's life required a private income. Life in a regimental mess meant participation in sports such as polo, hunting and racing, in addition to other young men's pursuits such as gambling, dinners, drinking parties and balls. This kind of life could not be sustained on an officer's pay alone. Despite the abolition of purchase, the officer corps remained the preserve of the wealthy. Mess life encouraged snobbery and exclusivity but, since the system was funded by the participants rather than by the nation, there were few dissenting voices. The state of affairs was recognized in a report issued by a committee under Lord Stanley in 1903, which concluded that 'many otherwise entirely suitable candidates are precluded from entering the Service by no other consideration than the insufficiency of their private incomes'.[8] In the last years of the nineteenth century about one-half of all generals were still of aristocratic birth. As recently as 1912 over 40 per cent of officers were from either the peerage or the landed gentry.[9]

Lord Carnarvon described regimental life as he experienced it in India in 1917:

It was Mess kit each evening and dining off silver plate. We drank the health of the King and the pages of my boyhood reading came alive with every new experience. Our style of life was truly superb. Each bachelor cavalry officer had five indoor servants: a dogboy to keep his dog free from ticks, to help with the kit cleaning, to frighten away snakes and to walk before his master at night with a hurricane lamp; a man to sweep, clean and empty the latrine; a boy to fetch and carry water and prepare the morning and evening bath; a butler to stand behind his master's chair at meals to see he had everything he wanted; and a bearer responsible for cleaning and pressing the mountains of kit.[10]

Like so many 'traditional' institutions that we are encouraged to believe had their origins in ancient times, the gentlemanly, etiquette-ridden regimental mess was a Victorian creation. Under the purchase system, colonels of regiments ran them much as they pleased. Once the Army became a national institution, regimental life became more ordered: garrison towns such as Aldershot were created and flashy dress uniforms were designed for each regiment. The familiar county regiments were formed as recently as 1881 by Cardwell's successor Hugh Childers. The regimental traditions so fiercely defended in the 1980s and 1990s in the face of 'peace dividend' amalgamations and other defence cutbacks are in most cases barely a century old.

The sobering experience of the First World War changed little. Wartime conditions clearly didn't impinge on Lord Carnarvon and his fellow officers. Despite the existence of a few scholarships, rising fees at Sandhurst limited the intake to those from prosperous families. A substantial proportion of cadets continued to be the sons of serving officers, and their fees were discounted.

The novelist John Masters recalls his fellow cadets when he attended Sandhurst:

At the RMC there were scores of titles and heirs to titles . . . Their only common denominator was that few had any intention of permanently pursuing a military career. They were here on their way to spend a few years in the Guards or the cavalry, because it was traditional, or because it passed the time while they were waiting to inherit estates, or because it was their only hope of an introduction into decent society. One young lord was sent a bottle of brandy and half a dozen pints of champagne every week by the peer his father, and had, besides, an inordinate amount of pocket money. Another cadet, much higher in the peerage than the first, was as broke as – as a Masters . . .

At the other end of the social scale there were some young men from the lower-middle and working classes. These had enlisted in the ranks, had been selected as officer material and had been sent to the RMC as 'A' (for Army) cadets. Of course they varied as much as the aristocrats, the brewers or the bourgeoisie, but this was a considerable discovery to most of us, for we had never before been exposed to such people on equal terms.[11]

At this time the British Army was clearly more socially flexible than, say, the German Army. In 1932, just before Corporal Hitler came to power, almost half of all German cavalry officers and one-fifth of staff and infantry officers were drawn from the nobility.[12] World War II, no more than the previous world war, did not greatly alter the social composition of the British officer corps. The officers' mess of the Royal Marines, as described by Evelyn Waugh, made no concessions to wartime privations in December 1939: 'We drank out of splendid silver goblets; the food is absolutely excellent . . . lobster, fresh salmon, cold birds, hams, brawn . . . Afterwards several rounds of excellent vintage port.'[13]

Many potential recruits were given their first exposure to military *mores* at the cadet corps run at most public schools. My own school, scarcely a hotbed of militaristic values, had a cadet corps, although participation was not obligatory. Many of us preferred alternative activities such as play-reading or – well, nothing much at all. The corps was certainly taken seriously by those peculiar enough to join it. During the 1960s there were still teachers commanding the cadet corps who had had military, indeed wartime, experience. By the 1990s that was far less likely to be the case.

In 1997 there were 198 corps in private schools and forty-five in state schools. The system was boosted in January 1997 when the Conservative government announced it would be spending more money on cadet corps in order to expand a force that stood at 130,000. The then Defence Secretary, Michael Portillo, told Parliament: 'The cadets are a good thing because they help young people to develop self-discipline, self-motivation and qualities of leadership.'[14] Neither Mr Portillo nor John Major, who fervently supported the idea, had joined the cadet corps when they were at school. Portillo preferred Scouting, the future Prime Minister played cricket.[15] That did not seem to diminish their qualities of leadership.

As recently as the 1960s, military stereotypes of callow, drawling lieutenants, choleric, red-faced colonels and bluff portly generals did not seem far from the truth. I recall a school prize-giving when for some obscure reason the visiting speaker was an air vice-marshal (we were more accustomed to archbishops). This was a time when the Campaign for Nuclear Disarmament was attracting considerable popular support, and many of the boys listening to the officer were sporting the familiar black and white lapel badges. This absurd character chose the occasion to launch into a diatribe against CND and even uttered the words 'Trust in God and keep your powder dry.' The censorious air vice-marshal may have been a splendid officer and commander, but to us he seemed an antediluvian figure whom we mocked and impersonated for months after.

As Corelli Barnett – a writer hardly indifferent to military values – has pointed out:

> Alone among the officers of Western nations, the British officer was still a 'type' recognizably distinct from the industrial executive. The social gulf – the gulf in status – between the British officer and his NCOs and men equally remained far wider than in European or North American armies.[16]

He was writing about the 1960s, when this was unquestionably the case; clearly, this tendency is less marked thirty years on. Part of the problem was that the armed forces, as a career, could scarcely compete with industry or the professions. Young men with ambition and drive were not likely to turn to the Army or Navy as a career of first choice; and consequently the officer corps remained dominated by upper-class recruits, often of the dimmer sort. Nor did the coming to power in 1979 of the avowedly right-wing Margaret Thatcher prompt any re-emergence of military values, let alone a surge in recruitment.

Recruitment officers scoured state schools in an honourable attempt to broaden the social base of future officers, but with limited success.

By the 1980s not even the public schools with traditional links to Sandhurst or the RAF college at Cranwell – schools such as Eton and Wellington – were continuing to supply a steady stream of recruits. Until the mid-1950s Wellington could be counted on to supply about forty cadets a year to Sandhurst, with Eton not far behind. From the 1960s onwards that figure would dwindle. There were still links between public schools and the smartest of regiments, but they only accounted for a handful of officers. By the 1970s a steady proportion of officers had been promoted from the ranks, and at present the figure is about 20 per cent. Army schemes to allow recruits to combine a university education with a cadetship have enjoyed some success. None the less by the late 1980s only about 40 per cent of cadets at Sandhurst had attended state schools – a figure not markedly different from the intake of many Oxbridge colleges. Many of those who trained as officers did so only on short-service commissions, which by the late 1980s accounted for about three-quarters of recruits. Very few young men were considering army command as a long-term career.[17]

The reforms and cutbacks initiated in the 1980s meant that the comfortable career trajectory that a senior officer could take for granted twenty years earlier was in jeopardy. The chances of ending one's career as a brigadier or general occupying a spacious official house and enjoying numerous perks were shrinking.

In recent decades promotion among commissioned officers has been organized along meritocratic lines, with regular advances through the ranks until that of major is achieved at about thirty. Then the officer will spend time engaged in further study at the Staff College in Camberley and, if he performs well, can expect to be a lieutenant-colonel by his late thirties.

As in other spheres of British life, the royal presence may well be a stultifying force. When each June the sovereign presides, as titular head of the armed forces, over the ceremony known as Trooping the Colour, she reinforces all the stereotypes about a fancy-dress army obsessed with ritual and form. Everyone knows that Trooping the Colour has no military significance, but it is arguable that it has retrograde psychological force in presenting an image of the Army utterly disconnected from the realities of daily soldiering. The purpose of the ceremony is to instruct the soldiery in the look of their regimental colours so that they would know where to rally on the confusion of the battlefield. As a ritual it dates from 1755 and has evolved into an elaborate ceremonial review of the Household Division by the sovereign, who is its commander-in-chief. The occasional sight of horseback princesses taking the salute as colonels-in-chief of various regiments does not foster an image of the British armed forces as a professional modern fighting force.

However, one undoubted benefit of the association with the Crown is that the Army has (at any rate since 1688) been essentially apolitical. It is unlikely that its officers' messes harbour many ardent Labour Party supporters, but for all that the Army has never been perceived as partisan. Nor has there ever been, except in the looniest circles, any question of the armed forces intervening in political matters, though of course the senior officers lobby hard to maintain their status and their role. In this they do not differ from other groups within society that feel their influence is waning.

Social life in the Army revolves around the mess, whether the sergeants', the NCOs', or the officers'. Each operates its own codes of behaviour, stipulating appropriate dress and other matters of social convention. It was the expense of participating in the officers' mess that obliged officers until fairly recently to have a private income. Dress uniforms, the cost of regular formal dinners, subscriptions and miscellaneous mess bills can add up to a sizeable sum. Each regiment establishes the character and exclusivity of its own messes, so there are no hard and fast rules about cost. Those with aristocratic traditions tend to be more conservative, rowdy and expensive to run than those organized more as pleasant retreats from military preoccupations.

The formal officers' mess may soon be a thing of the past, and not only because the background of its members has become more varied. There is less leisure time than there used to be, and many officers would rather spend time with their families or girlfriends than subscribe to another expensive, bibulous dinner at the mess.

If the mystique of the aristocratic officer and the mess bedecked with silver and crystal survives anywhere, it is in the five Guards regiments and two cavalry regiments of the Household Division, the élite corps of 450 officers charged with the responsibility, among others, of guarding the sovereign. The Guards are divided among the Grenadier, Cold-stream, Scots, Irish and Welsh regiments, while the Household Cavalry is divided between the Life Guards and the Blues and Royals. Each regiment claims to have its own unique character, its own brand of superiority. The Grenadier, Coldstream and Scots Guards have heritage on their side, as they were all created during the Civil War. The Life Guards, the senior cavalry regiment, dating from 1674, are said to excel at show-jumping; the Blues and Royals are reputed to display unusual skill at polo. The Life Guards are marginally the more aristocratic of the two. There are also smart infantry regiments such as the Royal Green Jackets, whose officers are so self-confident that, according to an unreliable source, they don't even bother to rise when the loyal toast is proposed in the mess.

The ancient snobberies and legends are less pertinent today than they ever have been. It is no longer acceptable or prudent to recruit officers primarily on the basis of their family connections or backgrounds. None the less, the fact that these regiments all perform ceremonial duties does set them apart and heap glamour upon them. They do, of course, participate in more mundane military duties, serving just like any other troops in conflicts such as the Falklands War and military patrols in Northern Ireland. The Life Guards and the Blues and Royals are, most of the time, armoured combat units based in Germany as well as in Britain, and selected members of the regiments are dispatched to the Hyde Park Barracks for spells of ceremonial duty.

Yet the lingering importance of ceremonial – on such occasions as Trooping the Colour and providing escorts for members of the royal family during state visits – marks out the Household Division both as an élite group and as an anachronistic standard-bearer for the Army as a whole. The Household Cavalry in particular retains strong connections with the Court, through intermediaries such as the quaintly named Gold Sticks in Waiting and Silver Stick, who organize escorts and other ceremonial matters in conjunction with the Lord Chamberlain's office.

To concentrate one's attention too strongly on those sectors of the Army where class and social background are still factors, however contentious, is to ignore the undoubted fact that in most parts of the armed forces, hungry for able, conscientious servicemen whatever their background, class has become irrelevant. Armies have become professional and managerial, and technical skill will count for more than fine horsemanship. The antiquated rituals of the cavalry regiment's officers' mess may be perpetuated, but they will be seen as increasingly marginal.

TEN

The Identity Crisis of the Working Class

To an American, the English working classes are impressive because of their fundamental conservatism; they are not, as a whole, aggressive, and insolent like the same people in America.

T. S. Eliot, *Letters*, letter to Eleanor Hinkley, 23 March 1917

In April 1996 an absurd but telling row broke out. The ebullient John Prescott MP, then deputy leader of the Labour Party, observed, in responding to an interviewer: 'I can tell you, I'm pretty middle-class.' Since John Prescott lives in an eight-bedroom house in Hull and drives a large car, his remark seemed unexceptional. But in Britain any comment involving class is guaranteed to cause a furore, and this was no exception.

The debate was spiced up by the contribution of none other than John Prescott Senior, a former railway signalman. He was having none of it. 'He is the son of a railwayman and the grandson of a miner. How can he be anything other than working-class? John worked as a steward on ships serving drinks to well-to-do passengers. If that's not working class I cannot think what is. When I see him I shall ask him what he thinks he's playing at. He should be proud to be working-class.'[1]

The ensuing discussion focused on the burning question: Which of the two Johns had got it right? Much unnecessary newspaper space and interview time was wasted on the matter, since it was fairly obvious that both men were right because they were using 'class' in different senses.

Junior clearly found it hypocritical to place himself on the same social level as a rubbish collector or dockworker because he was relatively well-off and could, should he wish, take foreign holidays in Tuscany and go to smart restaurants. In other words, in terms of *occupation* Junior, the successful career politician, is decidedly middle-class. Senior, however, also has a point, since in terms of his background and upbringing and inherited values Junior is undoubtedly working-class. He comes from a working-class culture and, for all I know, still adheres to it, eschewing Siena for Skegness and claret for bitter.

Myself, I find Junior's candour refreshing. It used to be obligatory within the Labour movement to stress one's membership of or deep empathy with the working class. The management committee of my local Labour Party in the 1980s was, in class terms, a mixed bag, and included feminist firebrands, a *Times* social affairs correspondent, a *Sunday Times* print worker, a QC whose brother was a Tory MP, a touchie-feelie psychotherapist, the works. This reflected the constituency, which stretched from the noble terraces of South Kensington, up over the leafy lanes of Campden Hill, through trendy Notting Hill to the impoverished and ethnically jumbled council estates of North Kensington. Our committee deliberations often struck me as very class-conscious. Those urging us to recapture the commanding heights of the economy were middle-class acolytes of Tony Benn. We always listened respectfully to the rantings of some of the more paranoid representatives of the black and Asian communities, even when many of us knew perfectly well that they were talking nonsense.

The miners' strike of 1984 was an exceptionally bitter struggle, with a ruthless government deploying thousands of police to combat infringements such as secondary picketing. Our committee was routinely addressed by visiting miners, who reported on what was happening at their pits, their villages. Afterwards collections were taken for their families. I did occasionally voice my opinion that although one sympathized with the plight of miners in a declining industry, the fact was that National Union of Mineworkers president Arthur Scargill had called the strike at the worst possible moment, namely when coal stocks were high and there was no pressure on the government to make concessions. In short, the strike was doomed to failure. It not only failed, but it split the union, provoked irreparable rifts within mining families and communities, and did nothing to prevent pit closures.

But miners were icons, and their cause, in Labour circles, was sacrosanct. That they were being led to disaster by Scargill was apparent to anyone who analysed the situation, but to say so would have been construed as gross disloyalty. So sentiment overcame rationality. The miners' strike brought out the worst on all sides: the brutality of a government, the ineptitude of certain trade unionists and the sentimentality of the left. When the strike was over, the left may have felt warmer inside for having supported the miners, but at the end of the day, the pits were still closed.

Here was class as culture operating with a vengeance. Our sympathy for the miners' plight took no account of the fact that most were earning handsome salaries. Miners were heroes; their jobs were dangerous, their health imperilled, their dignity unimpeachable. Their almost mythic centrality to the Labour movement ensured that their class status was not blurred by their relative prosperity. Yet for most workers the distinction between class strata had become blurred by the higher incomes enjoyed by many within the skilled working classes.

That coalminers maintained, and exploited, their loyalty to their historic class did not alter the fact that the post-war years have seen an astonishing degree of fluidity between the classes. To pretend that one is predetermined by upbringing to remain allied to a particular class is either sentimentality or snobbery. During *l'affaire Prescott* a newspaper reporter canvassed opinion at the Hull Trades and Labour Club. 'We all know what he is,' declared one member, 'and we all know what he pretends to be. He's working-class but unfortunately he's gone up the ladder and got pretensions and forgotten.'[2]

Going up the ladder is what people have always done, and often aspire to do. The daughter of George Walker, as working-class a figure as you could possibly imagine, has, through adroit marriage, become a marchioness. She has adopted aristocratic style and *mores*, and her children, who have a smidgin of royal blood in their veins, will no doubt be brought up like the privileged lords and ladies they are. So it is hardly surprising that working-class people of more modest social aspiration manage to 'climb the ladder', in some cases inadvertently, to middle-class status.

Moreover the rise need not be a slow upward shuffle over generations; it can be swift. If the owner of a car dealership, a man of unimpeachable working-class origins, now earning £100,000 a year and living in a substantial detached house in north-east London and sending his children to private school, insists that he remains working-class, then there is no arguing against it. This is a cultural rather than occupational identification. If, on the other hand, a working-class youth starts his career by cutting hair in Deptford, and ten years later is the proprietor of a Mayfair salon and earns £200,000 a year; if that young man, by his choice of friends, home, car, restaurants and clothing, happily divorces himself from his working-class roots, then it would be absurd to insist that he remains working-class, when his way of life is entirely consistent with upper-middle-class status. Even the retention of a working-class accent would not pose an obstacle to his rise through the class system.

The substitution of low-paid work in service industries for low-paid manual labour does not mean the working classes have evaporated. A move into areas of employment such as catering, hotel night portering and hospital cleaning can hardly be seen as a progression into the middle classes. Even those in unequivocally middle-class occupations such as teaching may hesitate before opting to *define* themselves as middle-class. A specific occupation may be a necessary condition for *embourgeoisement*, but not a sufficient one. Other factors such as accent, lineage, upbringing and cultural assumptions will also play a part.

Whether or not one defines 'working-class' in terms of occupation – what some sociologists call 'stratum consciousness' – depends on your angle of vision. For the middle classes in particular, it is easier to consign certain occupations – road sweepers, bus drivers, miners, dockhands – to the working class. The workers themselves take a less focused view, and I have often heard the simplistic definition that the working class is composed of those who work by selling their labour. This classic Marxist definition has the advantage of being infinitely pliable, embracing not only the 'traditional' working-class occupations but employees of all kinds such as clerks and shopworkers.[3] None the less, more conventional and realistic appraisals of the class structure would place shopworkers and clerks within the lower middle class.

These somewhat arid attempts to produce strict definitions of what it means to be working-class ignore the subtle gradations within any class, especially when that class composes a single community. As Richard Hoggart pointed out some years ago:

> To isolate the working-classes in this rough way is not to forget the great number of differences, the subtle shades, the class distinctions,

within the working-class themselves. To the inhabitants there is a fine range of distinctions in prestige from street to street. Inside the single streets there are elaborate differences of status, of 'standing', between the houses themselves.[4]

Robert Roberts, early this century, divided working-class Salford into tradesmen, artisans, semi-skilled workers and various grades of unskilled labourers. He noted class divisions *within* the community. 'At all times there were naturally many unsnobbish people in the working class who remained indifferent to the social effects of affluence or poverty on those about them and who judged others not at all by their place and possessions. On the whole, though, most families were well aware of their position within the community.'[5] Although what Roberts calls the 'working-class caste structure' remained 'complete and inviolate' many families were eager to win social gains for their children if not for themselves:

> Very many families even in our 'low' district remained awesomely respectable over a lifetime. Despite poverty and appalling surroundings parents brought up their children to be decent, kindly and honourable and often lived long enough to see them occupy a higher place socially than they had ever known themselves: the greatest satisfaction of all.[6]

In her breezy way, Jilly Cooper makes a similar point, distinguishing between 'the Respectable and the Rough', between the skilled, semi-skilled and unskilled, between the working and the unemployed. The historian Harold Perkin elaborates:

> The most important distinction within the working class was that between the 'respectable' and the 'roughs'. This was not a horizontal division between the affluent and the poor; it was a diagonal frontier running right through the working class from top to bottom but taking in more at the top and progressively fewer towards the bottom.[7]

Income alone does not define class status, even though most people who would identify themselves as working-class would not be particularly well-off. My plumber tells me cheerfully about the Caribbean holiday from which he and his family have just returned, and I have little doubt that his income far exceeds mine. In the 1980s some miners and newspaper printers were earning up to £40,000 a year. Yet most of them would have shrunk from the suggestion that they were middle-class. Famous entertainers with working-class roots often retain their class purity despite their wealth. The muse of the Lancashire working classes, Gracie Fields, may have retired to Capri and a life of luxury and servants, but she remained identified as working-class, because her career might have suffered had she done otherwise. Class loyalty is valued among the working as among the upper classes.

The journalist Tony Parsons, who sentimentalized the aristocracy in his television series on class, did the same for the working class. He alighted on a dairy manager and his wife, a hospital administrator, as exemplars of the upwardly mobile working class. By picking a couple that most of us would regard as middle-class, whatever their background, Parsons could make some ironic points, pointing to this couple, with their two cars and daughters destined for private schools, as confirmation that 'The working class no longer know their place,' that cloth caps and whippets are a thing of the past, that 'they are living proof that the working class can't be patronized'. Except, that is, by the likes of Tony Parsons. He concluded: 'The future is bright but the future is middle-class,' which is merely a pat way of saying that bright people, from whatever background, aspire to better themselves. Parsons dug up a copybook working-class couple (no doubt still keen on the whippets and the cloth caps) on the deprived Blackwood Leys estate in Oxford, which inspired a spate of mournful clichés: 'We won't see their like again. The salt of the earth have been scattered to the winds.'

It is inevitable that many individuals have been elevated out of the traditional working class for the simple reason that the class is shrinking. It has always had its roots in manufacturing industries and in manual-labour occupations such as mining or dockworking. With all these industries in decline, and replaced by service industries mostly staffed by middle-class people, 'working-class' becomes increasingly a matter of subjective identification rather than a description of a body of workers. Skilled manual workers, according to Bob Worcester of the polling organization MORI, have shrunk from 33 per cent of the population in 1979 to 23 per cent in 1996.[8]

The militant as well as the sentimentalist left resist the notion that the working class is dwindling because in the past it was only through class solidarity that workers could improve their pay and conditions. To concede that the working-class bloc is disintegrating would be to admit that its power base is weakening. As recently as 1988 Tony Benn could still be writing in his diary: 'I think many intellectuals . . . look down on the working class and think of them as yobbos who read the *Sun* and go to football matches and cause trouble. They have none of that confidence in the working class which is what we need if we are going to mobilise sufficient strength to defeat the system.'[9] The notion that the working class still constitutes a bloc that can be mobilized against the capitalist system sounds positively quaint.

But for a general practitioner in north London such as Dr Ron Singer, there is no doubt that the working class is a real and identifiable entity, definable in socio-economic terms.

'Class is not about fixity, but reflects socio-economic status. I use a classic Marxist definition. There are two classes, based on ownership of property and means of production. I'm not particularly interested in this, as I believe the only point in labelling something is in order to do something about it. The merit of the Marxist position is that it's clear. Classifying people by profession or earnings is tricky, as, for example, it ignores women. Those moving into a different class may bring their culture with them but not their health determinants. Ethnicity plays a role too. Middle-class blacks can have the same status in health terms as working-class whites.

'Of course there are healthy, well-regulated working-class families. But that doesn't refute the statistical evidence, any more than the existence of octogenarians who've always smoked sixty a day doesn't refute the argument that smoking damages health. The fact is that there's a difference between most working-class families and middle-class people who can not only make informed choices but have the income to implement them.

'In cultural terms class is a way of life. But you also die according to your class. Class helps to determine when and how you die. There is still a vast gap in death rates between the two ends of the social spectrum. However, the main determinants of health, such as poverty, lie outside the remit of the NHS. We can only react to them.

'Introducing the market factor into medical care will have its ramifications in terms of class. In other words, the big issue in the future will be who gets what. That decision will often be class-based, as working-class people will be less likely to argue forcibly that they should benefit than will well-informed middle-class patients.'

Another London GP added: 'I can't recall many patients who clearly identify themselves with the working class in an overt way. I have a trade union official with very rigid views, and he often comes in for a moan about the health service. He knows I share much of his unease with recent developments, but he doesn't seem to realize that I have better things to do during surgery hours than moan about how awful the government is. He's a passive character, a class victim. He has no sense of how to alter the world he so disapproves of. It's easier to be a victim, then you don't have to take responsibility for your plight.

'I don't like to generalize, but the working-class patients seem more accepting of disability and sickness – probably because they encounter it so often.'

Upward mobility is nothing new. Prosperity fuels aspiration, not revolution. To read Marx and Engels one would imagine that the Victorian working classes were chafing at the bit, eager for revenge on their capitalist oppressors. William Cobbett observed in the 1820s: 'In the mean while I see, and I see it with pleasure, that the common people *know that they are ill used*; and that they cordially, most cordially, hate those who ill-treat them.'[10]

Yet grievance did not translate itself into militancy. Of course there were poweful reformist movements such as the Chartists that were indeed perceived as a threat to the established order, but once Chartism was defeated, as Gareth Stedman Jones has pointed out

> working people ceased to believe that they could shape society in their own image. Capitalism had become an immovable horizon . . . The main impetus of working-class activity now lay elsewhere. It was concentrated into trade unions, coops, friendly societies, all indicating a *de facto* recognition of the existing social order as the inevitable framework of action.[11]

Electoral reforms such as the Third Reform Act of 1884, which empowered a substantial proportion of working-class voters, and the Redistribution Act of the following year, both strengthened the hand of the working class and undermined any revolutionary impetus its more radical leaders were hoping to arouse.

Numerically, the Edwardian working class was immense. About three-quarters of the working population were manual workers. Yet numerical strength did not transform itself into political strength. Despite the activities of labour organizers, only about 15 per cent of the workforce of about 14 million persons were union members, since a substantial proportion of the working class did not toil in factories or workshops, but was employed in domestic service.

Some historians doubt whether this group was ever permeated by 'class consciousness':

> There was that vast and unnumbered race who worked for themselves or others on a catch-as-catch-can basis: vendors of all kinds, porters, carters, operators on the doubtful fringe like bookies' runners, and even to some extent, dockers. In many ways they had what we take to be the essential characteristics of the Edwardian working class, yet in them a collective sense of class was aetiolated almost to non-existence: on the contrary, a jaunty and attractive individualism was essential to their lives.[12]

McKibbin also postulates that the sheer physical demands of labour left little time or energy for political activity:

> The instability and overcrowding of lower working-class domestic life, however affectionate family relations were, discouraged a sense of collectivity . . . Poverty also implied mobility, which implied votelessness; the poorer the areas the more gross the disfranchisement . . . The somewhat monolithic appearance the working class presented to strangers concealed divisions which were at least as intense within communities as they were within the work-force. Communal loyalties were, therefore, ambiguous; they were inert rather than active, and defensive rather than aggressive.[13]

Robert Roberts corroborates this:

> Despite the increasing population, trade union membership during the first six years of the century had remained static at about two millions . . . At that time one had to work hard indeed to convince the unskilled labourer of the need for trade unions at all. An individualist, he was simply not interested in easing the common lot, but concerned entirely with improving his own.[14]

None the less, the political leadership of the working class was overwhelmingly drawn from that same class. Since the 1930s the

Labour Party has usually been led by upper-middle-class politicians such as Clement Attlee, Hugh Gaitskell, Michael Foot, John Smith and now Tony Blair. Harold Wilson, whatever his class origins, was an Oxford don. The handful of working-class leaders of the Labour Party, such as James Callaghan and Neil Kinnock, were not conspicuously successful. But almost all the pre-World War I Labour MPs were working-class, although a handful, including Ramsay MacDonald and Philip Snowden, were quite well educated. The nascent Labour Party did succeed in consolidating the various strands of working-class political consciousness; most importantly, it harnessed the organizational power of the unions. Robert Roberts recalls the day in 1924 when the constituency in which he lived returned a Labour MP for the first time. That night

> simple socialists like my mother wept for joy and we, the young, felt ourselves the heralds of a new age . . . Not only the poor but the working class as a whole had somehow grown far bolder and more articulate. A street discussion took progressively a more intelligent political turn; labourers were no longer grateful to their masters . . . Old deference died; no longer did the lower orders believe *en masse* that 'class' came as natural 'as knots in wood'.[15]

Yet despite all the rhetoric, the Labour Party, and even the trade union movement, were not actively confrontational. There were exceptional moments, notably the General Strike of 1926, arguably the last expression of class struggle in modern British history. But the overall tenor of the Labour movement was not revolutionary, even in the face of repressive action. Richard Hoggart fine-tunes the point:

> There has been plenty of violent action by the authorities in England, especially during the first half of the 19th century. But on the whole, and particularly in this century, the sense of 'Them' among working-class people is not of a violent or harsh thing. This is not the 'them' of some European proletariats, of secret police, open brutality and sudden disappearances. Yet there exists, with some reason, a feeling among working-class people that they are often at a disadvantage, that the law is in some things readier against them than against others, and that petty laws weigh more heavily against them than against some other groups.[16]

This last point is confirmed by a jaunty portrayal of working-class attitudes published in 1911:

> The police do effectively divide the country into two classes, an upper and a lower – those above them, whose servants they are, and those beneath them, who are under their thumb . . . Unless the police have a thoroughly good case, it does not do for them to proceed against those who can hire good lawyers in defence, and furthermore retaliate. Gentry, therefore, are not arrested on suspicion; but working people are. The police are charged not only with the prevention and detection of crime among them, as among other people, but with the enforcement of a whole mass of petty enactments, which are little more than social regulations bearing almost entirely on working-class life. At the bidding of one class, they attempt to impose a certain social discipline on another.[17]

The Labour movement was not only shy of revolutionary action, it was scarcely even ideological. David Martin and Colin Crouch summarized its tone well:

> It is quite wrong to suggest that English socialism derives from a betrayal of proletarian revolution by its leadership: that leadership is the direct expression of a cultural tradition compounded of liberalism, religious dissent, and a pragmatic temper that rejects all total ideologies and utopian changes for whatever localized gains are to be had.[18]

It was different elsewhere in Europe. The Catalonian workers' movement in the 1930s was split between factions, variously allied to Soviet Communism or anarchism and other ideologies. Communism attracted the support of millions in post-war France and Italy; but not in Britain, where, for instance, the newspaper of the Communist Party, the *Daily Worker*, achieved modest sales, more because of its sports coverage than because of its hard-line stance. Support for the party itself was statistically insignificant. Trotskyist tendencies and other splinter groups have had no serious impact on British political life, even on the left wing of Labour Party politics.

In 1956 the Labour intellectual Anthony Crosland noted the discrepancy between rhetoric and action:

Some militants still occasionally speak in the accents of the class-war; but their social attitudes often belie their words. It is characteristic of a genuine class-war period, when the masses are rebelling against real oppression and exploitation, that the leaders identify themselves with their followers, not only intellectually and emotionally, but in their private and social lives. They embrace a severe austerity, decline to mix socially with the governing class, and dedicate their entire lives, their hours of leisure as well as of work, to the prosecution of the struggle. The more amiable and sociable attitude of contemporary leaders, even on the 'militant' wing of the Left, is a significant sign of the change of mood – and, of course, a well-justified symbol of greater strength and self-confidence. And so far as the rank-and-file are concerned, their attitude is described in a prophetic remark of Engels: 'the masses have got damned lethargic after such long prosperity'. But unlike him, not everybody would consider this a bad thing.[19]

In 1980 the former prime minister James Callaghan told a parliamentary Labour Party meeting:

I have never been ashamed of being a Party man . . . We joined it out of our experience. We didn't express that in class terms, we joined the Party because of inequality – the theory came later. The Workers' Educational Association, the TUC and the National Council of Colleges opened my eyes to Harold Laski, to G. D. H. Cole, to the Webbs, to Tawney, to Shaw, to Wells, and to Brailsford.[20]

Indeed, Labour politics have always been pragmatic. Some of the party's right-wing politicians even argued that too close association with the working class could actually jeopardize electoral success. Using language strikingly similar to that which would be employed by 'New Labour' politicians in the 1990s, Christopher Mayhew, admittedly an atypical figure, argued at a party meeting in 1959 'that the image of the Party at present was that it is the party of the working class, of the underdog and of nationalization. This was an image that would get us an ever declining number of votes. We must dissociate the Labour Party from this narrow class connection.'[21] It would soon come about. After the 1966 general election which returned a large Labour majority, Richard Crossman noted that the new intake was overwhelmingly middle-class: 'Of fifty new Labour MPs only four or five are genuine trade unionists; the rest are lawyers, scientists, teachers in technical colleges – overwhelmingly intellectuals.'[22]

The ideological inertia of the British working class could be irritating to those who hoped for a more radical assertion of socialist ideals. R. H. Tawney wrote in 1931:

> What the working-class movement stands for is obviously the ideal of social justice and solidarity, as a corrective to the exaggerated emphasis on individual advancement through the acquisition of wealth. It is a faith in the possibility of a society in which a higher value will be set on human beings, and lower value on money and economic power, when money and power do not serve human ends. But that movement is liable, like all of us, to fall at times below itself, and to forget its mission. When it does so, what it is apt to desire is not a social order of a different kind, in which money and economic power will no longer be the criterion of achievement, but a social order of the same kind, in which money and economic power will be somewhat differently distributed.[23]

Seventeen years earlier Tawney had upbraided the working classes for aiming at comfort rather than rights, but perhaps an ardent trade unionist might have responded that you can't eat rights.[24]

In terms of *mores* and culture, many working-class leaders were profoundly conservative. James Callaghan, George Brown and Ray Gunter may have represented their working-class constituencies (whether as union officials or MPs) admirably; radicals they were not. In 1962 Anthony Crosland expressed his exasperation with union obduracy when he wrote:

> The other special factor is the extreme conservatism . . . of the British working-class movement. The resistance to change (as I also found when trying to propagate radical reforms inside the Cooperative Movement) is sometimes stupendous. It is surely depressing, and would be true of no other country in the world, that a proposal to re-write a forty-year-old constitution should arouse such acute suspicion and resentment, even amongst some who like to think of themselves as radical. Traditionalism in Britain is no monopoly of the Right.[25]

Labour Party reformers of the 1990s will no doubt echo his words to the letter.

Trade union leaders may weary of being referred to as dinosaurs, but it remains true of some of them that their attitudes to race, gender and sexual liberation are entirely outmoded. Tony Benn encountered working-class reactionaries when speaking in 1980 to some train drivers.

> I talked to a couple of ASLEF drivers who were full of anti-working-class stories about scroungers on the welfare state, Pakistanis queuing up for supplementary benefit, etc. The press do a brilliant job. Here were two old trade-unionists who had been on the railways for forty-odd years, near to retirement, pumping what they had read in the *Mirror* and the *Sun* and the *Mail* and the *Express*.[26]

To Benn it was inconceivable that train drivers could arrive at their unpalatable views without having been brainwashed. It is part of the incorrigible sentimentality of the middle-class left to refuse to take on board that racist views are not the monopoly of the Conservative far right.

In the 1980s, though it pains me to write it, the Thatcherite Conservatives were more in touch with working-class aspirations than their traditional champions on the left. The old certainties were crumbling: union solidarity, the manufacturing sector, the contract with the welfare state, the acceptance of notions such as that home ownership and foreign holidays were middle-class preoccupations, and so forth. Labour policies seemed rooted in the past, while the Conservatives promoted diversity, 'choice' and materialism. It was all very well for traditional Labour politicians such as Dennis Skinner, Tony Benn and Margaret Beckett to defend socialist values and the interests of the working class, but their fervour no longer mattered in a world in which the organized working class was fragmenting. It took a new generation of Labour MPs, the often reviled 'Modernizers', to realize that the traditional Labour Party was appealing to an ever diminishing constituency, and that new ground had to be occupied if there were to be an electorally enticing alternative to the crude self-interest of modern Conservatism. The process has involved the near-destruction of 'Old Labour', and it is not hard to see why it has provoked such bitterness. But Britain has been kicked and manhandled into new territory, and Labour had to choose between gradual self-destruction or accepting that the terms of the debate had been changed utterly.

ELEVEN

Broken Biscuits Sold Here

As a rule there is no one so out of sympathy with working-class life as
the man who has just climbed above it.
                    Stephen Reynolds and Bob and Tom Woolley, *Seems So!: A*
                                Working-Class View of Politics, 1911

Accounts of working-class upbringings such as Richard Hoggart's, and
earlier portrayals such as Florence Bell's account of Middlesbrough in
At the Works, give an impression of working-class culture as somehow
unitary. Of course there were the gradations and subtleties that
Hoggart himself refers to, but there was always, as it were, a common
language. Physical proximity played its part. You may have disliked or
envied your neighbour, but you couldn't help knowing who your
neighbour was. Recreational activities helped unite communities,
whether games of football in the streets of the East End, or Friday-
night drinking sessions in the pub. The best of these descriptive writers,
however, take great pains not to sentimentalize the working classes, and
do not make light of the hardships, nor of the suffering wrought by
drink, gambling and illness.

The essentially unitary character of working-class life was cultural
more than class-conscious. To be class-based is not the same as to be
class-obsessed:

> Because manual workers chose to wear cloth caps and support
> football teams it does not follow that they saw the social order in
> terms of class ... It is perfectly possible to have a culture which can
> be defined as 'working class' but yet for the consciousness associated
> with this culture to have little or nothing to do with class.[1]

The institutional basis of working-class culture was always strong. It was often political – trade unions, co-operative societies, Labour clubs – but also encompassed sports and games, the pub and the music hall, the football match and the racecourse. According to some historians it was not until the early twentieth century that middle-class observers were even prepared to acknowledge that there was such a thing as working-class culture: 'The terms, "working classes" or "toiling masses" carried no positive cultural connotations, for they signified *ir*religion, *in*temperance, *im*providence or *im*morality. Indeed, it was often difficult for these strangers from the "civilized" world to discover where the "working classes" ended and where the "dangerous classes" began.'[2]

The political bias was often to the left – socialism – yet this did not necessarily preclude a social conservatism, a love of empire and a suspicion of foreigners. Education was both welcomed and feared. Victorian reformers such as the Tory John Ruskin and the socialist William Morris were active in workers' education, but the working classes often resented those who sought material benefits from that education. This attitude has persisted until quite recently. At my Cambridge college in the 1960s there were one or two students from unequivocally proletarian backgrounds who were unable to cope, I assume, with the social demands of Cambridge, for which nothing in their earlier life had prepared them. They either dropped out or faded into invisibility. Of course they were in a minority, yet for many there must have been a yawning gap between the closeness and shared assumptions of, say, a working-class community in the north-west and the cool, aristocratic, upper-middle-class ambience of a smart Cambridge college, with its servants and rituals.

Who knows what subtle pressures were imposed on those unhappy students by their conservative communities, where intellectual gifts may well have been viewed with suspicion, and the slightest social pretensions squashed: 'Talking posh', 'giving yourself airs' or having 'a lah-di-dah accent' were unacceptable. Such attitudes, understandable though they were, encouraged class inertia. Indeed, working-class culture has become ossified in the sense that it is not always easy to distinguish a genuine survival from a bogus revival. Yesterday's Welsh pit community is today's heritage centre.

What is one to make of Pearly Queens, or attempts to revive the music-hall tradition by aficionados such as Roy Hudd? I recall the genuine article, dimly, as transmitted in radio programmes such as Wilfred Pickles' *Have a Go* and *Workers' Playtime*. They vanished decades ago, and their very titles make one squirm today. Yet their cheerful coarseness attracted a huge following, even though their humour always eluded me. The humour has survived, in the form of comics such as the late Les Dawson, Bernard Manning and Jim Davidson, only it finds limited acceptance because of its parochialism, jingoism and (sometimes) racism.

The music hall, observes Gareth Stedman Jones, 'appealed to the London working class because it was both escapist *and yet* strongly rooted in the realities of working-class life . . . Working-class music hall was conservative in the sense that it accepted class divisions and the distribution of wealth as part of the natural order of things.'[3] That, emphatically, is no longer the case, so the revival of the music hall is probably, and inoffensively, an act of sentimentality. Other features of working-class life are probably doomed to extinction, notably allotments. There were 1,500,000 during World War II; today only a quarter survive, since much of the land has become too valuable to be preserved for hobby agriculture.[4]

Some features of working-class culture are less obvious, but at one time were no less deeply rooted. Childbirth and child-rearing were tackled in a different way in working-class households; as recently as 1963 sociologists could devote a book-length analysis to the subject. The average age at which mothers gave birth to their first child, the incidence and duration of breast-feeding, toilet training – all these matters seemed to follow class-based patterns. Because breast-feeding provides free milk, one might have supposed its popularity to have been greater among working-class than middle-class women. Not so. The authors deliberate:

> The answer seems to lie in the feelings and attitudes of mothers towards breast feeding, rather than in economic considerations. The wives of professional and other white-collar workers appear to be strongly influenced by the demands of 'duty' and 'principle'; and breast feeding, often referred to in books and magazines as 'baby's birthright', has the flavour of a moral obligation that they ignore only at the risk of painful guilt feelings. It is 'natural' to breast feed, therefore it must be right . . . One major reason for giving up breast

feeding was the mother's reluctance to expose her breast, even within the family circle. Here again, our impression is that there is a marked class difference in attitude. The middle-class mothers whom we interviewed seemed to be much less prudish in this respect than were mothers from lower down the social scale.[5]

Although sociological research does reveal pronounced cultural differences of this kind, sweeping generalizations are dangerous. Jilly Cooper indulges in them with such zest that one barely pauses to consider whether they are true:

> Because they dislike the management, the working classes don't like people saving their money or getting on through hard work. They put a premium on enjoying pleasure now, drinking their wages, for example, or blowing the whole lot on a new colour telly. Traditionally the only legitimate way to make a lot of money was to win it. Hence the addiction to gambling, football pools, racing, bingo and the dogs.[6]

This somewhat patronizing sketch is, I admit, recognizable, but it now seems like pure stereotyping, especially after a decade of Thatcherism. Margaret Thatcher did manage to persuade the working classes that they could free themselves from the stereotypes of their culture. For a start, they could make that crucial leap into middleclassdom by buying their own home. The lower classes were no longer expected to know their place; they were encouraged to claw their way out of it. With Thatcher's denigration of communal responsibility, the greed long practised by the middle and upper classes was now acceptable among all orders.

The decline of working-class culture began, of course, much earlier. Indeed, the introduction of the welfare state greatly levelled the distinction between the classes, by offering security to all. Robert Roberts recalls the chronic insecurity of the Edwardian working class: 'Men harboured a dread of sickness, debt, loss of status; above all, of losing a job, which could bring all other evils fast in train . . . Fear was the leitmotif of their lives, dulled only now and then by the Dutch courage gained from drunkenness.'[7]

The introduction of the welfare state meant that the poorer classes gained far more than they paid into the system – as was intended.

Pensions, hospital care, libraries, clean water and good education were no longer the preserve of those who could pay for them. Modern communications also evened out class distinctions: everybody listened to the same radio programmes, and later everybody watched the same television programmes. Taxation was used not to redistribute income, but to distribute essential social services evenly among the population.

Thus the welfare state, and the increasing freedom of working-class women to go out to work, enriched the working classes. Televisions, cars, foreign holidays and other delights became commonplace. Less and less was class related to income. The factory worker or the printer might well bring home twice as much money as the schoolteacher or local government officer. The acquisition of previously unaffordable material possessions was not an expression of striving to enter a higher social class, but a simple act of hedonism: a wish to make daily life more enjoyable and to ease physical hardships.

Harold Perkin notes:

A team of sociologists who studied a group of affluent workers in the motor, ball bearing and chemical industries in the then thriving town of Luton in the 1960s found that, on the contrary, despite their enjoyment of material gains such as house and car ownership and foreign holidays, they were just as solidaristic in support of the trade unions as more traditional workers.[8]

Thatcher changed all that, and the principal beneficiaries of her invitation to join the scramble for wealth – exemplified by 'Essex Man' and his consort – threw themselves at her feet. But their loyalty proved short-lived. When by 1990 the dream had begun to turn sour, they were loudest in their protestations, as though the two-car garage and the fortnight in Majorca had become theirs by right. Whether upward mobility had turned a segment of the working class into the middle class is, in the end, a matter of self-identification. With two incomes in the 1980s, it was not difficult to adopt an essentially middle-class way of life. But if that same family, a decade later, had experienced job loss, negative equity and ever rising bills, they might question whether income and spending alone were sufficient to alter class identification and allegiance within a matter of years.

It does appear that the Thatcher years made class solidarity obsolete. The welfare state provided a structure of benefits and a minimum level of economic security that obviated the need for solidarity and co-operation, while Thatcherism extolled individualism at the expense of community. Solidarity still exists, but among interest groups – abortion campaigners, gay activists, anti-roads lobbyists – rather than classes. Even thirty years ago the political scientist Eric Nordlinger was arguing that as far as most workers were concerned the notion of solidarity had no political, social or economic meaning.[9] In British trade unions sectionalism – which had its origins in ancient distinctions between craft, industrial and general unions – often seemed more important than solidarity, leading to demarcation disputes and the multiplication of unions within a single trade.

Thatcher won many working-class votes, but this in itself was not novel. Working-class Tories were assiduously wooed by Benjamin Disraeli, and there have always been Conservative trade unionists. In the 1960s it was estimated that one-third of manual workers voted Conservative. This was partially the politics of deference, of respect for one's betters, of assuming that an individual of breeding, education and wealth must be better suited to rule than someone of more humble origins. The political scientists Robert McKenzie and Allan Silver concluded after considerable research in the mid-1960s:

> Even in the highly industrialized urban areas from which this sample is drawn, it appears that political and social deference of working class people to the elite predisposes a significant part of the working class to vote for the Conservative party ... as the party of their natural social superiors who are, by inheritance, tradition, and training, better equipped to govern than men who have risen from the working class itself.[10]

But deference is not the same as submissiveness: 'Deferentials tend to assume that there is a certain reciprocity in the relationship: that those of elite origins will behave in a way that merits respect (and hence deference).'[11]

Tony Benn takes a more robust view. 'Every country's got people who think they're better than anybody else but it's only in Britain that most people can be persuaded they're not as good as somebody else. It's inseparable from the monarchy, the Lords, the honours list. We are absolutely an hierarchical society and that – very, very cleverly – is used to defuse class. You make the Communist Frank Chapple a lord. The

British ruling class withdraw under pressure and co-opt the leaders of the revolutionary movements. Then when there's a pause you recover the territory you've lost. The whole gain of the post-war period is now being taken away.'[12]

The Labour Party was always class-based, while the Conservatives (although you are at liberty not to believe them) present themselves as a party of nation rather than class. Eric Nordlinger pondered the passivity of so many working-class voters, and concluded:

> The evidence then indicates that notwithstanding feelings of personal political powerlessness on the part of more than one-quarter of the workers, these workers are not politically alienated. Rather, it seems as if they accept their impotence as an inevitable consequence of the individual's weak position and limited resources in contrast to the resources and complexity of the government.[13]

It is hard to say whether the essentially unideological nature of the trade union movement was, in the long term, a benefit or a liability. Given the Labour affiliations of many unions, it has always suited the Conservatives to demonize British trade unionism. The truth is, however, that until quite recently trade unionism was organizationally srong and ideologically feeble. As long ago as 1872 Hippolyte Taine was observing:

> It is a remarkable fact that these unions do not deviate from their original object: they have no other aim but wage increases, and do not think in terms of seizing political power, which they most certainly would do in France. They are in no way political, are not even social; they envisage no utopias, do not dream of reforming society, putting down usury, abolishing the hereditary principle, of equal pay for all or of making every individual a partner in the State.[14]

In the century that followed, little changed.

Graham Parkin sits alone in a small terraced house in the Derbyshire village of Bramley Vale, facing the allotments and the pigeon huts. He grew up here, left school at fifteen, worked down the local pit, and also worked for a builder's merchant. In 1974 he started attending the Co-operative College, and then went to Hull University to study economics. He does not look in the best of health. Indeed, a bout of encephalitis in 1984 nearly killed him. But he recovered, and since 1985 has represented a local district as a Labour councillor.

'This is a working-class community, but even within it there's a consciousness of those who are better-off. Most of the miners lived in Dole Lea, where I also grew up. Many of the pit gaffers lived in Bramley Vale, but up the hill is the village of Glapwell, where people think they're superior because they live higher up. When I was a boy we would never walk in front of the gaffers' houses. Just wouldn't.

'The pit – the colliery entrance is just across the road from Bramley Vale – closed in 1974. Some of the men went to other collieries or found work elsewhere. But for many miners it was the end of their working life. Unemployment here is still about seventeen per cent. There are people here in their thirties who have never worked, and their kids have no future either. It's not that they don't want to work. I know families that only buy food once a fortnight when the giro comes. They have no luxuries. Unemployment causes a lot of stress and many health problems.'

The local collieries at Williamthorpe and Holmewoode were mostly converted into industrial parks after the pits closed in the 1970s. There is plenty of light industry here now, but not enough to compensate, says Parkin, for the loss of jobs in the mines.

'There's certainly less community identity here since the pit closed. And the sale of council houses was in my view divisive. People adorned their houses and they took on middle-class overtones. It's a cultural shift – there's a nice cliché for you. Crime has increased. Until a few years ago the local community policed itself. We left our doors open during the day. But the crime rate has shot up over the last few years.'

Walking through Dole Lea, we encountered a former miner, who told us his windows had been forced the other night. Parkin introduced me as someone who had come to investigate whether the notion of class still existed. 'Does class still exist, Jim?' Parkin asked the old man, who just roared with laughter.

I asked Parkin whether there was still a culture of deference in the area.

'No. But, then I never knew a single Tory, Not one. Loyalties don't change round here. People react very emotionally to political issues.'

The churches reflected the class divide. 'The Methodist church was the working-class church. The gaffers went to the parish church. I only went to the church at Ault Hucknall for weddings or funerals. That's changed now. Today vicars are much more involved with the community, more oriented to the working class and their problems. The Methodist church closed when the pit closed, but I expect there are still lay preachers around. I wouldn't really know. I've never believed in religion.'

At Dole Lea there are rows of modest former council houses clustered around the large Miners Welfare Social Club, known rather grandly as the Institute and today serving as a community centre as well. Up in Glapwell are larger, more prosperous estates from the 1940s. These communities seem frozen into a time when work was orderly and secure. Class and stratification mark every brick. Near Stainby Mill stands a war memorial to World War I, but Parkin says the mining communities argued against having anything to do with it. They perceived it as being patronized by the upper class. Above the hamlet are the towers of that proud architectural marvel Hardwick Hall, but Parkin says he has never set foot inside the house.

As the afternoon wore on, Parkin said he had to leave. 'I have to go off with my pigeons. Can't get more working-class than that, can you?'

Graham Parkin still inhabits a world of working-class solidarity. The estrangement from the middle and upper classes that he clearly feels is none the less far from the yawning gulf that was commonplace fifty years ago. In those times the only working-class people that their social superiors would encounter were their servants, mechanics and gardeners. Despite the passivity of the British working classes, they were still regarded with deep suspicion by those who ruled over them. Their acceptance depended on their deference.

Quentin Crewe, in his survey of the upper-class journal *The Queen*, quoted from an Edwardian issue of the magazine: 'The lower classes are, as a whole, unambitious and incurious; they seldom realise the advantage of improving themselves by further education and they do not learn either to use their hands, to read steadily and with purpose, or to think.'[15] The poor were regarded as an unsightly and unwholesome nuisance, an alien species.

The Edwardians . . . blamed the poor even more severely than the Victorians had done, believing that poverty was the result of idleness and improvidence, and therefore the only effective method of dealing with it was coercion. In 1905 about one person in six belonged to the slum class. There were at that time 14,470 paupers on the books of the London unions every Saturday, and the cost of pauperism for the year 1902–3 was 3.5 million pounds. 'Of course, this is far too high a proportion, but the noise they make and the trouble they cause is largely in excess of their numbers. However, it is chiefly for them that the rest of the community has to provide policemen, workhouses and prisons, and all the paraphernalia of repressive, remedial and philanthropic organisations . . . Dramatic measures will be necessary before the greater part of the evil can be stamped out. In the first place, let it be accepted as an unbreakable rule never to give money to beggars nor food or clothes to tramps.'[16]

The Queen saw no reason why 'the hard working thrifty classes' should work all the harder 'to support and continue a class and system of which they disapprove'.

The socialist historian R. H. Tawney noted this same phenomenon in 1912:

Class-ethics are a most curious thing. It is the ineradicable assumption of the upper classes that a workman should be primarily a good productive tool. He is always judged from this point of view, from the assumption that all he wants or ought to want, is not to live but to work. The slightest extravagance in him is condemned by the very people who, even though far from wealthy according to modern standards, never dream of denying themselves small pleasures and luxuries.[17]

Jessica Mitford recalled relations between aristocrats and the deferential rural working class during her childhood: 'Labour Party supporters were virtually unknown in Swinbrook. Only once was a red rosette seen in the village. It was worn by our gamekeeper's son – to the bitter shame and humiliation of his family, who banished him from their house for this act of disloyalty.'[18]

Naturally the upper classes liked to pride themselves on their easy rapport with those who worked for them. Lady Redesdale was immensely shocked when her radical daughter Jessica stigmatized her as 'an Enemy of the Working Class':

Muv was genuinely stung.

'I'm *not* an enemy of the working class! I think some of them are perfectly sweet!' she retorted angrily. I could almost see the visions of perfectly sweet nannies, grooms, gamekeepers, that the phrase must have conjured up in her mind.[19]

Lady Redesdale may have been benign, but we have already seen from Ronald Blythe's *Akenfield* that relations between aristocrats and servants could be repellently feudal. Despite tales of faithful retainers, there is little evidence for the myth that there was a special bond between the mightiest and the poorest in the land. The journalist Louis Heren grew up in the East End of London in the early decades of this century:

I do not subscribe to the fond old Tory theory that the people at the top of the social heap get on well with those at the bottom. When I was growing up the gap was so wide that we did not even think of the well-born and powerful as fellow citizens, but the lower-middle class despised, perhaps even feared us. We were what they had been or might have been, but, as they probably saw it, for their hard work and thrift.[20]

The traveller and writer Freya Stark was scarcely a conventional woman, yet she succumbed to élitist prejudice when, lying in hospital in 1934, she wrote:

My ideas are changing rapidly in one way as I lie here and see the masses at close quarters – eleven of them in the other beds, ranging from what I take to be a charlady to a lady-typist. Not *one* of them with a *personal* idea in her head; not one of them *vitally* interested in anything that is not material and tangible; not one of them using her leisure to do anything but read the most appalling rubbish and look at cinemas and shops.[21]

In an interview with Dennis Skinner MP, who represents the former mining constituency of Bolsover in Derbyshire, I asked whether the modern working class formed an economic interest group, in the Marxist sense, or whether it had turned into a kind of cultural association.

'It's always been a bit of both. People in this country used to dirty their hands in industries such as mining, steelworks and shipbuilding – very difficult physical jobs. There used to be a million miners in this country between the wars. Now people mistakenly think that because they by and large have a different style of work that somehow or other those classes have disappeared. All I'll say to you is go into any hospital and you'll see class all over the place. You'll see a lot of very poorly paid workers at one end and increasingly you'll see a lot of bosses on the other. So the economic divide is quite stark.

'Just because the pits have gone, or most of them, don't imagine that the divide of economic interests has disappeared. I would have thought there was more low pay now than there was when I first started work as a teenager in the mines after the war. At least there were some limited regulations. Now it's a total free-for-all. In the areas of total deregulation, people are below the poverty line by a mile.

'And now of course you've got an underclass as well. You've got about four million people who haven't got a job. The official unemployment figures are a nonsense. I've got ex-pit villages in my constituency where half the male population is unemployed. You can count them. So when I hear people – middle-class people in the main – talking about how classes have disappeared in Britain, I just smile. I come from a background and I live in an area where I'm surrounded by the class divide.

'There's another way in which you can measure things. Jumble sales are back again. I've seen shop signs saying "Broken Biscuits Sold Here". That's going back to the 1920s and 1930s. It's a far cry from Benidorm, isn't it? And then you see the homeless on the streets of London and other large towns. That's absolutely new. There used to be meths drinkers, older men in the main, around Euston Station. But that was the sum total of it. Now it's young and old, men and women. That's all part of the class system in Britain. People don't see it as old-fashioned class, but it's there.'

Scargill's new Socialist Labour Party is an old-fashioned Marxist-style party. But it's clearly attracting virtually no support. Why not?

'The instincts of most working-class people, even in Arthur's own area, is that they want to see the back of this government. The first thing they have to do is derail this Tory train.'

And splitting Labour was not the best way to do it.

'Absolutely.'

Isn't it also that the rhetoric just doesn't appear relevant any more? The kind of language Scargill uses doesn't seem appropriate to most people.

'He does give the impression that he wants to see the fall of capitalism in the morning. I mean, I'll settle for it, but I know it's not on offer.'

Do working-class people want to escape their class, perhaps by finding jobs that pay enough for them to afford a foreign holiday, a larger house, a better car, whatever? People want to better themselves, have a better life for their children.

'That used to be the phrase when I was growing up. I went to a grammar school and won a scholarship, and the whole idea was that you bettered yourself. And you could. I had no need to go into the coalmines. I had all my school certificates at that time, but I wanted to be with my mates. The trouble today is that very few kids have got the chance to better themselves. I represent a constituency where the teachers couldn't really say that with any conviction, because a kid of fourteen could turn around and say: "I've got an older sister and brother at home, and they've never had a job. That's what you said to them – get a job and better yourselves. But it hasn't done them any good."

'That's why the social fabric is breaking down. Thirty years ago one would leave the doors open at night. Now they lock them and they get kicked in. It used to be unheard of, robbing one another, friends, relatives.'

But thirty, forty years ago there was poverty as well.

'They also had a job. They had to get up in the morning!'

Are there still working-class Tories?

'Of course. There's always been large groups of people who believe that there are others in society who are better than they are. When I speak, as I do, at meetings all around Britain, one of the messages I leave people with is that they shouldn't feel inferior – to MPs, to doctors, to lawyers, to those who have a job that doesn't mean clocking in and clocking off. That sort of deference still exists and I try to smash that down wherever I go. I try to conduct myself as an MP to give people the impression that there's no need to bow and scrape. It's not egotism. When I don't bow to the Speaker, I do it because I don't want to be hypocritical. I don't believe in paying due deference to those supposedly more important. That's why I dont stand up for people either.'

TWELVE

Overclass and Underclass

I am acutely conscious of and amused by class distinctions. I love them
and hope they endure for ever. They are part of the spice of life.

James Lees-Milne, *Another Self*, 1970

Dennis Skinner referred to the underclass, which has become such a
controversial concept that it needs clarification. Since the 1970s two
new concepts in the analysis of class have been created and debated: the
underclass and the overclass. 'Underclass' has been around for a while
but was given a new lease of life by the controversial American academic
Charles Murray. Such eminent thinkers on social policy as Ralf
Dahrendorf and Frank Field MP have contributed to the debate. Just as
the underclass is that body of the poor and/or dependent who eke out an
existence outside the traditional labour market, so the overclass ignores
traditional boundaries of social origin.

It is sometimes hard to discern how the term 'overclass' differs from
the more traditional term 'Establishment'. The political journalist
Peter Kellner, in an enthusiastic article published in 1994 in the *Sunday
Times*, made the following distinction:

Instead of a tight, mainly hereditary Establishment, we now have a
more porous, sometimes meritocratic, overclass. It sports no uniform
and obeys no single set of rules. It is a diverse entity, whose members
occupy Whitehall offices and City dealing rooms, discreet clubs and
garish advertising agencies, judges' chambers and (from time to time)
open prisons. It is as daft to generalise about members of the
overclass as about members of the underclass.[1]

But if you can't generalize about them, then how do you recognize
them? If it's as diverse as Kellner suggests, then does the concept have

any more usefulness than 'the Establishment'? And it is surely an exaggeration to think of the Establishment as 'hereditary': the peerage, yes, but not the politicians, the bishops, the senior civil servants and diplomats, the judges.

Kellner attributes the growth of the current overclass to the Thatcher reforms. Policies such as cuts in taxation and social security benefits, council house sales and the toleration of high unemployment have, he argues, benefited the overclass, leading to 'a significant increase in inequality'. He continues: 'The charge against the dominant faction of the overclass is that its culture has generated policies that have driven Britain in the opposite direction and created Murray's underclass.' In other words, the overclass is not the consequence of certain political and economic policies, but the driving force behind them, a definable group of individuals whose common interest acted as the spur to Conservative radicalism. Thus the overclass must have been in existence before Thatcher came to power, in which case Kellner is describing an embedded feature of our social structure rather than a recent development.

The remainder of his article is an analysis of growing inequality. However, although mounting inequality may well be a deplorable development, you don't need to posit an 'overclass' to explain it. In short, Kellner's article doesn't make a convincing case for the existence of an 'overclass', nor does it distinguish it sufficiently from the standard view of the 'Establishment'.

A year later the same newspaper printed another article on the same topic. The authors came up with a definition of the group in question: 'a group of wealthy individuals who are separated from the rest not by birth but achievement'. That doesn't sound much different from the upper echelons of the business élite. The authors identify 'a troubling side to the trend':

> Like other elites before them, this one does not mix with those they leave behind. They do not use state schools, they go private. They do not need to worry about the vagaries of the NHS, they have private health insurance. They can choose to live on exclusive estates, in some cases with private guards. They isolate and insulate themselves from society's mainstream. So while they influence public policy – they include lawyers, company directors, management consultants,

top doctors and the most senior broadcasters and journalists – they do not participate in much that it has to deliver.[2]

These 'troubling' signs of alienation from 'society's mainstream' are, however, shared by countless other people. Seven per cent of the nation's children are educated privately; millions contribute to private health schemes. They cannot all be members of an overclass. The majority are undoubtedly middle-class people in a growing panic about the deteriorating quality, as they perceive it, of state-provided services. The guarded estate is far more a feature of American suburbia than of its British counterpart. The lawyers and senior journalists I know tend to live in pleasant but by no means sumptuous houses in Notting Hill or Islington, and many of them have a country retreat as well. But in no sense are they isolated from the rest of the community. I dare say there are parts of the country where many well-heeled and over-rewarded executives, their incomes plumped up with handsome share option schemes, opt for the neo-Georgian house within the wire-fenced estate, but they can hardly be said to constitute an entire class. Moreover, it would be a fair guess that a substantial proportion of the Great and the Good, who earn overclass-size incomes, are the very same people who sit on the boards of quangos and hospital trusts. They may be criticized for some of their activities, but they are hardly isolated from the community as a whole.

The authors quote from various surveys, by Hay Management Consultants and the Joseph Rowntree Foundation, to support their assertion that the 'acceleration of executive earnings contributed to the fastest-growing gap between rich and poor of any industrialized nation apart from New Zealand'. This may well be the case, but in terms of class analysis the only significance this has is further to marginalize the traditional upper classes, which does not greatly trouble the majority of people. The extent to which the growth in top salaries is deserved or a manifestation of greed is a moral rather than a class or sociological issue.

The only significant difference between the so-called 'overclass' and the rest of the middle class is that its members, being richer, tend to be spared the insecurities that nag at the average middle-class household, troubled by negative equity, school fees, rising insurance premiums and so forth. A segment of the professional middle classes has always been sufficiently rewarded to be free from financial anxieties, so this is nothing new. No doubt there are also some well-paid directors or journalists who fritter away much of their income on E-type Jaguars, expensive restaurants and wines, mistresses and luxury holidays, and end up just as insecure as the rest of the middle class.

An American definition of the overclass was offered in the same article by an editor of the *New Republic*, Michael Lind:

> The overclass is the managerial-professional elite that has almost completely replaced older aristocracies as the dominant social group in every industrial democracy. As the robber baron was the typical figure of 19th-century capitalism, so the overclass professional or manager is the typical figure of post-bourgeois managerial capitalism.

However tenacious some aristocracies have been in clinging to their way of life, they ceased to be a 'dominant social group' almost a century ago. World War I dealt them a severe blow throughout Europe. Except in Britain, their political power and influence as a group or class has been negligible. Europe's most powerful economy, that of Germany, is directed at political and commercial levels by a managerial-professional élite, exactly as one would have expected.

Lind argues that earlier 'aristocracies and patriciates' had a paternalistic conception of *noblesse oblige*, which is lacking in the contemporary overclass. Well, it's arguable whether *noblesse oblige* was the guiding principle of absentee Irish landowners or Hungarian magnates. It's also arguable, as has already been suggested, whether the overclass lacks any sense of communal responsibility. It may be true of America, as Lind writes, that 'the American overclass is devoted to shirking civic obligations in order to pursue private interests', although the numerous foundations and charitable organizations established and maintained by rich American families suggests that his generalization is far too sweeping. Moreover, America is a more individualistic society, embracing equality of opportunity rather than *noblesse oblige*. In Britain, there seems little evidence that the rich and successful are shirking their civic obligations, whatever they may be, more than in the past.

So it seems hard to justify the legitimacy of the term 'overclass', at least in a British context. It is too vague and is insufficiently differentiated from previous élites. Whether or not there is an overclass ends up as a semantic quibble. Whether or not there is an underclass has greater implications. There is a distinct moral edge to discussions about the overclass, and at the heart of assertions about the underclass is a distinction not far removed from Victorian notions of the deserving and undeserving poor.

The distinctive feature of the underclass as defined by Charles Murray and others is its cultural difference from the poorer working class. Factors such as single parenthood, lack of education and long-term unemployment create welfare dependency and a more or less permanent severance from the labour market. The underclass has, in effect, dropped out of the social consensus, which is why levels of drug-taking and crime are disproportionately high among its members. Illegitimacy is the central issue, argues Murray, especially in his apocalyptic essay 'Underclass: The Crisis Deepens'.[3] Because children model themselves on the behaviour around them, if their father is absent, their mother feckless and their peers disposed to criminality, then in all likelihood, he suggests, they will follow suit.

There is no agreement on the composition of the underclass; different writers formulate different criteria. Christopher Jencks in 1989 discerned a dozen different definitions. If there is widespread agreement that a woman of seventeen with no partner and two chidren, living solely off benefits, is a fully qualified member of the underclass, there is less agreement about, say, the 'blameless' individual who is equally dependent.

The Murray-model underclass is characterized by its 'deplorable behaviour'[4] – criminality, drug-taking, irresponsible parenting – but no effort is made to establish how this underclass has come into being. Social scientists rail at Murray because his vivid description of the underclass posits, but does not prove, a causal connection between the condition he describes and the behaviour of those in that condition. Because Murray does not shrink from ascribing blame to the under-class, the term has become a useful shorthand term, a code, for slack journalists and manipulative politicians. Right-wing intellectuals such as John Redwood seize on Murray's prescriptions in order to plead for a return to traditional morality in which there are economic as well as moral sanctions against illegitimacy. Authoritarian politicians such as Michael Howard, the former Home Secretary, are at pains to insist there is no correlation between crime and high unemployment; nor, by extension, with poor housing and lousy schools. If this is so, then there has to be something inherently vicious within the underclass that predisposes them to antisocial behaviour. It follows, then, that society need not concern itself unduly with the welfare of the underclass, who have largely brought their misfortunes on themselves. Murray, for example, offers 'the definitive proof that an underclass has arrived is that large numbers of young, healthy, low-income males choose not to take jobs'.[5] He does not ask why this should be so, but contrasts them with an earlier generation that was prepared to take on any job, however poorly paid, rather than remain idle. They have not, he writes, been 'socialized into the world of work'. The reader is left free to condemn modern young males as feckless or, in Murray's pretty word, 'barbarians'. He does have an explanation for the increase in lone parenthood: until the 1970s a combination of moral disapproval and low benefits made it economically unfeasible for a young woman to rear a child on her own. That has ceased to be the case over the last twenty years.

With a clear conscience the underclass – at any rate its 'feckless' division – can be isolated, most effectively in prisons, and we can sit back in moral disapproval. This highlighting of an underclass plays on the widespread fear of crime and violence. It directs our anxiety and ire at the alleged perpetrators, without requiring those trusted with the management of our society – politicians – to do anything about it, other than take draconian measures which pander to the fear in the first place. It seems no accident that writers such as Charles Murray have used images of plague zones and disease in their journalistic writings, a pathological rhetoric that stokes up anxiety and encourages readers to think of the underclass, labelled by Murray in his 1994 essay 'The New Rabble', as not fully human.

However, the fact that authoritarian politicians have exploited the notion of an underclass does not mean that the term is without meaning. Having spent some time in the black and Hispanic slums of Los Angeles, I can understand how a culture of joblessness, crime, drug profiteering and violence can become a kind of norm to which there seems to be no realistic alternative. It's hard, *pace* Murray, to find comparable sloughs of despond in Britain. When he writes, 'See photos of the South Bronx, commonly compared to post-blitz London, for a glimpse of the future',[6] he is simply scaremongering. Lone parenting may give rise to a number of problems, but it has not yet turned large tracts of our major cities into war zones. And if there are war zones in Brixton or Toxteth, it is self-evident that countless other factors have made their malign contribution.

What seems odd is that those politicians and social scientists who espouse the concept most eagerly also seem the least disposed to do anything about it. It is as if they revel in social inequality, which allows them to feel morally superior to the 'feckless' poor, whose alleged amorality enhances the observer's own sense of virtue. Frank Field, in his book *Losing Out*, accepts that there is an underclass in Britain, but argues that it is the consequence of policies, ferociously pursued by Thatcher governments, that fostered greater social inequality. Murray dismisses this line, saying that the underclass was detectable as far back as the 1950s. However, Murray's underclass is misguided at best and delinquent at worst, whereas Field's includes such characters, absent from Murray's ne'er-do-wells, as frail elderly pensioners, of which there are some two million on means-tested income support in modern Britain. Clearly, the two men are talking about very different population groups.

In general, it does seem to be the case that societies with a belief in social equality – e.g. Japan, Germany, the Netherlands – have enjoyed a steadier economic performance and greater social stability than those without it. As a report in the *British Medical Journal* argued:

> Cumulative measures of lifetime social circumstances – such as wealth, family assets, lifetime earnings, and occupational careers – are the crucial socioeconomic predictors of longevity . . . The current government . . . continues to pay no heed to the growing evidence that increasing income inequality is bad for the economy, bad for crime rates, bad for people's working lives . . . and bad for health – in both the short and the long term.[7]

Right-wing sociologists and politicians have argued that the poor are growing richer at a faster rate than the rest of the population, but this is a minority view, contradicted by numerous reports, such as those published by the Joseph Rowntree Foundation. An article by Nicholas Timmins seems to summarize the state of play succinctly: 'The evidence that the poor are worse off in *absolute* terms than they were in 1979 is beginning to look shaky. The evidence that they are *relatively* poorer, however, remains.'[8]

The demonizing of the poor is an unwelcome trend in British politics. It was this kind of rhetoric that justified such abominations as eighteenth-century laws aimed at preventing vagrants from becoming a liability to a parish in which they chose to settle, 'the policy being to punish the vagrant for his wandering and yet deny him the means of obtaining a permanent habitation and the chance of regular employment'.[9]

Of course it is wrong to 'scrounge' off welfare, but one searches hard for the same heat of moral disapproval directed towards, say, middle-class tax evaders or perpetrators of million-pound scams in the City. There seems little evidence that there is a swathe of poor people who, as a matter of firm conviction, have no wish to have a job (or a job that earns an income greater than that provided by social security benefits), no wish to live in attractive surroundings and no wish to end a cycle of continuous indebtedness. The fact that those living off benefits are in effect prohibited from taking on part-time work that might boost their earnings and make them more self-reliant has only contributed to the problem of enduring poverty in Britain.

If it is difficult to substantiate claims that there is a morally pernicious stratum of British society that corresponds to notions of an 'underclass', there certainly does seem to be a large band of no-hopers. Dr Ron Singer is aware of such a group: 'The underclass as a term is supposed to take in the permanently disadvantaged: the permanently unemployed, the disabled, the HIV-positive, families whose homes have been repossessed, those in chronic ill-health, those released from prison with no hope of steady employment. As a GP I don't even come into contact with much of the so-called underclass, as they aren't even registered, especially if they are street or hostel dwellers. Many of those people are simply alienated. I have one patient who lives in his car. He used to have a house and family, but he fell on hard times and is now completely at odds with everything around him. I don't like the term "underclass" because it's entirely negative and suggests people are irredeemable.'

Another general practitioner finds the issue confused by ethnicity: 'There's a large ethnic population in this part of London, blacks and Asians, but also refugees and immigrants who mostly fall into the category of the underclass. I can't help feeling that ethnic issues sweep aside considerations of class and power. I have refugees coming through my surgery – Kurds, Angolans and others – who have been, many of them, through torture, malnutrition and chronic illnesses that will never disappear. What's more, they have a tenuous grasp of the social system in which they now have to live. The generation that comes here never fully recovers or adapts, but their children do, and fast.

'The real underclass here is composed of the mentally ill and the single, elderly poor. These are the most desperate cases I see. Single mothers may not be having a wonderful time, but they know how to work the system. But a seventy-year-old widow or widower on a state pension – for them it's cyanide time. What kind of future, other than a diminishing income, do they have ahead of them? It's very grim. It depends on the borough, but some councils release mentally handicapped people "into the community", which in their case means a shared flat in a tower block. The working-class families that used to live in the tower blocks around here have mostly moved out into small terrace houses that they have been able to buy. That leaves the tower blocks as run-down, malodorous homes of last resort for single mothers, the mentally handicapped, the single elderly. Unfortunately, in many cases, they can't cope, and the benefits they receive are clearly inadequate, so they live in squalor. The smell can be appalling.'

What the doctors are describing as an underclass is a sea of human misery, brought about by a multiplicity of causes. In some cases the misery and squalor may have been self-inflicted, but in general the underclass as they describe it deserves compassion rather than demonization.

THIRTEEN

Majesty

Monarchy in Britain . . . stands in a class by itself, uniquely popular
and secure.

Kingsley Martin, *Crown and Establishment*, 1962

Classes in themselves do not depend for their existence and survival on a
monarchical system, but a class structure would be deeply modified in
the absence of such a system. The network of protocol, hierarchy and
precedence embedded within a class system would not make sense
without a summit that shelters and sustains all the gradations that lie
beneath it. Barons and marquesses and dukes could still rub along, as
they do in France and Italy, without any monarch, but in Europe they
have no power, whatever the private pretensions of those aristocracies.

In Britain, however, the very existence of a court perpetuates a
plethora of institutions. Britons, as has often been remarked, are not
citizens but subjects. Our governments are conjured into being by the
head of state, the monarch. Newly appointed ministers, although
chosen by the prime minister of the day, must kiss the hand of the
sovereign. Judges, civil servants, members of the armed services and
others required to swear oaths of allegiance offer those oaths to the
Crown, not to Parliament: 'I swear that I will be faithful and bear true
allegiance to Her Majesty Queen Elizabeth the Second, her heirs and
successors, according to law.'

Parliament each year is opened, and the legislative programme read
out, by the sovereign. The House of Lords, largely composed of
hereditary peers, is surely untenable without the monarchy. The
monarchy may have limited power in practice, but it has extraordinary
authority, and all manner of things are done in its name. Without it,
hierarchies would dissolve; the honours system, at least in its titled

upper reaches, would lack all justification; the aristocracy would be reduced to a purely ornamental status; and the Church of England would have to look elsewhere for a Defender of the Faith.

For at least nine centuries the monarchy has leaned down to pull up those it favours. It has been a kind of government by puppetry. Genuine democracies, of which the United States has to be a prime (if flawed) example, generate their energies – social, cultural, economic – from below. Wealth may be a tawdry goal, but no more so than security and status conferred entirely through an accident of birth.

In Britain enterprise and achievement have usually had to be validated from above. American baseball players are enshrined in a Hall of Fame. British actors and actresses can't rest until they have a knighthood or damehood, conferred from on high, to attest to their talent and success. The British monarchy is at the decadent core of a system that rewards its subjects with baubles and titles, that lifts the favoured ones gently from rung to rung through a system permeated with class values.

None of this is good for the psychological health of a nation. In a previous century we proudly, if arrogantly, invaded other nations, both to enrich ourselves and to confirm our own cultural superiority over less enlightened peoples. Nowadays we count ourselves lucky if we can persuade Asian countries to take advantage of our low-cost labour. It's a skewed vision of the world, in which we welcome the colonial status we once inflicted in others, and without a monarchy and the hierarchical, class-imbued values that it validates we might be less complacent about the dwindling of our economy and of our international status.

It seems, paradoxically, that our veneration of the monarchy burgeoned rather than declined in the face of the loss of imperial power. As recently as 1981, with the marriage of the Prince of Wales, the monarchy seemed unassailable. Its woes, partially self-inflicted, are no more than a decade old. In terms of public esteem its heyday probably spanned the years from 1920 to 1980. As Britain found itself increasingly unable to sustain its imperial role, our people seemed to take refuge in an exaggerated respect for the monarchy.

Our Georgian and Victorian ancestors had few qualms about criticizing the monarchs of their day. But in the twentieth century criticism of the monarchy became unacceptable. A combination of modesty and remoteness proved a winning formula. The nation wanted to be reassured rather than dazzled. We didn't require to be ruled – the franchise had taken care of that – but we needed the avuncular touch, the quiet certainty that those who represented the summit of British-ness were, after all, not so very different from the rest of us. Elizabeth II confirmed this when the first television documentary to chronicle royal life showed that she too watched television, enjoyed jigsaw puzzles, could drive a car, and couldn't decide what to wear. The monarchy was remote and untouchable but our own concerns were mirrored by theirs. Their stolidity was our comfort. And their moments of pomp were potent reminders that once we had been great.

Glued into popular affection, the monarchy performed another role. By affirming values that corresponded to those of the nation, by retreating from the Belle Epoque, from King Edward's cigars, champagne and twelve-course feasts, the Windsors created a stability that seemed imperishable. The aristocracy, all beneficiaries of royal patronage, shared the limelight of public esteem. The royal family became role models. For generations Queen Mary – thin, Germanic, truly regal and unsmiling – lived out her role of rectitude, and in our own day the Queen Mother, a softer, more maternal figure, has won a place in the nation's affections by an extraordinary act of novelistic self-creation. In her flowing dresses, babyish colours and large floppy hats and veils, she bears no sartorial resemblance to any other living woman. Some may find it risible, but she has refashioned herself as a timeless icon, a rock-like symbol in a time of transience, a perpetual aunt. Her daughter, in contrast, merely looks tweedy and only appears to smile at Commonwealth conferences and when within twenty yards of a racehorse.

The monarchy, by definition, stands above other classes. Protocol ensures that even the wealthiest duke is made aware that he occupies a different planet from a royal duke or princess. The outrage of Princess Margaret whenever she felt insufficient respect was being paid to her royal status has been well documented.

This, it has long been recognized, poses a psychological problem for a modern monarchy. While it is essential that a monarchy retains some of the mysteriousness that Walter Bagehot wrote of, it makes no sense for a late-twentieth-century royal house to isolate itself in a self-enclosed world of pomp, protocol and imperiousness. 'Its mystery is its life,' wrote Bagehot; 'we must not let in daylight upon magic.'[1] Indeed, by admitting light, especially in the form of television cameras, the royal family confirmed what in previous decades was merely suspected: that they are as subject to foibles and weaknesses and moral dilemmas as the rest of us.

Despite the game-show antics of Prince Edward or the excursions into the televised confessional of Prince Charles and Princess Diana, this is in no sense a populist monarchy. The children of the Queen may occasionally yearn to be simple folk (only with lots of money), but a glance at the royal household confirms that the Court is in all respects an expression of class superiority. Its members are drawn from a narrow band of families, often with a tradition of royal service. The head of the Court is the Lord Chamberlain, since 1997 Lord Camoys, a leading Catholic peer and businessman. His department of 195 people has overall responsibility for ceremonial, the organization of state visits, receptions and parties at the palaces and their gardens, the royal collections and stables, the Crown Jewels, the appointment of some one thousand warrant holders and the Poet Laureate, and for the medical and ecclesiastical households attached to the Court. A few of the grandest state occasions, such as coronations, funerals and state openings of Parliament, are delegated to the Earl Marshal, the Duke of Norfolk.

The Lord Chamberlain's office is separated, however, from the Queen's household, though the Lord Chamberlain is a senior member of that household. Within her household are Gold Sticks and other military dignitaries and aides-de-camp, the mistress of the robes (Duchess of Grafton, DCVO), a squadron of attendants titled either women or ladies of the bedchamber, and twenty-seven equerries. Keeping an eye on the royal budget and estates is the Keeper of the Privy Purse and Treasurer to the Queen. Most of the other immediate members of the royal family, the royal princes and dukes, have their own personal households, stuffed with equerries and ladies-in-waiting.

The Lord Chamberlain's Office is staffed by fifty-six persons – or fifty-six persons sufficiently senior to warrant a listing in *Whitaker's Almanac* – most of whom are 'gentlemen ushers' drawn from the higher ranks of the armed forces. Other dignitaries include Gentleman Usher to the Sword of State (General Sir Edward Burgess, KCB, OBE), the Bargemaster (R. Crouch) and the Swan Marker (D. Barber). The ushers are dripping with CVOs, KBEs and GCBs, but poor Messrs Crouch and Barber must do without. (In the 1880s the Radical MP Henry Labouchere took a dim view of such court appointments, referring in this instance to the Master of the Buckhounds and the Lord Chamberlain: 'One noble Lord gets a salary for galloping after Her Majesty's dogs, another receives £2000 a year for walking about with a stick.')[2]

The class stratification of the royal household is further enforced by the Royal Victorian Order, an order of chivalry at the personal disposal of the sovereign. Thus the Queen can reward her trusted servants, and presumably let her less trusted ones know that they need to pull their hose up, by elevating them to the various ranks of the order, from the lowly Member (MVO) to the loftier GCVO (Knight Grand Cross).

The Queen has no fewer than forty chaplains, though it appears that a chaplain would be lucky to find himself preaching more than once in the royal presence during his tenure. The medical household comprises fourteen members, including a surgeon oculist, a surgeon gynaecologist, a surgeon dentist and an orthopaedic surgeon, and there are separate apothecaries for the households of Windsor and Sandringham.

The Lord Chamberlain also oversees royal warrants. Standing recently in the reception room of the champagne house Perrier-Jouet in Epernay, I amused myself by checking their royal warrant, which dated from the early years of the reign of George V. It is a wonderful document, full of scratchings-out and emendations, suggesting the King and his officials couldn't quite make up their mind whether Perrier-Jouet had the edge over Moët and Pommery. This warrant was issued by the Board of Green Cloth. The board still exists, with six officials at its command, and today it occupies itself with the nationally important task of licensing taverns within a twelve-mile radius of the Palace of Whitehall.

Until 1968 the Lord Chamberlain was also responsible for theatre censorship, which usually meant little more than governessy objections to strong language or representations of Important Persons on the stage. It was impossible to discern what qualified the Lord Chamberlain to undertake this delicate task. When the Wilson government let it be known that it proposed to abolish these powers, the Court voiced its displeasure. The Prime Minister had to explain to his colleagues: 'I've received representations from the Palace. They don't want to ban all plays about live persons but they want to make sure that there's somebody who'd stop the kind of play about Prince Philip which would be painful to the Queen.'[3] Fortunately the Court's attempted intervention proved fruitless.

The Lord Chamberlain also keeps his eye on the Ascot office, housed in St James's Palace. The Queen has her own official representative at Ascot, Colonel Sir Piers Bengough, KCVO, OBE, and he is assisted by his secretary, Miss L. Thompson-Royds, who has had to content herself with an MVO. It is their job to sift through the thousands of applications received each year for admission to the Royal Enclosure.

In Scotland the household is stiff with hereditary bearers of their offices: the Lord High Constable, the Master of the Household, the Bearer of the Royal Banner, the Bearer of the Scottish National Flag and five hereditary keepers of various palaces and castles. There's a hereditary carver, Major Sir Ralph Anstruther Bt, GCVO, a botanist, painter and limner, and even an astronomer.

The Queen has her own ecclesiastical and medical households for Scotland, numbering twenty-five and six respectively, and her own bodyguard for Scotland. This, the Royal Company of Archers, consists of a few dozen captains, lieutenants, ensigns and brigadiers, all ceremonial titles. The ensigns include the Earl of Elgin, and the Duke of Montrose is tucked among the brigadiers. The bodyguard has its own chaplain and surgeon. In addition to its ceremonial function, the Royal Company operates as a prestigious private club, bringing together the titled and the rich from all over Scotland.

The Queen Mother has her own household, numbering twenty-eight. In addition to her ladies of the bedchamber and equerries, she enjoys the attentions of an apothecary and a separate surgeon-apothecary. Prince Edward has a private secretary in the shape of Lieutenant-Colonel S. G. O'Dwyer LVO, who is assisted by Mrs R. Warburton MVO; and a paltry clerk, Miss L. Bugge, as yet unrewarded. However, the Princess Royal has an entourage of twelve.

Of course many of these appointments are honorary, which is another way of saying that the holders of these titles do little more than put in an occasional appearance on great state occasions. None the less, this core of over four hundred courtiers constitutes a formidable administrative machine that, in addition to keeping the Court ticking over, immures the monarch within an aristocratic ghetto.

The monarch's sense of privilege and distance must be further reinforced by the military squads at her disposal. The ancient court positions of Gold Stick, Silver Stick and Colonel Foot Guards act as liaison between the monarch and the regiments that form her Household Division. Other regiments and corps also have duties associated with the sovereign: the Royal Corps of Transport provides the Queen's Baggage Train; the Queen's dispatch rider is a member of the Royal Signals.

The Court naturally wishes to remain in touch with the monarch's subjects throughout the land, which is the primary role of the lords lieutenant. Although their appointment falls under the aegis of the Secretary for Appointments at 10 Downing Street, the Queen is directly consulted before appointments are made, and many, probably most, of the office holders are known personally to her. Lords lieutenant are overwhelmingly male and aristocratic. In 1985 their number included a duchess, two marquesses, two earls and three viscounts out of a total of forty-six.[4] In 1990 one-third of the male lords lieutenant in England were Old Etonians.[5]

Their most serious duty requires them to chair the local committees that recommend to the Lord Chancellor, in this context the representative of the Queen, those who should be appointed magistrates in the county. They also make recommendations to the Prime Minister for honours and draw up lists of those worthy of invitations to royal garden parties. When the monarch honours his county with a visit, the lord lieutenant acts as host.

Lords lieutenant are unpaid, though given a little help with the purchase of their ceremonial finery, and their basic expenses are covered. Although the financial demands of the office may not be particularly onerous, they do need to give up a fair amount of time. So perhaps it is not surprising that the landed aristocracy has been singled out for the honour of representing the monarch at local level. None the less the whole institution, as presently constituted, continues to isolate the Court as an upper-class enclave, remote from the preoccupations of the vast majority of the sovereign's subjects.

Because courtiers are drawn from a narrow social circle, they find it difficult to understand that the rest of the population, however patriotic, may not wish to be at the beck and call of the Court. Richard Crossman recalls a meeting of the Privy Council at Balmoral in September 1966:

As Lord President I had to go and see the Queen first with the papers for the meeting. We chatted for a few moments, then the others came in and lined up beside me and I read aloud the fifty or sixty Titles of the Orders in Council, pausing after every half a dozen for the Queen to say 'Agreed'. When I'd finished, in just two and a half minutes, I concluded with the words, 'So the business of the Council is concluded.' The Privy Council is the best example of pure mumbo-jumbo you can find. It's interesting to reflect that four ministers, busy men, all had to take a night and a day off and go up there with Godfrey Agnew to stand for two and a half minutes while the list of Titles was read out. It would be far simpler for the Queen to come down to Buckingham Palace, but it's *lèse-majesté* to suggest it.[6]

Tony Benn recalls how in October 1969 he was summoned to Balmoral, where the Queen was then in residence, to be sworn in as a minister. He strenuously objected, to the displeasure of Prime Minister Harold Wilson and the Privy Council Office, but eventually got his way, arguing that he had previous commitments at Telford which it would be impolitic and impolite to break. So his swearing-in took place at Buckingham Palace instead. The Clerk of the Privy Council, Sir Godfrey Agnew, mentioned to Benn that the Queen had been very upset 'at the newspaper story that other Ministers who had gone up there had not enjoyed it and had thought it a waste of time'. Agnew added that 'the comments by a Minister undermine the respect for authority'. Clearly this official had not the remotest sense that ministers might have more important things to do than travel to Scotland and back for a swearing-in ceremony.[7]

Ceremonial is inextricably related to the life of a court. By its very nature, it highlights the social or political transaction at the expense of the paltry individuals involved. The format for a state occasion never varies, suggesting that an opening of Parliament or a coronation is a timeless occasion, not only reaching back into the remote past but stretching forward into an infinite future of ceremony and pomp. The anachronism of the ceremony is its point. Capable of endless repetition over the years, it gathers authority with use.

Because ceremonial is public and carries symbolic weight, it is quite different from etiquette. Despite restrictions, until relatively recently, on who could be admitted to the royal presence, the British Court has never been as devoted to antiquated etiquette as many European courts. In the 1890s the Duchess of Marlborough, visiting the Spanish Court, recalled that she 'managed to acquit myself with dignity and, on reaching the royal presence, to drop the three ceremonial curtsies Spanish custom required'.[8] Queen Mary, herself no slouch when it came to etiquette, was awed by Spanish formality when as a princess she attended the wedding of King Alfonso XIII in 1906.

> She and Prince George were lodged in 'cathedral-high' apartments, to and from which they were solemnly conducted by a Spanish Duke before and after every meal and every ceremony or entertainment. Vast marble colonnades stretched before them in every direction. The doors of each room were guarded by halberdiers with pikes. As the Prince and Princess of Wales left their apartments an official would clap his hands, and every halberdier would present arms, passing from one to another the cry: '*Arriba Princesa! Arriba Príncipe!*'[9]
>
> She loved it.

Ceremonial is also an exercise in public relations, in wowing the populace and stirring patriotic fervour. During the heady days of imperial power in India, Queen Victoria's assumption of the title of empress was celebrated at an elaborate durbar in Delhi in 1877. The exercise was repeated for King Edward VII in 1903, when Lord Curzon himself created an orgy of pageantry and ceremonial that far outshone the Victorian effort. (Its extravagance also attracted considerable hostility from both the British and the Indian press.)[10]

The State Opening of Parliament was another piece of Edwardian stage management. During Victoria's reign, the Queen's Speech had been read out on her behalf. King Edward astutely realized that the monarchy needed something of a boost after the prolonged and often dour reign of his mother. The result was a royal descent on Parliament in honour of its opening.

Its manufactured pomp is solemnly described by Julian Paget in his book on pageantry:

> The Sovereign is received by the Earl Marshal, and the Lord Great Chamberlain who, as bearer of the hereditary title of Keeper of the

Royal Palace of Westminster, has a significant part to play on this occasion. He wears a scarlet Court dress, incorporating the emblem of the gold key of the office of Chamberlain, while at his hip hangs the actual golden key to the Palace of Westminster. As the Queen moves up the Royal Staircase to the Robing Chamber, she passes through two lines of dismounted Troopers of the Household Cavalry, in full dress with drawn swords.[11]

The monarch enters the House of Lords. The best seats in the chamber are occupied not by government ministers but by peers. Peeresses are requested to wear tiaras, high-court judges are robed and bewigged, the Lord Chancellor bends before the sovereign and removes from a silk bag the speech which she will read to Parliament. First, however, the 'faithful Commons' are summoned. But not without another dose of confected ritual.

The Lord Great Chamberlain lifts his wand of office, whereupon the Gentleman Usher of the Black Rod, in his capacity as the Sovereign's Messenger, makes his way to the House of Commons. As he approaches, the Serjeant-at-Arms there carefully slams the door in his face. Black Rod then knocks three times with his rod, the Serjeant-at-Arms looks through the grill, to identify the caller, and only then is the door opened. The Sovereign's summons to the Commons is thereupon conveyed to the Speaker by Black Rod.[12]

In 1901 Sir Edward Cadogan witnessed the King's procession from the Long Gallery of the House of Lords. The Duke of Devonshire, wrote Cadogan,

was carrying an elaborate tray . . . and upon it rested the Crown of England. He seemed not altogether appreciative of the solemnity of the occasion or his own important part in the proceedings, and adopted towards this function of his an amused but rather scornful tolerance . . .

By his side stood another equally dignified figure, with the same reputation of insensitiveness to trappings and meretricious adornment. This was the Prime Minister, Lord Salisbury, who was obviously regarding the whole proceedings as an infernal interruption to the business of Parliament. These two leading patricians habitually exasperated King Edward with their indifference to the more decorative side of our existence.

In this noble and glittering throng I waited it seemed hours – and then of a sudden a blast of trumpets rent their air, the doors were thrown open, and across the threshold came King Edward and Queen Alexandra, hand in hand in all the panoply of state, leading a retinue of bedizened courtiers in their wake.[13]

King Edward's innovation is with us still, and as bogus now as it was almost a century ago. When as a Cabinet minister Richard Crossman decided to skip the State Opening, he told the Prime Minister he would plead diplomatic illness. A few days later the Duke of Norfolk huffed and puffed in a letter to Crossman 'that he was deeply alarmed and disturbed by what I had said about not going to the State Opening and that only the Queen could relieve me of the obligation to go'.[14] Crossman went to see the Queen's private secretary, Sir Michael Adeane, who told him he should simply have written to the Queen asking to be excused; to have involved the heralds was asking for trouble. Adeane smoothly added, 'Of course, the Queen has as strong a feeling of dislike of public ceremonies as you do. I don't disguise from you the fact that it will certainly occur to her to ask herself why you should be excused when she has to go, since you're both officials.' With this splendid piece of flattery, Adeane persuaded Crossman to attend.[15]

Coronations are ceremonies of greater antiquity, but it sometimes seems that the only people who fail to take them seriously are the participants. Lady Diana Cooper whooped it up at the coronation of George VI. Her husband, Duff Cooper, was a serving government minister at the time, and she had weightier credentials as the daughter of the Duke of Rutland:

The Coronation! . . . Clothes, uniforms, robes, ermine, miniver, rabbit, velvet, velveteen. Where were the coronets? In the bank, at Carrington's, or in the attic? There were fears for bad places behind stone pillars, absurd fretting over starvation and retiring-rooms . . .

Our places we found to be behind the Viscounts, not all I hoped but good enough. The many hours of expectation were relieved by exquisitely funny comings and goings. Peers without pages in a crowded tribune cannot cope with their velvet robes. One hand holds the coronet, the other gathers up the heavy folds in the most impudic fashion. Retiring-rooms dotted all over the Abbey are magnets. Our Viscounts were dodging in and out like water-carriers. Hunger obsessed them. One, returning from retirement, brought from some first-aid booth an enormous box of mixed chocolate-creams. He naturally stumbled (his velvet brought him down) and the silver-papered chocolates went careering down the steeply built-up tribune. There was an ugly rush to catch them by any Viscount within reach of their rolling.[16]

There was another ugly rush when the Coopers made an unseemly dash for the exit by jumping the queue of viscounts.[17]

On the same occasion the Duke of Bedford was present as a Gold-Stick-in-Waiting.

Although I received a medal for it, it actually meant that you acted as a peeresses' lavatory attendant. We had rehearsals for weeks and weeks before in which we did absolutely nothing . . .

On the great day we had to turn up in Court dress, velvet breeches and agonizing new pumps at about half past three in the morning. It was five hours or so before any of the guests arrived, and by the time the ceremony started my feet were in such agony that I forgot all about my duties. To make things worse somebody had lost the key to the lavatories, and for about half an hour they all had to use buckets until we broke down the doors.[18]

Ceremonial is for external consumption. It doesn't matter that the peers and peeresses were creased with laughter, bored rigid or groaning with enforced constipation. What mattered was that the populace was suitably impressed by the grandeur of the occasion, in which they could participate vicariously. This pomp by association increased immeasurably during the television age, and mine was one of the countless households that first acquired a television set in order to watch the coronation of Elizabeth II. That ceremony was every bit as obscure, long-winded and anachronistic as those that had preceded it, but its very impenetrability contributed to its awesomeness. It was a ceremony performed by a cast almost exclusively aristocratic in its composition, and the nation gawped, peering through the bars at a world it could never experience first-hand.

*

Although entrenched within aristocratic life, the monarchy recognizes that it cannot always remain aloof from its subjects. It must participate in ceremonies of national mourning and attend, after a seemly pause, scenes of national disaster. Even that grandest of royal figures, Queen Mary, knew the value of a comprehensive display of the common touch. In 1912 she and George V visited South Wales.

> Mary flustered the officials by demanding to see the interior of a typical Welsh miner's cottage. When, after some hesitation, her request was granted she refused to confine herself to Mrs Thomas Jones's best parlour in the tiny house in Bude Street, but penetrated into the kitchen where she perched herself upon a kitchen chair. After drinking a cup of tea, and accepting the gift of an old mug, the Queen proceeded to examine the rest of the cottage, which she pronounced airy and clean. The news of this perfectly natural behaviour spread like wildfire through the valley.[19]

Even those of radical instincts were co-opted into the fervour. It comes as no surprise that some of the most loyal supporters of the monarchy have been politicians of the left. The reasons for such conformity are not hard to fathom, and were well captured in Kingsley Martin's account of the 1924 Labour Party conference, where eight

> resolutions were tabled, sorrowing over photographs of Ramsay MacDonald and some of his colleagues, wearing 'blue gold-braided tailcoats and white kneebreeches with sword' at Buckingham Palace. The instinct of the critics that much more was involved here than a trivial issue of manners was correct. The readiness of Labour ministers to fall in with court protocol foreshadowed their future attitude to the Establishment. Not only MacDonald, but working-class members of the Government thoroughly enjoyed the novel sensation of being received by the King, dressed as their aristocratic predecessors had been; they were glad to give the lie to newspaper charges that they were wild revolutionaries.[20]

Of course Conservatives were every bit as obsequious as their socialist counterparts. Sir Godfrey Agnew, president of the Privy Council, the same gentleman who had lamented to Tony Benn that it was deplorable of ministers to complain about royal protocol, indiscreetly related to Barbara Castle that Tory ministers were reduced to fawning idiots in the royal presence: 'Everything was a shambles: "The worst swearing-in I have ever seen." The five came streaming in and every one of them flopped on to one knee on the floor! He indicated that they should move nearer the Queen on to the stools and to his astonishment everyone moved towards the stools on his knees!'[21]

Admittedly the ceremony is more demanding than ballroom dancing. Richard Crossman had to endure it in October 1964 as an incoming minister: 'I don't suppose anything more dull, pretentious, or plain silly has ever been invented. There we were, sixteen grown men. For over an hour we were taught how to stand up, how to kneel on one knee on a cushion, how to raise the right hand with the Bible in it, how to advance three paces towards the Queen, how to take the hand and kiss it, how to move back ten paces without falling over the stools – which had been carefully arranged so that you did fall over them.'[22]

To be sure, in the days before the royal family became megastars in a soap opera which they themselves scripted on a daily basis, they did inspire a curious awe (if not in Crossman). We all knew they were creatures apart. When I was about eight, my school was informed that Her Majesty would be driving through our corner of London. A thousand schoolboys, all in short grey trousers and caps, lined the streets, clutching paper Union Jacks. No doubt the royal limousines cruised past some distant intersection, but I have no memory of actually seeing the Queen. None the less, we all claimed to have done so. Hers was an auspicious presence and we longed to be, however briefly, in its aura.

Some years later, there was another royal visitation at my secondary school. We adulatory schoolboys were corralled behind a rope and invited to view the proceedings from a distance of about two hundred yards. Awe was soon replaced by boredom. Television reports of royal walkabouts give the impression that the royal family routinely mingle with their happy subjects. In practice such excursions into the hoi-polloi are carefully controlled.

Tony Benn – a useful witness, being one of the few persons with regular access to the Queen who was not rendered mute and obsequious by the experience – observed this process when, in 1975, the first oil was brought ashore from a North Sea field.

The first thing I noticed was that the workers who actually bring the oil ashore were kept behind a barbed wire fence and just allowed to wave to us as we drove by. We arrived at a huge tent, constructed at a cost of £40,000, and laid with an extravagant red carpet. The tent was about the size of two football pitches and held 1000 people, most of whom had been brought up from London . . .

The day was a complete waste of time and money, and when you see the Queen in action, everything else is just absorbed into this frozen feudal hierarchy. All the old big-wigs are brought out into the open as if they were somehow responsible for a great industrial achievement, while the workers are presented as natives and barbarians who can be greeted but have to be kept at a distance . . . I know there is a security problem but there was no need for this.[23]

Given the present disenchantment with the monarchy, it is worth noting what a recent phenomenon that is. On the wedding day of the Prince of Wales, I was considered highly eccentric in preferring to spend the day exploring the Kent countryside rather than glued to a television set. A friend of mine involved in the wedding ceremonial later observed to me, 'St Paul's Cathedral is built on a site of a Roman temple, and as I watched the young couple proceed up the aisle towards the altar I could smell the scent of sacrifice in the air.'

He knew of course, as I did not, that the wedding was a piece of breathtakingly clever stage management that had the nation as well as the bride fooled for years. I am not sure that the rot now busily undermining the plinth of monarchy set in with the maladroit television appearances by members of the royal family. I suspect it was the duplicity of that royal wedding – the careful selection of the virgin bride and her gradual betrayal, the icy wars between the courtiers, the stage-managed dishing of the dirt by the aggrieved couple – that undermined the image of the Perfect Family so painstakingly nurtured by the Windsors.

Until then, the royal family occupied a pinnacle of rectitude. It took seriously its role as head of the Church of England and Defender of the Faith, it shunned the centuries-old tradition of royal philandering, it avoided the company of divorced persons, it resisted debauchery of all kinds, it adopted, in short, all the values of the most sober and self-denying segments of the middle class. At the same time the political neutrality of the royal family, as well as its religious role, provided a defence against extremism and a guarantor of social stability. The sovereign, despite a strong coursing of German blood in royal veins, exemplified Britishness. Britons of all classes could identify with the sovereign as a personification of national identity. Especially in times of war, the sovereign merely had to *be*, not to do, in order to win respect and admiration.

The symbolic stability could not, and did not, last for ever. The British upper classes have never been reluctant to behave disgracefully, and it is ironic that the only group to which the aristocracy feels subservient – royalty – should have accepted values that were always alien to much of the upper classes. It has been tough luck on the heir to the throne and his siblings that they were required, at least initially, to pretend that they shared the moral rectitude of low-church vicars.

The deception is over, the frailties laid bare. What remains is a shell, a kind of aristocratic satellite slowly circling above us, utterly remote, wittering on, poor dears, about their *annus horribilis* and expecting a grovelling nation to fork out tens of millions because the owners of royal palaces believe they are exempt from fire regulations, plus £60 million for a new yacht. If ever a class were hurtling towards self-destruction, a *premier grand cru* that is oxidizing fast, it is the House of Windsor.

The British monarchy may well owe its survival hitherto to Benjamin Disraeli. After the death of the Prince Consort, Queen Victoria became a grumpy recluse. It was Disraeli, ever the astute politician, who gave her a new lease of life as matriarch and empress. The wilful old woman may have been a model of propriety, her ghillie apart, but she felt few constraints about trying to get her way with the parade of governments that passed before her during her long reign. She even tried to veto ministerial appointments, which was definitely out of order. Constitutional monarch or no, she liked to rule. Despite her autocratic tendencies, Victoria shared, perhaps exemplified, many of the values espoused by her subjects. One of her prime ministers, Lord Salisbury, observed, 'I have always felt that when I knew what the Queen thought, I knew pretty well what view her subjects would take, and especially the middle class of her subjects.'[24]

Her libertine son Edward may have offended public morals, but politically he behaved himself. After all, it was in the course of his reign that other monarchies trembled, and these anxieties were all the more troubling for George V, who looked on as his cousinhood toppled from their thrones in 1917 and 1918, leaving five imperial thrones and eight royal ones vacant. Even though in the course of George V's reign there were Labour administrations in Whitehall, the monarchy had nothing to fear. Labour ministers, as we have seen, could match in obsequiousness anything that courtiers and Tory peers could offer.

Given the veneration felt for the monarchy throughout much of the twentieth century, it is sometimes difficult to recall that this was the exception rather than the rule. The eighteenth and early nineteenth centuries tolerated ferocious criticism of the sovereign. On the day George IV was buried, *The Times* commented: 'There never was an individual less regretted by his fellow creatures than this deceased King. What eye has wept for him?'[25] Victoria's Prince Albert may not have been a barrel of laughs, but he was a model consort, thereby offending the pleasure-loving aristocracy with his seriousness and genuine concern for social issues such as housing.

His early death and Victoria's saintly widowhood did not still opposition to the monarchy on the part of some politicians. The Liberal MP Sir Charles Dilke, for one, harboured republican sentiments, declaring in 1871: 'If you can show me a fair chance that a republic here will be free from the political corruption which hangs about the monarchy, I say, for my part – and I believe that the middle classes in general will say – let it come.'[26] Pioneering socialists such as Keir Hardie felt it was more important to change the system than the figurehead. 'Until the system of wealth production can be changed,' he wrote in 1897, 'it is not worth exchanging the queen for a president. The robbery of the poor would go on equally under the one as the other.' None the less, he stoutly declared, 'I owe no allegiance to any hereditary rule' and refused in later life to stand when the national anthem was played.[27]

The left remained indifferent to republicanism. In May 1936 Harold Nicolson noted in his diary that H. G. Wells 'becomes more of a republican every day, and is in fact the only political thinker I know in England who seriously believes that it would be desirable or possible to abolish the monarchy'.[28] After the abdication crisis of December 1936, a republican amendment was offered to Parliament but received only five votes. The Labour Party echoed Keir Hardie's view that republicanism was a distraction from more important issues. By taking enormous care to act with complete propriety in all constitutional matters, the monarchy gave no ammunition to its few ideological opponents. George V and George VI may have expressed in private views that were stoutly right-wing, but they were careful not to seek to impose them on the government of the day.

When in 1969 there was one of the regular rows about the financing of the royal family, prompted by Prince Philip's lament on American television that the family would soon be in the red, the Cabinet discussed the issue. In his diaries Richard Crossman revealed that he was a republican, as were Barbara Castle and (surprisingly) Roy Jenkins, but other senior ministers, including George Brown and Jim Callaghan, were staunchly royalist. 'Roughly speaking,' noted Crossman, 'it is true that it is the professional classes who in this sense are radical and the working-class socialists who are by and large staunchly monarchist. The nearer the Queen they get the more the working-class members of the Cabinet love her and she loves them.'[29] It is hardly surprising that Labour politicians have been as wary as their Conservative counterparts about even considering reform of the constitutional monarchy. Even though the right-leaning *Economist* has come out in favour of abolition, republicanism is a taboo subject, at least in political circles.

The discretion of successive sovereigns does not disguise the fact that the Crown enjoys considerable powers, especially in the appointment of prime ministers. Where there is no consensus within the dominant political party, it is the monarch who, after taking advice, must decide who is to be the next prime minister. There are times when this right has been exercised. King George V summoned the inexperienced Stanley Baldwin rather than Lord Curzon to head the new government in 1923. He was swayed by Balfour's advice that it was better for the new prime minister to be a member of the Commons rather than the Lords.[30] Other contentious cases arose in 1957, when a choice had to be made between Harold Macmillan and R. A. Butler on the retirement of Sir Anthony Eden; and in 1963, when Elizabeth II sought a successor to the ailing Harold Macmillan. There are other, hitherto mercifully untested, 'residual powers', such as those that would allow the monarch, in an emergency, to ignore Parliament and govern 'by order of council'.[31]

The Crown has never been short of panting defenders rallying round whenever the most modest attempt at reform is proposed. When in 1952 the House of Commons debated whether or not to reduce the Civil List (in the absence, as some MPs pointed out, of any information about the income of the royal family), the proposal drew only twenty-five votes in favour. Emrys Hughes MP contrasted the Queen's Civil List income of £475,000 with the £14,000 that the Queen of the Netherlands took off the Dutch state.[32] Such arguments have continued to the present day, inevitably obscured by the guesswork concerning the wealth of the royal family.

In 1995 the Crown estate of 250,000 acres generated an income of £94.6 million. These revenues derived from agricultural estates and from London properties that include most of Regent Street, much of Haymarket and Trafalgar Square and the Strand; twenty-three acres along Millbank, Kensington Palace Gardens and Victoria Park in Bethnal Green. However, since 1760 these revenues have been handed to the state in exchange for the Civil List (currently £8.9 million), which is not a particularly good deal so far as the monarchy is concerned. However, the sovereign does not relinquish the (unknown) income from the fifty-thousand-acre Duchy of Lancaster, nor does the Prince of Wales hand over the income from the Duchy of Cornwall.[33] There are other costs, estimated at about £50 million, of running the monarchy which do not come from the Civil List but are financed by various government departments; these include the royal household, and the royal aircraft, train and yacht. Moreover, nobody knows the true worth of the Queen's jewels and investments.

In recent years concessions have been made to assuage public concern that the nation is underwriting one of the world's richest families. The Queen announced that from 1995 she would henceforth pay income tax.

A few trimmings here and there do not, of course, alter the strangulated nature of the Court and its elaborate structure of sinecures, antiquated titles, excessive luxury and insider pampering in the form of grace-and-favour apartments in royal palaces.

Yet the monarchy has its defenders. R. K. Massie robustly wrote in 1981, 'Nothing in American life or in the history of its political institutions, for instance, can match the awesome ring of the statement: "Queen Elizabeth II is the fortieth monarch of England since the Norman Conquest."'[34] Massie also offers the familiar argument that by its mere existence, the monarchy is doing us all a terrific favour: monarchy 'is theatre and pageantry, bringing glamour and colour into the lives of millions of citizens. And, to succeed, monarchy must also have a touch of mystery.'[35]

Others take a Burkean view, extolling the monarchy as a token of continuity within a sea of change, a mystical notion of a single family linking the past with the unborn future. At the emotionally overwhelming time of the Coronation in 1953, *The Times* became incoherent: 'The Queen also stands for the soul as well as for the body of the Commonwealth. In her is incarnate on her Coronation the whole of society, of which the State is no more than a political manifestation.'[36] Who could expect to live up to such a billing indefinitely?

A mere half-century later, such views seem decidedly quaint. In the 1950s and even 1960s any criticism of the monarchy was considered provocative and close to treasonous. Lord Altrincham's mild strictures, which were directed more at her courtiers than at Her Majesty, caused a scandal in the 1950s. As recently as 1985 even I, a republican, was taken aback when a friend of mine, a former chaplain at Eton, declared that in his view the entire royal family should be put against a wall and shot – the Romanov solution, we may call it. Admittedly this cleric's proposal was a trifle extreme, but it made me realize that it was no longer necessary to keep republican sympathies concealed.

Perhaps the monarchy will survive, but it doesn't deserve to. Not because the present occupant of the post has performed poorly – on the contrary – but because the job itself has become an affront to a democracy. It seeks to impose ethical, religious and cultural values to which the majority of the population no longer adhere. It insists upon maintaining itself in a luxurious style of life that would make any other European monarch blush. Governments tell us we are so close to penury as a nation that we can no longer afford adequately to educate, house and nurse our citizenry, but there is an endless source of money to sustain duplicated royal households and palaces, trains and yachts, and all the other perquisites of royalty.

The monarchy has shown itself incapable of more than cosmetic change. Criticism is deemed disloyal or cruel, on the grounds that They Cannot Answer Back. But any structure of state that has the power to choose prime ministers has to be held accountable, and has to justify its existence. The monarchy insists on maintaining a preposterous and teeming court, kept subservient with personal orders of chivalry, grace-and-favour apartments and other forms of patronage. By so doing it sustains a culture of deference, which in itself bolsters an antiquated and harmful class structure. Our social arbiters fritter away their energies arguing about whether divorced princesses retain the right to the title 'Royal Highness'. This is a momentous issue, we are informed, as a Diana or Sarah without the handle HRH would be required to curtsy to her own children. Arguments will be raised about the difficulties of switching from a constitutional monarchy to a republican democracy, but this is not the place to consider the means by which the change can be effected. Despite the difficulties – how the president is to be elected, what will replace the Queen's head on postage stamps, how to rename the Royal Mail – the imperative is greater than a matter of mere practicalities. As the millennium approaches it is indefensible for Britain to be governed according to an accident of birth, however admirable the present sovereign may be.

None the less the major political parties will not even consider the issue. The Labour Party discourages any talk of constitutional reform that may affect the role of the monarchy. In August 1996 a parliamentary candidate (a self-declared royalist, though of a peculiar kind) wrote a Fabian Society pamphlet, *Long to Reign Over Us?*, that proposed the abolition of the Civil List, the transfer of the royal prerogative to the Speaker of the Commons, and the creation of a rotating presidency for the Commonwealth; he proposed that the Queen's political role cease and her only duties be ceremonial. Annual parliamentary scrutiny would review the expenditure of the royal household. Such proposals fall far short of abolition, but were dismissed by the Labour leadership, no doubt for the understandable reason that this particular can of worms was best left unopened until well after the 1997 general election.[37]

After the Fabian pamphlet was published, Conservative newspapers such as the *Daily Telegraph* expressed shock, and Cabinet ministers such as Michael Portillo warned sternly about the dangers of meddling with the constitution. Backbench Tory MP Teresa Gorman called the author of the pamphlet, Paul Richards, a 'nutcase', and Labour MP Frank Dobson dismissed the pamphlet as 'silly'. A week later it became known that the court itself had for twice a year been convening a conclave called the Way Ahead Group, composed of senior members of the royal family and leading courtiers. And what had they been discussing? Much the same issues as those Paul Richards had been airing, plus that of primogeniture. As Richards himself pointed out in an article: 'When the *Sun* revealed that the royals themselves had been discussing reform, did Portillo warn them of the dangers of meddling with the constitution? . . . By proving their willingness to adapt, the royals have wrong-footed those Tories who seem incapable of countenancing change.'[38] I draw a different conclusion: royalism is closely allied to sycophancy, and it is intellectually dishonest for politicians to slag off reformist proposals when they come from a partisan source and to maintain silence when similar proposals, albeit still at a preliminary stage, come from the Palace.

The abolition of the monarchy would not cause the British class system to vanish overnight, but it would strike a mighty blow against the mode of deference and obsequiousness that is hindering the development of Britain as a modern political culture. Our twittering preoccupations with the trivialities of who bows to whom, who walks backwards and who does handstands, which national organization has the right to be dubbed Royal, who is bugging whose telephone, how to sort out which army officer is snogging which princess – all this idiocy, which makes for congenial gossip but has been elevated to the stuff of national obsession, would come to a precipitate end. And if, by implication, the abolition of the monarchy calls into question the House of Lords, the Royal Assent and the whole nature of our government, *tant mieux*.

FOURTEEN

Laws of Heredity: The House of Lords

It is not enough that a political institution works well practically; it must be defensible, it must be such as will bear discussion, and not excite ridicule and contempt.

Rev. Sydney Smith, 'Four Speeches on the Reform Bill', 1831

Some years ago I was visiting the Caucasian enclave of Nagorno Karabakh as part of a group led by Baroness Cox, who had championed the Armenian cause in that nation's struggle with neighbouring Azerbaijan. Also in the party were four congressional aides from Washington DC. While we were waiting for a helicopter to arrive, one of them asked me whether Baroness Cox was an aristocrat. I explained that she was a life peer and Deputy Speaker of the House of Lords, but not an aristocrat.

This left them baffled, and, as we had a few hours to spare, I sat them down and explained the British parliamentary system to the four aides. They greeted with astonishment my revelation that our upper chamber is dominated by hereditary peers.

Their bewilderment at a self-proclaimed democracy giving political powers to an unelected and unaccountable bunch of aristocrats confirmed the sheer oddity of the system. The British have grown up with it and seem to regard it as a lovable foible, a way of keeping some elderly gentlemen out of harm's way for a few afternoons a week. It is certainly true that the powers of the Lords are very limited. None the less we are talking about the upper chamber of the mother of parliaments.

In February 1997 the House of Lords was composed of 1203

members, of whom 1060 are eligible to attend and vote (the remainder are on leave of absence or haven't taken their oath). The House consists of 766 hereditary peers, 411 life peers and law lords, and twenty-six archbishops and bishops. Of the hereditary peers (as of October 1996) 318 were Conservative, 15 Labour, 24 Liberal Democrat, 201 sat as independent crossbenchers and 68 were 'others'. Of the life peers 142 were Conservative, 96 Labour, 32 Liberal Democrat, 118 crossbenchers and 21 'others'. The bishops profess no party affiliation.[1] In some respects the Lords may be an efficient body, but its members are under no compulsion to turn up, let alone contribute to its deliberations. Many life peers are created as 'working peers', but this is often no more than wishful thinking. As for most captains of industry or businessmen elevated to the Lords, their attendance record is, for understandable reasons, poor.

Despite the introduction of life peerages in 1958, the membership of the upper chamber remains skewed in favour of the Conservative Party. Among the crossbenchers, the voting record is approximately two to one in favour of Conservative governments. The chamber's Conservative leanings are hardly surprising, since aristocracies are not usually given to radical tendencies.

The average age of the peers is sixty-five – which seems to dispose of the argument sometimes offered in defence of the Lords that the arbitrariness of the hereditary principle brings in younger men who can make fresh and zany contributions to debates. This can certainly happen, and in April 1996 Lord Gretton became eligible, on turning twenty-one, to take his seat. However, he declined to do so on the laudable grounds that he was still at college.[2] Moreover, the argument that the Lords, topped up occasionally with an elderly trade union leader or former Labour minister or musician, can represent a broad social spectrum looks rather dim in light of the fact that as recently as ten years ago over one-quarter of the membership consisted of Old Etonians.[3] Indeed, half of all hereditary peers had attended that one school.

Certainly the Lords is no longer an extension of White's Club for the wealthy landowners who dominated the chamber until the late nineteenth century. In the twentieth century recipients of hereditary titles were more likely to be distinguished professional men than landowners. Between 1901 and 1957, 16 per cent of new creations were industrialists, 18 per cent professional men, and only 8 per cent were landowners.[4]

Lord Mancroft, a third-generation peer, points to himself as an example of a hereditary peer who none the less makes no claim to be an aristocrat. 'Indeed, the Lords is not so much a chamber composed of the aristocracy as the rump of the ruling class, a class that has always been partly embodied in the hereditary peerage. None the less our great political leaders have rarely been aristocrats. Men such as Peel, Gladstone and Asquith had private incomes, but were not aristocrats.

'I count myself a member of this rump, but I am not an aristocrat. My grandfather was Lord Mayor of Norwich, became an MP and minister and was given a peerage. He went to a local grammar school, I was sent to Eton. That's a typical story of the British ruling class, and the way it is flexible enough to absorb new recruits, whatever their background.'

By the early 1980s, calculated the historian Donald Shell, the occupational background of members, expressed in percentage terms, was as follows: landowner/farmer (44), public service/administrator (30), industrialist/service/manufacturing/retail (23), military (15), political work (14), banking/insurance (10), legal (10), civil and diplomatic service (10), authors/publishers (10), teachers and dons (9), arts (4), Church (3), advertising/PR (2), accountant/economist (2), engineer (2), others (22). The excessive totals occur because some peers have more than one occupation.[5] Elevations to life peerages have broadened the background of the membership, yet peers remain overwhelmingly prosperous, male and the products of public schools. Any claim, insists the usually dispassionate Donald Shell, that 'peers by succession being in the House of Lords through the accident of birth (and death) are a cross-section of society ... is nonsense'.[6]

Succession to a hereditary peerage at a relatively young age can give a welcome boost to the politically ambitious, enabling them to obtain ministerial office without having to go to all the trouble of finding a constituency and standing for election. Lord Melchett became a minister in the Labour government of 1976–79 at the tender age of twenty-eight. Now a stalwart of the Green movement, he is opposed to the hereditary principle in government. That devoted student of the aristocracy Hugh Montgomery-Massingberd interprets this as double standards, commenting: 'The obvious comment is that his own career has illustrated the advantages of such a system for if he had not been a peer he would have been nowhere near ministerial office at such an age.'[7] If that is so, then it is surely a scandal that ministerial office should have been offered to anyone merely because a hereditary peerage had provided a short cut to government membership.

There are other goings-on at this branch of the Palace of Westminster that strike me as close to sharp practice. When in 1992 Lynda Chalker lost her seat in the Commons, John Major promptly ennobled her and she continued to serve in government. Mrs Chalker may have been an excellent minister, but her constituents had favoured her opponent in the general election. Major's response was perfectly legal, no doubt, but hardly reflected the wishes of the electorate.

It also seems odd that the Leader of the House of Lords should be Lord Cranborne. Cranborne is the son of a peer, the Marquess of Salisbury, and thus ineligible to sit in the Lords in his own right. It transpires that John Major had a writ of acceleration issued, which allows the son of a peer with a secondary title (in this case Baron Cecil) to be 'summoned' to the Lords and thus to dodge the usual rules. Again, it's legal, but it's a fudge.

There are a few restrictions on membership. Minors and bankrupts are excluded, but lunacy, thanks to a lacuna in the Mental Health Act, offers no legal hindrance to a peer taking his seat in the House of Lords. Lord Bicester, who has spent most of the past thirty-two years in mental institutions but is no longer considered dangerous to himself or others, took up his seat in the Lords in 1997.

Rogues are also welcome. The 6th Earl of Effingham inherited a title but no money. His career got off to a poor start when in 1932 he drove over a labourer and killed him. His subsequent career included being declared an official bankrupt; going into business, so to speak, with the Kray twins; and conviction on a drink-driving charge. It was not until 1967, by which time he had presumably recovered from the bankruptcy, that he first honoured the Lords with a maiden speech. He attended the house regularly, pocketing his expenses but neglecting to make any contribution to the business of the House. His main reason for hanging around the Palace of Westminster was to drum up business for a travel agency. When he died in February 1996, *The Times* drily noted, 'It would be difficult, therefore, to claim that, whether in his lawmaking role or his general way or life, he represented a shining advertisement for the hereditary principle.'[8]

A similar observation was made by Henry Labouchere, a Radical MP – only in the 1880s. He was a consistent campaigner for the abolition of the House of Lords and remarked of Lord Ailesbury: 'It is rather ridiculous that a man who has been warned off a racecourse and expelled from the Jockey Club should come down here to legislate for the people of England by hereditary descent.'[9]

Another of today's peers, Lord Monkswell, has enjoyed a spell in prison. The title was granted to an ancestor who served in one of Gladstone's governments, and eventually passed to a doctor whose socialist principles prompted him to disclaim the title. The doctor's son, Gerard Collier, worked in middle management until he inherited the title. His contributions to the House have been few but memorable, and he helped four lesbians to gain access to the galleries during a debate on the so-called Clause 28, which allowed local councils to ban activities that could be construed as promoting homosexuality. The lesbians abseiled into the chamber, to the dismay of their lordships and the delight of the public. Lord Monkswell gained further disapproval after he took the extreme measure of assaulting his mistress's psychotherapist, and ended up in prison. After his release, he described himself as an unemployed parliamentary consultant, and supplemented his dole money with his stipend from the Lords.[10] A peer is entitled to £33 per day, plus £32 for secretarial expenses, and an overnight subsistence payment of £74 if his or her home is so distant from the House that accommodation in London must be found if the peer is to attend on successive days.[11]

By now it should be apparent that government according to the hereditary principle is equivalent to government by lottery. This parliamentary aberration is legitimized by a ceremonial memorably described by Matthew Parris as 'a good deal of to-ing and fro-ing and bowing by people dressed in carpets'.[12] The ceremony for the introduction of new peers was created in 1621. Today it seems like the first step in that anaesthetization that afflicts most new members of the House, reducing even Labour peers to a coy and chortling geniality. Lady Longford, in her prelude to her husband's history of the Lords, spells it out:

> The ornate doors at the northern end of the Chamber open and the figure of Black Rod appears. He is an officer of the Order of the

Garter, founded by Edward III, and carries a black rod in his black-gloved right hand and wears a white satin bow on each shoulder of his black tail coat; he is undoubtedly the smartest figure in the House. Behind him come Garter King of Arms in a splendid tabard of red, blue and gold with the arms of England, Scotland, Ireland and Wales; there are scarlet satin bows on his shoulders. In his right hand is his silver-gilt sceptre of office, in his left the new peer's patent of creation on a vellum scroll. Then follow in single file behind Garter the new peer himself supported by two peers of his own rank . . . All three wear their scarlet and ermine parliamentary robes . . .

Meanwhile our three peers have reached the Bar of the House . . . All three bow. I used to think they were bowing to the Lord Chancellor, but on learning that they were bowing to the 'Cloth of Estate', I made the further mistake of imagining that the Cloth of Estate was the Throne itself. For there it stood on the shining dais with a fitted cover of red cloth piped in yellow. Not so. The Cloth of Estate marks the position which the Sovereign, if present, would occupy, beneath the carved canopy glittering above the Throne . . .

The new peer approaches the Woolsack, where the Lord Chancellor is awaiting him in the white wig, black tricorne hat, black breeches, stockings and buckled shoes and a black gown.

And so it goes on, for a considerable while longer.[13]

The powers of the House of Lords are, of course, limited. The primary power is that of delaying legislation and of scrutinizing and proposing amendments to bills under consideration by the Commons. In the late 1980s and early 1990s, when the Conservative government grew in arrogance in inverse relation to the talents of its ministers, the Lords displayed unwonted vigour in honing and refining legislation, on some occasions returning badly drafted bills for reconsideration by the Commons. The Lords had stern things to say about the Major government's plans to introduce nursery education vouchers and to deny benefits to asylum seekers who do not claim asylum within minutes of disembarkation, and has objected to measures that would dangerously extend the powers of the police.

The only actual veto retained by the upper chamber is over any bill to extend the lifetime of a parliament. This has only arisen in wartime, and the Lords accepted the proposals made by the Commons in 1915 and 1940.[14] If the argument for the continued existence of the House of Lords as presently constituted is that it's a fairly harmless institution that has virtually no power to deflect the will of the people as expressed in the Commons, then it is fair to ask whether it is worth preserving an archaic body with such paltry powers and influence.

The Lords as a parliamentary body (of sorts) dates back to the reign of Edward I (1272–1307), who summoned sixteen parliaments during his reign. Already during the fourteenth century the Lords and Commons were meeting as separate bodies, and by the end of the century the former were headquartered in the Palace of Westminster, the latter in the chapter house of Westminster Abbey. In those days membership of the House of Lords was not a hereditary right, but by 1500 every peer of the realm could expect to be included in any summons to Parliament. In medieval times the Lords were paramount but gradually surrendered much of their authority to the Commons. Only during the reign of Henry VIII did the House of Lords come to be known as such, and the hereditary right of peers to receive summonses to the chamber only became law in 1625.[15] In 1692, the Lords accepted the Commons' claim to financial control.[16] Thereafter the balance of power between the two chambers remained essentially unaltered until the Parliament Act of 1911.

The current debates about the merits of the hereditary principle as a basis for government are not new, and even some aristocrats have expressed grave reservations. A reformist bill was introduced by the Earl of Dunraven, a Conservative, in 1888, and in the same year the Commons discussed a resolution questioning the hereditary principle. The future Lord Curzon, as a Conservative MP in the 1880s, urged the House: 'Why should we not, by means of life peerages, make the House of Lords representative of the middle classes of this country, and even of the labouring classes too, and of the dissenting denominations, and, more than that, of every branch of industry and business?'[17]

Gladstone was also keen to reform the House of Lords, but was dissuaded from pursuing the matter in 1893. In 1907 Lord Newton, also a Conservative, introduced a bill, subsequently withdrawn, that would have eliminated a peer's automatic right to a seat in the Lords. A select committee, appointed in 1908 by the Earl of Rosebery, came to much the same conclusions as Lord Newton.[18] Winston Churchill, newly hatched as a Liberal MP in 1906, dismissed the Lords as 'an institution absolutely foreign to the spirit of the age and the whole movement of society'; it was 'one sided, hereditary, unpurged, unrepresentative, irresponsible, absentee'.[19] Even a grandee such as the Duke of Bedford voiced his opposition to the hereditary principle, and proposed a system in which life peers were appointed to the chamber.[20]

Such debates were timely, as the Lords and the Commons were frequently at loggerheads, especially in 1906 and 1908 when the Lords trashed two education bills passed by the Commons; the bills had to be abandoned by the Liberal government. Other legislation was obstructed or rejected in 1909. It was inevitable that the Commons should lose patience with such high-handed behaviour, and in February 1909 the Liberal MP Arthur Ponsonby introduced proposals for reform. 'The principle of hereditary legislators', he declared, 'will not hold for a moment because it is really not defended anywhere.'[21] But the measure was roundly defeated as it lacked the support of the Asquith government. Emboldened, the House of Lords rejected the Liberal Budget that year, provoking a dissolution of Parliament and a general election in January 1910. The Liberals were returned to power but continuing difficulties with the Lords led to a second election in December.

Perhaps Lord Redesdale was not typical of the reactionary tendency in the upper chamber, but his daughter Jessica Mitford's account of his furious opposition to any reforms gives some flavour of the more colourful defences of the rights of the peerage. His

> deepest ire, however, was reserved for a proposal to reform the House of Lords by limiting its powers. The Lords who sponsored this measure did so out of a fear that, unless such a course was taken, a future Labour government might abolish the House altogether. Farve angrily opposed this tricky political manoeuvre. His speech was widely quoted in the Press: 'May I remind your Lordships that denial of the hereditary principle is a direct blow at the Crown? Such a denial is, indeed, a blow at the very foundation of the Christian faith.' To Farve's annoyance, even the Conservative Press poked fun at this concept, and the Labour Press had a field day with it. 'What *did* you mean to say?' we asked, and he patiently explained that just as Jesus became God because He was the Son of God, so the oldest son of a Lord should inherit his father's title and prerogatives.[22]

In 1911 Asquith introduced the Parliament Act that would replace the absolute veto powers of the House of Lords with the power to delay legislation by up to two years. The Lords gave the bill a second reading but amended it heavily. Asquith forced the issue by threatening, with the acquiescence of the King, to create a sufficient number of new peers to assure a government majority in the truculent Lords unless the amendments were removed. On 9 August the bill was debated again in the Lords and eventually passed with a government majority of seventeen. The House retained its right to initiate and to amend legislation, being compelled to stand back only if that legislation was passed by the Commons in three successive sessions. So-called 'money bills' could only be delayed up to one month. The Parliament Act weakened the more autocratic features of the House of Lords, but by no means stripped it of all its powers. With a few amendments, those powers are still in place.[23]

The preamble to the Parliament Act made it clear that the government had never intended it to be the final word on the composition of the upper chamber. The Bryce Commission, set up to consider the matter further, in 1918 proposed an upper chamber partly elected by MPs and partly chosen by a joint committee. Proposals based on the commission's report were made to Parliament in 1922 and 1927 and broadly endorsed, but no legal changes were made.[24] In 1925 the Duke of Sutherland proposed restricting the eligible peers to 350 or 400 and introducing life peers. The consequences were predictable: 'Following the Lord Chancellor, many other Peers spoke in support of my motion,' the duke recalled; 'the motion was carried; and the Lord Chancellor then announced that a Cabinet Committee would be appointed to consider the matter. At last, it seemed as if something really would be done – but, I need hardly add, my optimism was soon damped and has since been extinguished . . . Nothing further has been done to this day, thirty-two years later.'[25]

Even Labour governments were reluctant reformers, and the Attlee administration merely resorted instead to promoting Labour supporters to the peerage so as to correct, slightly, its pro-Tory balance. Decades after it had been widely recognized, even by Conservative peers, that the House of Lords was democratically indefensible, successive governments decided instead to let sleeping dogs lie.

In 1958 life peerages were created, a development welcomed by much of the hereditary peerage. The idea had been mooted back in 1910, and even the King had told Asquith that he was 'strongly in favour of them as I believe are most sensible people'.[26] Life peerages were also conferred on women, helping to redress another imbalance in the Lords.

It was the death of Viscount Stansgate in 1960 that renewed debate about the House of Lords. His heir was a Labour MP called Anthony Wedgwood-Benn. The Speaker of the House of Commons and the Commons Committee of Privileges ruled that 'Wedgwood-Benn' was now translated into 'Stansgate' and thus the bearer of the name was ineligible to retain his Commons seat. Instructions were given to bar the member from the House. Wedgwood-Benn received little support from his leader, Hugh Gaitskell, who both encouraged the new peer to take his seat in the Lords (which as always was short of Labour members) and banned him from meetings of the parliamentary Labour Party until he did so.

This kind of thing had happened before. In 1894 three MPs, St John Brodrick, Lord Wolmer and George Nathaniel Curzon – all heirs to peerages – jointly introduced a private members' bill to enable a sitting MP to retain his seat on succeeding to a peerage. It received a first reading, but thereafter floundered for lack of parliamentary time. The following year Lord Wolmer's father died, and Wolmer became Lord Selborne. The Speaker required the new peer to withdraw from the Commons while the chamber discussed his desire to retain his seat. To no avail: Selborne was ruled ineligible, just as Wedgwood-Benn would be sixty-five years later.[27]

In 1961 Wedgwood-Benn, henceforth referred to as Tony Benn in accordance with his own preference, introduced the Peerage Renunciation Bill, which would allow a peer to give up his title during his lifetime, but permit his heir to take it up again on his father's death should he so wish. Benn, readopted by his constituency, forced a by-election in May 1961; he doubled his majority to over thirteen thousand votes. But he was still barred from the House of Commons, and even his own party excluded him from its annual conference as an *ex officio* member. Meanwhile, his Conservative opponent sat in Parliament as the member for Bristol South-east.

It was an extraordinary situation. Parliament had upheld the anachronistic hereditary principle and overruled a democratic electoral mandate. There was no doubt that the voters of Bristol South-east wanted Mr Benn to represent them, but were being denied that right. Only in Britain, of all democracies, could an electoral decision be regarded as an irritant in the face of the near-mystical powers of the aristocracy.

Parliament did at least acknowledge that this was a bizarre and unsatisfactory situation, and set up a joint select committee to consider the matter. In 1963 the committee voted in favour of permitting peers to renounce their titles and the Peerage Act subsquently became law. Benn renounced his title in July 1963. Another by-election was held, which the other political parties chose not to contest, and Mr Benn, his title consigned to the attic for the rest of his lifetime, was re-elected. The right to renounce was to prove handy for Conservative peers too, allowing Lords Hailsham and Home to put themselves into considera-tion for leadership of their party. (After they completed their service in the Commons, they were kindly returned to the upper chamber as life peers.)

The 1963 Peerage Act also allowed women who had succeeded to peerages to take up their seats in the Lords, and extended the same right to all holders of Scottish peerages, who had previously been represent-ed by a group of sixteen elected from a total of thirty-one Scottish peers. These measures may have sorted out anomalies, but if anything they reinforced the hereditary character of the chamber.

When Labour was voted into government in 1964, Prime Minister Harold Wilson took the same view as Clement Attlee about reforming the House of Lords: he didn't want to touch the issue with a bargepole. When Lord Longford raised the matter, he was supported only by the Lord Chancellor, Gerald Gardiner, and Wilson dismissed the proposal by saying, 'I can imagine nothing quite so divisive as an attempt to reform the House of Lords.'[28] But two years later Longford won the support of Richard Crossman, the new Leader of the House of Commons. Lord Carrington, then the Conservative Leader of the Lords, was also sympathetic.

If the Labour leadership in the 1960s was reluctant to initiate radical reform, it was for sound tactical reasons. Labour ministers knew well that the Lords was an absurd institution, but it suited governments nicely to have an upper chamber with very limited powers. Reform the Lords, and it might gain some teeth, which could inflict damage on government legislation. If some doubters became converts to the cause it was because they felt that, if Labour didn't deal with the issue, other parties would. Barbara Castle expressed this view in her diary entry for 12 October 1967:

> I think the position of doing nothing and keeping the Lords impotent by keeping them ridiculous is no longer tenable. We should either abolish the place or reform it. And it is clear that the Liberals – and Tories too – will come out with proposals for reform even if we do not, and it would be unwise to let them get the initiative.[29]

Later that year an all-party conference tried to work out a deal: the composition of the Lords would be reformed with some increase in its powers, but the specific powers to delay legislation would be curtailed. The reformed composition would consist of non-voting hereditary peers, who would be welcome to contribute to debates, and voting peers, who would be appointed for life and expected to attend regularly. The proposal left the hereditary system intact (even though Crossman noted in his diary that both Tories and Liberals with whom he had been in discussion favoured a House made up solely of life peers),[30] but denied the peerage its automatic right to a vote. The life peers would include a substantial portion of crossbenchers so as to boost the independence of the upper chamber.

Initially ministers could work up little enthusiasm for the proposals. However, in November 1968 the government published a White Paper entitled *House of Lords Reform*. It was modelled on the conference proposals, and would have introduced a retirement age of seventy-two and reduced not only the hereditary element but the numbers of law lords and bishops, giving a chamber with 230 voting members. The White Paper attracted wide support from ministers and shadow ministers but considerable criticism from backbenchers.

The bill, called the Parliament (No. 2) Bill, was put before Parliament. The House of Lords voted 251 to 56 in favour, with Conservative supporters outnumbering Conservative opponents by two to one. After its second reading on 3 February 1969, the bill ran into trouble during its committee stage. Eleven days and eighty-eight hours were spent arguing its merits; the bill was vigorously attacked by the bizarre combination of Enoch Powell from the Tory right and Michael Foot from the Labour left. The two front benches, although supporting the bill, failed to throw their weight behind it; on 17 April 1969, after a ferocious row in Cabinet, the government abandoned the bill.

It was not difficult to understand why Conservative traditionalists might be opposed to reform, but it is harder to explain why some radical Labour elder statesmen attacked it so savagely. Foot's objections came from his reluctance to increase further the powers of prime ministerial patronage. (Similar objections were raised in 1996 when Tony Blair proposed, in effect, to revive the bill were Labour returned to power.) Other Labour MPs feared that a reformed upper chamber would have greater powers than the cosy but usually ineffectual House of Lords with which they had cohabited for so many decades. Some MPs from both sides of the House argued for an elected component in addition to or instead of the appointed.[31]

So almost seventy years after the Parliament Act had successfully curtailed the powers of the House of Lords, and decades after repeated attempts – often initiated by the peerage – to modernize the upper chamber, Parliament, and Britain, were back to square one. In the years that followed the ignominious withdrawal of the Parliament (No. 2) Bill, there were sporadic attempts to revive the issue of reform. In 1978 a Conservative Review Committee, chaired by Lord Home, recommended a hybrid upper chamber on the basis of election as well as nomination. They envisaged a total membership of four hundred.[32]

But as far as the Labour leadership was concerned the issue was dead. In April 1979 Tony Benn and Eric Heffer tried to revive the long-standing Labour pledge to reform, but James Callaghan merely retorted, 'I won't have it, I won't have it.' And he didn't, although the election manifesto for that year made the watery statement that 'the House of Lords is indefensible with its power and influence'.[33] Nor was the indifference confined to the Labour Party. After Mrs Thatcher came to power in 1979, her government made no attempt to implement the proposals put forward by the eminent Conservative Review Committee of the previous year. During the 1980s a secret committee chaired by William Whitelaw pondered the idea of further reform, but once again no action was taken. Labour Party study groups continued to consider the idea, but never proposed anything more substantial than commitments to limit its power.

Harold Wilson had created 243 peers – a salutary reminder of the immense powers of patronage enjoyed by modern prime ministers –

but none bore a hereditary title. Margaret Thatcher in 1983 took the thoroughly retrograde step of reinstituting them. The beneficiaries, William Whitelaw and former Speaker George Thomas, had no male heirs, so their titles would die with them, but none the less, after decades of proposals for reform from both sides of the House, her decision sent out the wrong signals. Moreover in 1984 Harold Macmillan, who was 'traditionally' entitled to an earldom as a former prime minister, accepted the earldom of Stockton, which passed to his grandson on Macmillan's death in 1987. So thanks to Mrs Thatcher the hereditary principle, the arch-absurdity of British political life, has been perpetuated.

Her government was willing to go to any lengths to avoid defeat on any serious measure in the Lords. Her proposal to replace the supposedly unpopular rates with the 'poll tax', imposing a standard rate of local tax on all, whatever their income, was passed by the Commons in 1988. This was precisely the kind of issue on which the Lords, stuffed as it was with elderly lawyers, might prove a trifle awkward, especially since someone had put forward the unkind amendment that the new tax should be related to one's ability to pay it. However, the Leader of the House of Lords, Lord Denham, saw to it that five hundred peers, some of whom had probably not set foot in the Palace of Westminster in decades, turned up on the night to give the government an overwhelming majority of 317 votes to 183. Some of the richest landowners in Europe dutifully voted for a tax that would ensure that they paid the same sum as the council worker who swept the streets in front of their London houses.[34]

This time-honoured procedure, genially known as whipping in the backwoodsmen, provoked considerable derision in the country. The independent-minded Tory MP George Walden described it as 'an ignoble procedure',[35] but governments are less squeamish. So are certain peers. Lord Vestey, who naturally supported the government, was reported to have saved himself £4000 in taxes on his Gloucestershire estate alone.[36] In most institutions, such behaviour would have been regarded as blatant conflict of interest, but the Lords prides itself on its breadth of expertise, and no doubt Lord Vestey is a leading expert on tax matters as they relate to his own landholdings. (Indeed, there is no Lords equivalent to the register of members' interests in which MPs must confess all.)

As though it had become a ritual event for a bunch of Conservative peers to ponder their own parliamentary fate, another report, *Second Chamber*, was published in 1995; its author was the Earl of Carnarvon, assisted by Lords Selbourne, Bancroft and Tenby. It offered a defence of the Lords, paying tribute to the independence of its crossbenchers and the contributions made by the younger peers. The report warned that 'the worst upshot would be if reform of the House of Lords were to lead to years of constitutional tinkering and uncertainty'.

This seemed to be a reference to the Labour Party, which, revitalized under Tony Blair, was formulating its own proposals. These involved abolishing the voting rights of hereditary peers and creating up to one hundred life peers to restore the political balance of the upper house. There was no immediate proposal for any elected component. Recognizing that this proposal magnified prime ministerial patronage, Labour suggested that some kind of independent body would help draw up the list of the lucky one hundred, and it pledged itself to re-examine how to make the Lords more democratic sometime in the twenty-first century. Meanwhile, Jack Straw MP reassured the present membership of the House of Lords that some of the more active hereditary peers would be allowed to stay on in the reformed house after conversion into life peers; further, twenty-first-century stages of reform might provide for a partially elected upper chamber.[37]

The reactionary historian Andrew Roberts lamented that reform would mean that 'a fund of eccentricity and talent will be lost to future generations', including, no doubt, Lords Effingham and Monkswell. The Lords, Roberts continues, 'has traditionally shown indulgence to those of its members, such as Lord Montagu of Beaulieu, the late Lord Kagan and the Marquess of Bristol, who have fallen foul of the law'.[38] Precisely why those who have fallen foul of the law should be empowered to legislate over the rest of us is not clear to me. In an orgy of sentiment, Roberts laments that rationalism 'is to triumph at last over the natural romance and ancient elegance inherent in the hereditary principle. What has always been an organism will be turned into a machine'.[39]

William Waldegrave MP, the brother of an earl, offered an extraordinary defence based on the argument that the populace much prefers non-democratic to democratic institutions. He offers not a shred of evidence to support this view:

People despise democratic institutions in this country. If you look at
the institutions that have the greatest public support, they are
hereditary institutions. Peers are respected more than members of
the House of Commons, the Royal Family is respected more than the
peers. The further away you are from the democratic process in this
country, the more respect you have.[40]

In similar vein, Woodrow Wyatt, once, astonishingly, a Labour MP,
writes, with scant evidence: 'The country loves and values the House of
Lords, despite and even because of its eccentricities . . . Hereditary
dukes, marquesses and earls are more highly regarded by ordinary
people than they may merit. They are seen as live, romantic evidence of
a history we are proud of.'[41] Wyatt does conclude that life peers also
make a useful contribution, which is just as well, since he is one of them.
Indeed, for Wyatt the fact that peers are not accountable to constituents
(or anybody else) is, in some mystical way, a triumph of democracy: 'In a
sense, the Lords is the last bastion of democracy in Parliament. As they
cannot be dismissed by constituents, they have a habit, now unusual in
the Commons, to listen to debates and vote for whichever side they
think has won the argument.'[42]

A related line of defence was articulated recently by the Marquess of
Reading: 'When I first joined I was worried by the lack of democracy,
but I now see the wisdom of the Upper House. We are a wonderful,
eclectic mix who can talk on the most extraordinary range of subjects.
We have also been brought up with a sense of responsibility to
govern.'[43] Mark Bence-Jones and Hugh Montgomery-Massingberd
echo, in romantic and essentially fatuous terms, Lord Reading's self-
congratulatory view:

> Although the life peers are intended to broaden the membership of the
> House, it is in fact the hereditary element which gives the House of
> Lords its unique and most valuable breadth of outlook; bringing to the
> House younger peers and an extraordinary variety of distinguished men
> and women who have experience or expertise in particular fields far
> removed from those of the average political time server.[44]

When reform was debated in the Lords in July 1996, Lord Cranborne,
Leader of the Lords, declared that the amateur nature of the Lords was
one of its greatest assets.[45]

A more thoughtful conservative defence was given to me by a bishop: 'I don't think democracy should be confused with head-counting. The Lords brings into public life those whose voice might otherwise go unheard. There are some very gifted and useful members of the hereditary peerage. It also brings in the young. Were the hereditary element to disappear from the Lords, the average age of the chamber would rise. It's about sixty-five now. After reform I expect it would rise to seventy-five.

'I don't doubt that if Labour comes to power the Lords will be reformed. It's obvious that Tony Blair can only fulfil a few of his plans. Doubtless the easiest to deliver is some constitutional change. So no doubt he will make a sacrifice of us, and throw a few ducal coronets to the masses.

'As you can tell, I am not enchanted by the notion of constitutional reform. As a historian I find ancient wisdom enshrined in our historic constitution. But I dare say you won't find a single other member of the chamber, and certainly no hereditary peer, who will defend the *status quo*.

'I would justify my presence as a voting member of the Lords by arguing that although my vote can only be cast on a personal basis, I do none the less have a constituency. On issues such as asylum bishops do have considerable experience. We come into contact with individual cases, we make representations to the Home Secretary, we listen to what various agencies have to tell us, and so forth. I can't be partisan, of course, and the basis of my vote has to be an appeal to fundamental Christian principles. On an issue such as the poll tax, although there may arguably be a moral dimension involved, I do not think bishops should stand in the way of a fiscal measure approved by the lower chamber.'

Perhaps the most convincing defence of the Lords is that it functions well as an institution. Indeed, few would dispute that its debates and committee discussions can result in beneficial amendments to hastily conceived legislation; that the level of debate, conducted in a calmer and less antagonistic atmosphere than that of the Commons, is often more distinguished than in the lower chamber; that its running costs are remarkably low; and that the tally of 380 peers who in 1995 attended regularly is impressive. Alexander Pope's couplet is an appropriate summary:

For forms of government let fools contest;
Whate'er is best administer'd is best.[46]

Lord Pilkington, chairman of the Broadcasting Complaints Commission and a recently elevated life peer after concluding a career in education as High Master of St Paul's, agrees that the Lords can't be defended on rational grounds but finds some merit in the hereditary principle: 'Life peerages tend to go to men and women who have kept systems working, not to radicals. For the most part they are conferred on those reaching the end of their professional lives. So the maverick tendency in the Lords is represented by the hereditary peers. Moreover, much of the necessary work in the Lords is done by hereditary peers – certainly on the Conservative side. It also gives a forum to some highly individual characters such as Conrad Russell. It's very hard to see someone like Conrad standing for election, but he makes original and provocative contributions that might otherwise not be made. It is doubtful if many would question the system if hereditary peers were split more evenly between the parties.

'Life peers, on the other hand, are often a mirror image of the political party making the appointments. Margaret Thatcher elevated Thatcherites, Tony Blair elevates Blairites. So to some extent the appointees are under political control, which is far less true of the hereditary element. It's also less true of life peers ennobled because of their distinction as actors or musicians or publishers, but on the other hand they rarely attend.

'The presence of the hereditary element means that the Lords cannot be more than a revising chamber. We often have the time and expertise to give bills more careful consideration than the Commons. To give the Lords more clout, such as the right to reverse decisions taken in the Commons, you would need to have an elected element, which is just what the Commons is fearful of.

'Hereditary peers have a tradition of public service that continues to this day. Ever since George III our monarchs, with the exception of George IV, have followed a line of duty and public service. This has been echoed in certain aristocratic families such as the Salisburys. Of course it's an anachronism, but the alternative would be to confer greater power on those who support the political parties, whether financially or otherwise.'

Lord Mancroft has no problem with the hereditary principle: 'I don't see the hereditary principle as an anachronism. Inheritance is part of the structure of life. Businesses, houses, land, possessions, all are handed down through families from generation to generation. The peerage is one more facet of this. The House of Lords is just the last vestige of the hereditary principle that used to be the norm in this country. The Lords is not democratic, it isn't meant to be democratic, but other powerful office-holders, such as judges and bishops, aren't elected either. However, I am not opposed to reform, though it's hard to make constructive suggestions for how to achieve it until people decide what a reformed second chamber is supposed to do.

'In our defence I would argue that peers are untainted by political allegiance or other outside influence. You can't buy a peer. Our strength is that we only answer to our own conscience.'

The Lords' strongest argument against reform is the difficulty of replacing the House with a chamber that would satisfy the criteria of being more democratic while less dependent on political patronage. Moreover, there is a nervous feeling, not unjustified, that wholesale reform (or abolition) of the Lords could threaten other elements of our unwritten constitution. With the bishops ejected from the upper chamber, disestablishment becomes a more plausible option for the Church of England. What alternative forum, if any, would be devised for the law lords, who would also, one assumes, have a reduced (or no) role in a reformed chamber? If the most democratic option were pursued – an elected upper chamber – then how would its powers be balanced against those of the elected Commons, and would the Commons sanction a second chamber that would be a genuine rival to itself? And how could a mostly appointed upper house have any greater claim to democratic legitimacy than the present arrangements? These are not trifling issues.

The perpetual tactical difficulty in which the House of Lords finds itself is that if it is too effective in revising legislation, it lays itself open to the accusation that it is thwarting the will of the people as expressed by the Commons. On the other hand, if the noble Lords sit on their hands, then its very existence would be called into question.

The consequence is that the House of Lords places self-imposed limits on its powers of revision. Thus it is often reluctant to confront the government, and allows bad legislation to go through more or less on the nod precisely because it fears charges of obstructionism. In 1993, for example, the unpopular bill to privatize British Rail slipped through the Lords, despite the misgivings of numerous members. Curiously, the repeated run-ins between the often inept Major government and the Lords did not lead to Conservative MPs demanding changes in the composition of the powers of the Lords; indeed, the position of the Major government on Lords reform was that there was no need for it.

However, the self-proclaimed independence of the House of Lords must not be exaggerated. Despite the encomia directed at the cross-benchers, they have, since 1979, supported the Conservative line two times out of three: 'In the 1988/9 session, for example, 61% of crossbench votes went to the Government and helped produce 172 Tory victories and just 12 defeats . . . On average the post-1979 Conservative governments have lost 15 divisions per session; the 1974–9 Labour governments lost about 70 per session.'[47]

There is no avoiding the fact that the Lords has an overwhelming Conservative majority (Labour peers account for only 10 per cent of the membership), even though Lord Cranborne argues, unconvincingly, that this huge majority is a 'myth' because many hereditary peers never vote.[48] But, as we have seen, they certainly do vote when the government requires their votes on an issue crucial to its survival. Lord Skidelsky, a life peer who defends the hereditary principle, has argued that the issue of the Tory majority can be resolved by eliminating the surplus: 'This can be done by reducing the number of hereditary Conservative peers and increasing the number of Labour and Liberal Democrat life peers. A reduction of Conservative numbers could be effected by Conservative hereditary peers electing a proportion of their numbers.'[49]

Not that the Labour and Liberal Democrat peers are necessarily ferocious adversaries. Many Labour peers become heavily sedated once free to roam the tearooms of the Lords. They offer only the most gentle criticism, making ponderously coy allusions to 'the other place' where many of them eked out their political careers, and seem to lose in a sea of politeness whatever incisiveness they may once have possessed. In 1967 Richard Crossman despaired of Labour peers such as Frank Beswick and Gerald Gardiner: 'They've only been there a few years but they are already in love with the House of Lords and only want to see the mildest changes.'[50]

Tony Benn recalls meeting Dora Gaitskell, ennobled after the untimely death of her husband. She was in high dudgeon because Eric Heffer MP had attacked the Lords.

'Eric Heffer,' she fumed, 'wrote an article in *The Times* called "Who wants the Lords?" and I'm going to write back, "Who wants Eric Heffer?"'

I said the electors of Liverpool Walton want Eric Heffer, and off she stomped. When Labour people get to the Lords they love it; they don't want to move or change it; they can't see any problems with it.[51]

And it is surprising to see how the socialist Barbara Castle softened her stance when it was her husband Ted who, to compensate for disappointments in his own political career, was handed a life peerage. On the day of his induction into the Lords she wrote: 'Ideologically I hate the House of Lords, but, as a wife, I know what this means for Ted and I don't intend to let anything spoil it. It is his great chance to take part in Parliament and it is a poor socialism that leaves no room for the illogicalities of love.'[52]

Love might not need to be so illogical were it not for the irredeemably illogical nature of the House of Lords. It is refreshing to be reminded that some senior hereditary peers acknowledge the absurdity of the place. The Earl of Onslow recently declared: 'I find it extremely difficult to justify the fact that, because one of my ancestors got pissed with George IV, I can boss you all about. I would be totally in favour of deeply thought-out, root-and-branch reform of the second chamber.'[53] This view is echoed by none other than the Duke of Westminster: 'I fundamentally disagree with [the Lords'] present make-up . . . It is no longer appropriate today for someone to have a full vote in Parliament merely by virtue of an accident of birth.'[54]

Many peers favour reform but few have firm ideas about how it is to be accomplished. Lord Mancroft confesses to being perplexed: 'I don't have a clear idea of what a reformed Lords would be like. I certainly am convinced that an elected upper chamber is undesirable: it would be a nightmare. But things can't go on as they are because of the huge load of legislation in Parliament. I don't believe more than ten per cent of legislation coming from the Commons is properly considered. It's scandalous that the Commons deprives us of decent working conditions and research facilities. I know MPs are also badly off in this respect, but it's far worse in the Lords. I have to share an office with six other peers. But if all this legislation, including new European legislation, is going to pass through the system, then they will have to make more use of the second chamber, and that will require reform.

'But in the meantime I think we should leave well alone. The Lords is primarily a revising chamber, and very expert at it. That's our strength: warning the government that what is being proposed is not going to work. So much legislation from the Commons is badly drafted and we can help put it right. Our members are deeply experienced in government, the civil service, the law. The Commons is full of paid amateurs, and the Lords is full of unpaid professionals. The quality of our debates is superb and I'd even describe it, on certain occasions, as magical. Everyone's views are heard with courtesy, as there's no snobbery in a chamber where everyone is a peer. The sad part is that nobody listens to the debates, nobody gives a damn.

'Our hereditary peers put honour and nation before party. They are willing to be a thorn in the side of government and to tell them to think again, as they did with the War Crimes Bill and the Criminal Justice Bill. If you're going to get rid of us, and that day may eventually come, then you must ensure that we are replaced by something better.'

Given the difficulties of reforming the House of Lords, there remains the option of abolishing it altogether. This could give unchecked powers to the Commons, especially when a government commands an enormous majority. Dennis Skinner MP favours abolition: 'Here we are approaching the twenty-first century and half of our Parliament is not elected. We talk of this being the mother of parliaments and the kind of democracy that should spread to eastern Europe and everywhere else in the world – and the whole thing is a farce. But if in the next Parliament there is a measure to take away the voting rights of hereditary peers, I'll vote for it. It's not very much, but I'll vote for it, even though I believe in the abolition of the place.'

Tony Benn made a similar point in a radio debate with Lady Ellis, a Conservative peer. He castigated Britain as a hierarchical society that institutionalizes feelings of inferiority. People at the top, he argued, have often not earned their position, and when they are appointed to legislate in the Lords they add insult to injury by being immune from removal from office.[55]

Those who would see the Lords either radically reformed or abolished surely have an overwhelming case. It seems preposterous that anyone could even attempt to justify retaining the hereditary peerage as a parliamentary body. No matter whether its powers are great or limited, it cannot be acceptable in any democracy for an accident of birth to determine who shall legislate. Nor can it be acceptable for certain individuals to be given high ministerial office without any consultation of the electorate. There have undoubtedly been a handful of outstanding ministers who have originated from the House of Lords (as well as a good number of boobies and nonentities), but their appointment offends against democratic principles. Given that Britain operates a parliamentary democracy and not an American presidential system, it cannot be right that, out of the entire population, peers can be handed a ministry without ever presenting themselves to the electorate.

That peers cannot be held accountable constitutes another offence against democratic principle. But most indefensible of all is the domination of the House by the hereditary aristocracy. It is all very well to hold up this antiquated British system as quaint, quirky and altogether adorable, but democratic government should not be in the hands of a random collection of individuals whose only common feature is the possession of a title. Defenders of the system point to the diversity of age and experience which it offers, but if diversity in itself were such a paramount political virtue, one can only wonder why other democracies have not reached for a pin and the telephone directory in selecting their legislators.

If Britain is a mature nation, then it must give up the indulgence of being partially governed by an aristocracy. Apart from the offence against democracy, it encourages a culture of deference and sentimentality. If every other democratic state has managed to devise a reasonably effective system of parliamentary democracy without invoking the hereditary principle, then it cannot be too colossal an undertaking for the British system of government to do the same.

FIFTEEN

The Honours Market

After lunch Lord Harding [chairman of Plessey] looked in for a
moment to ask me for a knighthood for John Clark, Managing
Director of Plessey.

Tony Benn, *Office Without Power*, entry for 13 January 1970

We British revel in titles and orders. With a still-potent aristocracy in
place it is perhaps hardly surprising that we take such things seriously.
We criticize yet tolerate our fantastically complex system of official
rewards, each with its own delicate nuance, its own aura of reward and,
regrettably, often its own whiff of corruption. The system is not only
laughable but pernicious, helping to reinforce notions of class and
gradation.

It is fitting that a nation should reward individuals who have given
outstanding service or made some remarkable contribution to national
or international life. The United States has its Medal of Freedom, the
former Soviet Union had its Order of Lenin, France has its graded
Légion d'honneur. But to the best of my knowledge no other country has
a panoply of medals and ribbons to reward old men who help children
across the road, nor hands out titles of nobility to middle-aged men who
have made a great deal of money.

As always with British 'traditions' most orders turn out to be far less
ancient than we are led to believe. A few chivalric orders are of medieval
origin, such as the Garter and its Scottish counterpart the Thistle.
These tend to be reserved for senior aristocrats and courtiers, plus a
retired prime minister or two. They remain in the gift of the sovereign,
as does the Order of Merit, the only honour actually worth having and
limited in numbers to twenty-four.

Honours dispersed more widely are relative newcomers. The Order of the Bath was founded in 1725, but as an exclusive band of knights, not as the catch-all for civil servants and army officers which it subsequently became. The diplomatic order of St Michael and St George was created in 1818, and the Order of the British Empire was founded as recently as 1917 by King George V, to reward services to an empire that was still flourishing and to offer an all-purpose gong to anyone not entitled to a more specific order. The expansion of titles and orders paralleled the expansion of the peerage. With the aristocracy, old and new, obsessed by rank, it was not surprising that those lower down the social scale, but equally loyal servants of the state, should be eager for rewards too.

With honours at the disposal of the sovereign – or, in effect, of the government – they inevitably came to be used as an effective form of patronage. The honours system rewards good behaviour and discourages dissent. Civil servants, politicians and diplomats know that if they behave themselves and do as they are told they will sooner or later gain a knighthood or some other honour. The fact that the recipients take it as seriously as they evidently do merely adds to the power of patronage. As countless politicians' memoirs confirm, lobbying for honours is common.

In his biography of Lord Curzon, Kenneth Rose cites a fairly innocuous instance. The former Cambridge don O. B. Browning, aged eighty-two and living in Rome, wrote in 1919 to Curzon to bid for a KBE 'on the ground of propaganda, for which many have been decorated'. He pitched his request so cannily, as Curzon, the inventor of so many 'traditions', had also been the brains behind the Order of the British Empire. But his bid was only partially successful, and in 1923 he received the OBE instead, which he was apparently content with, as it chimed in so neatly with his own initials.[1]

It is difficult to know precisely how many individuals have ever declined an honour, but it is certain that Ramsay MacDonald refused the peerage that is 'traditionally' conferred on retiring prime ministers. ' "The King pressed me to accept an earldom. But I refused. Me an earl? How ridiculous." Or the garter? "Certainly not." '[2] Lord Longford can only think of five men who refused peerages since 1945: Winston Churchill, Isaiah Berlin, Kenneth Younger, Jack Jones and Robert Maxwell.[3] Tony Benn adds the name of Joe Haines, a political adviser to Harold Wilson and subsequently a newspaper columnist.[4]

The honours list performs numerous functions. It is a perk for senior civil servants and diplomats; it rewards Members of Parliament for long service and docility; it recognizes outstanding achievement in medical, scientific, artistic, sporting or academic fields; it rewards those who contribute handsomely to the governing party; it panders to popular taste by rewarding performers; it marks the end of a career; it bribes supporters of the governing party, such as newspaper editors and advertising and PR executives.

In 1996, one honours list conferred peerages on a retired medical professor, the former chairman of the BBC and a field marshal. All routine stuff. Twenty-eight new knights were created, of which six were for 'political service'. The sovereign's own order of knighthood, the KCVO of the Royal Victorian Order, was awarded to the Dean of St Paul's and a former lord lieutenant, presumably for unspecified services to the Queen. Opera did well, with a damehood for Felicity Lott and a knighthood for the director of the Royal Opera House, Jeremy Isaacs. Dora Bryan, at the ripe old age of seventy-two, had to make do with a mere OBE, and was outflanked by the broadcaster David Jacobs, who notched up a CBE. Ruth Rendell got the CBE, but another novelist, Joanna Trollope, had to content herself with the OBE. What do these distinctions reflect? Are they literary value judgements? Long-service medals? Reflections of sales figures? Or of political affiliation? And who decides? It does, after all, seem odd that the Conservative-leaning novelists P. D. James and Jeffrey Archer end up in the House of Lords, while Ruth Rendell is a mere Commander of the Order.

Astonishingly, awards for gallantry are directly related to military rank. Lists published in May 1997 awarded CBEs to colonels and brigadiers, OBEs to lieutenant-colonels, and MBEs to majors and lesser officer ranks. NCOs had to make do with QCBs and QCVSs.[5]

By 1997 the notion that merit had anything to do with honours was finally laid to rest. It is arguable that the peerage, no less, awarded to (ardent Conservative) Andrew Lloyd Webber was justifiable on the grounds of his immense worldwide popularity, even if it was hard to equate his artistic achievements with those of the only other musicians awarded peerages: Benjamin Britten and Yehudi Menuhin. However, Cilla Black also received a gong on the grounds – there could be no other – that she was popular with the viewing public. Singers sing, composers compose, actors act, cricketers score runs. Ms Black reads a script. The honours list, already discredited for innumerable abuses, is now used to pander to public enthusiasms.

How the system operates remains mysterious. There are various scrutiny committees (their membership not disclosed but formerly and perhaps still under the chairmanship of permanent secretaries from the civil service) that waste public money by sifting through countless lists, sorting them into the worthy and the unworthy, whittling and honing. The principal scrutiny committee, which vets candidates for life peerages, consists of retired politicians such as Lords Pym and Cledwyn.[6] Nominations from the Honours Nomination Unit are processed by unnamed 'advisers' whose identity is unknown even to the unit. Preliminary lists are also submitted by the higher ranks of the Foreign Office and other ministries, Commonwealth prime ministers who opt to participate (there's usually an MBE for someone in Antigua or Fiji), the Prime Minister and the sovereign. It's the Prime Minister who exercises the heady power of patronage, striking off the names of those who displease him or her, adding a few to reflect personal enthusiasms (a loyalist rabbi or long-forgotten cricketer). Now that the public is invited to make recommendations, presumably there are other committees that decide which of the two hundred hospital cleaners really deserve that MBE, and whether the enthusiasm for an obscure Welsh poetess reflects the ardour of her family and friends or the passionate appreciation of a sizeable segment of the Clwyd literati.

Until recently honours handed out to the civil and diplomatic service caused the least trouble, as they were the equivalent of long-service medals, awarded more or less automatically after promotion to the necessary grade. Ambassadors to medium-sized or politically sensitive countries can usually expect a KCMG, a Grade B knighthood within the Most Distinguished Order of St Michael and St George, or the grander Grade A knighthood denominated by GCMG on being dispatched to an indisputably major country. Anyone overlooked through some quirk in the system may benefit from a royal visit, when the sovereign may well dispense an MVO or CVO as a kind of thank-you note. Similarly, permanent secretaries will usually pick up a knighthood, though after John Major became Prime Minister they have had to wait a bit longer for it. It used to be automatic, but after rumblings in the press and elsewhere about the fatuousness of the system awards now tend to be slightly more selective. It is arguable that this is even worse, as the process of deciding who is worthy will usually favour the time-servers, the dogged, the merely competent. Despite this 'reform', civil and diplomatic service awards still accounted for about one-fifth of the honours announced in June 1996.

The whole system is distinctly reminiscent of the way in which rank, known as *chin*, was distributed in tsarist Russia. The Russian nobility was divided into hereditary and non-hereditary ranks, and codified in the Table of Ranks. On reaching a certain status, individuals were granted *chin*.

> Government dispensation of privilege contributed to, and then rewarded, upward social mobility through the system of higher educational institutions, through Tsarist bureaucratic service (military and civil), and through the world of commerce and industry. No matter what the route, the government's aim was to coopt the new elites into traditional positions of privilege rooted in the society of orders.[7]

However, because noble status was conferred on such individuals on a personal basis, it could not be bequeathed to descendants. The Russian system extinguished itself by 1917. Ours lingers on.

The honours system sustains heraldry, the ancient pursuit of busily creating absurd coats of arms and mottoes for life peers. Mark Bence-Jones and Hugh Montgomery-Massingberd make an interesting point in defining the character of British coats of arms:

> A coat of arms may be a badge of aristocracy; but it has never been necessary to have armorial bearings in order to be an aristocrat . . . The Heralds, down to the present day, have recognized this fact by defining a gentleman as a man entitled to bear arms – in other words, a grant of arms is given to a man on the assumption that he is a gentleman already.[8]

This merely underlines the nonsense of the whole business, since honours have been bestowed on individuals subsequently revealed to be rogues or criminals.

Nowadays a coat of arms is a purchasable commodity from the College of Arms. Anyone with a university degree or other professional qualification or a commission in the armed forces can apply to have a coat of arms. The fee of £2575 includes consultations with a herald on a suitable crest, and a sheet of vellum with beautiful calligraphy showing the crest and motto. An official at the college told me that the offer was open 'to all people of eminence rather than notoriety. A serial killer would not be acceptable.' If the heralds have any doubts, they may demand support from two referees to confirm that the applicant has reached 'a minor level of sufficient gentrification'. The college does not concern itself with mottoes (Sir Cliff Richard's is 'Sing a new song'), which may be changed at whim.

The College of Arms, incorporated in 1484, is now part of the Royal Household and headed by the Earl Marshal, the Duke of Norfolk. It is he who, in theory, takes final decisions on coats of arms, new titles and precedence, assisted by thirteen heraldic officers, the three kings of arms (Garter, Norroy and Clarenceux), six heralds and four pursuivants with the jolly titles Bluemantle, Rouge Dragon, Rouge Croix and Portcullis. Their annual pay, set in 1620 and unaltered since, is a generous £17.80 (£13.95 for pursuivants) but is supplemented by fees charged for genealogical research. The college awards about two hundred grants of arms each year, to corporate bodies as well as new peers.[9] One would imagine that heraldry as a sphere of activity would be in decline as we reach the end of the twentieth century. Not a bit of it: 'In Scotland, more coats of arms have been granted since 1930 than in the 300 years before it.'[10] It is all rather sad, a sure sign that we are as preoccupied by class as ever.

Harder to defend than automatic civil service honours is the distribution of political honours. These, and promotion to ministerial rank, are the two potent weapons every prime minister wields to keep backbenchers and constituency associations in order. From 1951 to 1964 the Conservative government gave knighthoods to over two hundred of its MPs, one-third of all Tories in the Commons during that period. Harold Wilson abolished political honours in 1966. This was welcomed by his Cabinet colleagues, but not by the party workers. As Richard Crossman noted: 'After I'd talked to Len Williams at Transport House and heard the reaction of our regional officers and Party agents I realized that excluding political Honours really meant excluding Party agents and regional organizers and virtually no one else.'[11]

None the less Wilson went ahead. He also sought to reduce the number of automatic knighthoods dished out to the civil and diplomatic services. Barbara Castle expressed her forthright approval: 'The most outrageous thing about [the honours system] was that it reflected the system of social stratification and snobbery in this country. One of my most embarrassing jobs as a Minister was to present the BEMs to railwaymen and other members of the lower orders with whom the Queen did not think it was worth her while to shake hands.'[12] (This did not, however, prevent her from lobbying Wilson for a peerage for her husband Ted.)

A few years later political honours were restored by the incoming prime minister Edward Heath. Heath never worked up much enthusiasm for this form of patronage and awarded only nine political knighthoods during his term of office. When Wilson returned to power in 1974 he again abolished political honours, but marred his record with the infamous resignation honours list of 1976, when he rewarded his cronies, both honest and crooked, for their loyalty. Margaret Thatcher reinstated political honours, but the Labour and Liberal leaders declined her invitation to make their own recommendations. Within ten years over one hundred Conservative MPs were knighted or ennobled.[13]

Margaret Thatcher imaginatively exploited her powers of patronage. What kind of signal did it send to Fleet Street when editors sympathetic to her cause, such as Larry Lamb, John Junor and David English, were knighted? It seemed astonishing at the time that serving editors could even think of accepting knighthoods, but since they were unapologetic Thatcher supporters, they were scarcely compromising themselves by accepting the titles. But if ever men deserved to be regarded as poodles of the ruling party it was those, broadcasters included, who accepted honours from the prime minister of the day. The message, doubtless, was not lost on other titans of the media.

Ever since Lloyd George peddled honours for cash, everyone has been aware of the potential conflict of interest inherent in a politically organized honours system. Lloyd George, aided by his fixer Maundy Gregory, specialized in the sale of baronetcies. The going rate for a knighthood was £10,000, for a baronetcy £40,000 and for a peerage £100,000. There were plenty of takers.[14] Ever since the public outrage at the Wilson resignation honours in 1976, the scrutiny committee has closely monitored the award of political honours to ensure that they are not granted in exchange for financial contributions. The prime minister, however, is at liberty to ignore its recommendations.

The Political Honours Scrutiny Committee has proved astonishingly ineffectual. Many of those who have contributed lavishly to Conservative Party funds have been rewarded with knighthoods or peerages. Sir James Hanson, Alistair McAlpine, Victor Matthews, Arnold Weinstock and Jeffrey Sterling were just a few of the industrialists and businessmen given peerages by Margaret Thatcher. Hanson donated £852,000, Sterling's P&O shipping company £727,500. Of the eighteen companies that contributed almost £2 million to the Conservatives between 1979 and 1983, the directors of fourteen of them were honoured.[15]

It may just be a happy coincidence that all the leading and most deserving entrepreneurs of the day were ardent government supporters, but to the dispassionate onlooker, it smacked of corruption. Not much changed under John Major. Each year an average of sixteen industrialists or businessmen were knighted. From 1990 to 1996 he awarded forty-five knighthoods and five peerages to businessmen, of whom two-thirds were contributors to party funds.[16] A further scandal erupted in April 1997 when it became known that a lobbyist was pressing for a knighthood for businessman Jeffrey Whalley on the grounds that he was prepared to contribute £100,000 to Conservative Party funds.[17] In June 1997 Tony Blair made it clear that his government would revert to the long-standing Labour policy of not awarding political honours.

There are defenders of the whole shabby system. The historian Andrew Roberts can be relied upon to put the reactionary view: 'As the "Fount of Honour"', he has written, the Queen

> has presided over a system remarkably free from corruption. It enables the state to save the taxpayer a fortune, by rewarding top people with enamel badges and new names rather than paying them more. And awards for charity work have an attraction when made by the unimpeachable Queen Elizabeth that they could never have if made by some compromise candidate of an elected president.[18]

The system institutionalizes toadying and political corruption. The way in which the system is stratified perpetuates class distinctions. John

Major's famous pledge to work towards a 'classless society' is not reflected in the honours lists he has overseen since 1990. It is true that more awards are nominated by the public than before, but these are invariably low-grade honours. Despite the occasional hand-outs to traffic wardens and other 'ordinary' people, the lists are still dominated, as they always have been, by functionaries, politicians, popular figures in the arts and sports, and party contributors. The wearying parade of actresses and pop singers proudly displaying their pathetic MBEs outside Buckingham Palace enlists popular heroes in a system that encourages gradation, hierarchy, forelock-tugging and social conformity. Nor is one greatly reassured by Prime Minister Tony Blair's declaration in July 1997 that outstanding headmasters and headmistresses would henceforth be eligible for knighthoods and damehoods – an exciting step backwards into the politics of patronage and hierarchy.

The honours system panders to and perpetuates snobbery. In E. F. Benson's delicious comic novel of 1931, *Mapp and Lucia*, Mrs Wyse tends to leave displayed on the refectory table 'an open purple morocco box in which reposed the riband and cross of a Member of the Order of the British Empire'. The visiting Lucia peers at the bauble, and asks what it is: 'Mrs Wyse hastily shut the morocco box. "So like servants to leave that about" she said. "But they seem proud of it. Graciously bestowed upon me. Member of the British Empire."'

We laugh, but no doubt such scenes are replicated in households throughout the land, as proud recipients flaunt their medals with engaging modesty and delude themselves that it means something more than the last, deeply condescending gasps of privilege. The whole system should be chucked away, retaining the Order of Merit, which does honour outstanding achievement, and awards for gallantry. Nothing else has any place in a modern democratic society.

SIXTEEN

The Elastic Season

In S'ciety, don' dey dress wid clothes on ebery day?
Ronald Firbank, *Sorrow in Sunlight*, 1924

The recent history of the Season illustrates how Britain is moving from a class-based society to a more complex hierarchy based on money as much as background. The Season began simply as a succession of events to divert the upper classes during the early summer when Parliament was in session. While the menfolk were supposedly busy at Westminster, their wives and daughters gathered to entertain each other, gossip and play the marriage market. They would arrive in May and disperse by 12 August, when they would head back to the country to start shooting birds. Although the aristocracy were the main participants in the Season, many events, such as the races, allowed people of all classes to divert themselves and gawp at the fashionable world.

Today the Season is more elastic. It begins with the Berkeley Dress Show in early April and continues until mid-September with Queen Charlotte's Ball. It takes in a variety of pleasures: sporting events, balls, races and oddities such as the open day at Eton known as the Fourth of June. The most prestigious events are those that attract royal patronage: Ascot, Goodwood, polo in Windsor Great Park and so forth. A handful of cultural events such as Glyndebourne have been incorporated into the Season, but that has more to do with two other factors associated with the Season – a chance to wear expensive clothes, and an addiction to champagne picnics – than with an abiding love of opera.

In the eighteenth century the Season was essentially the London staging post in a year-round quest for entertainment. At other times of the year, the aristocracy and gentry would congregate at spa towns such as Bath and Tunbridge Wells, where they could take the waters, play cards – and, of course, gossip and flirt. In the late eighteenth century Bath alone attracted over thirty thousand visitors annually. Noble families from northern England unable or unwilling to journey south would content themselves with the attractions of Buxton or Harrogate instead.

None the less it was the London Season that carried the greatest prestige. To rent (or buy) a London house, staff it and entertain the *beau monde*, and maintain a suitably lavish wardrobe, all this cost a great deal of money, and it must have been a relief to many a head of household when the London establishment could be closed up for the year and the family bundled back to the relative economies of the country seat.

By the mid-nineteenth century, when the Season had become an institution, it had developed its own rules and protocols. The participation of the Court gave it a grandeur and formality that the social whirl at the spa towns could not match. The entrance ticket to the Season was presentation at Court, which naturally restricted participants to the most socially eminent and respectable landed families.

Lord Cadogan, in his memoirs, recalls the Season as experienced in the 1880s as

> one of gentle occupations in a lustrous atmosphere. It was a very sedate routine of intermingled pleasure and duty which claimed the allegiance of the exclusive circle of friends and relations that formed London society of those days . . .
>
> Etiquette in those times prescribed very rigidly the precise hours when you might or might not do things. The men returned to their clubs or to their work, which never, even in the case of Cabinet ministers, seemed to be very exacting or long-enduring. The ladies went home to change into the smartest toilettes for their not very vigorous rounds of visits in Belgravia or Mayfair . . .
>
> There were no weekend exeats to the country in those days. Ascot was probably the only serious interruption to the flow of entertainment that, for three solid months, kept within the bounds of London's West End . . . It all seemed so durable, so secure, so timeless . . . Taxation was light, the cost of living was low.[1]

By the early twentieth century the entertainments were, if anything, even more lavish. Lord Carnarvon recalls the Season during the 1920s:

It was the fashion to hold large parties and balls in private houses such as Londonderry House, Norfolk House and even in my mother's lovely house at Seymour Place. The scenario was much the same on every occasion. There would be perhaps ten dances, then supper, and then another ten dances. Supper was generally a gargantuan meal with lovely fat Egyptian quails, lobster galore, various cold meats as well as mountains of hot salmon kedgeree.[2]

Because participation in the Season was restricted to the 'best' families, many *nouveaux riches* became desperate to penetrate its exclusive circles. By the early twentieth century the doors of the great London town houses did occasionally admit those not from the landed élite, but that was still the exception. One method of entry for such people was to enlist the help of a noble family who were feeling the pinch, as a German observer noted in the 1930s:

There are titled ladies, whose resources are inadequate for the heavy expenses of the Season, and who take money from prosperous families for securing admission to the sacred precincts of Buckingham Palace for a daughter who is not properly entitled by origin to presentation at court. For a consideration they will pilot this smuggled debutante through the whole Season, take her to their country house, introduce her into other Society families, and so obtain for her a place in the upper class which, in spite of all their money, is out of the reach of her parents . . . The sums paid by social aspirants for the launching of a daughter into Society are said to run into thousands of pounds.[3]

Jessica Mitford recalls her days as a débutante, when she and her sister Nancy were presented at Court:

A hairdresser came to the house to arrange the regulation white ostrich feathers in our hair, and we set forth in a hired Daimler for the hours-long journey down the Mall, inching forward in an endless procession of debs and their mothers. Crowds of Londoners traditionally turned out to appraise the new debs; one would hear their comments as they peered through the car windows:
   'Ow, ain't she a corker!'
   'That one ain't much. Lookee 'ere, there's a beaut for ye!' . . .

Clambering finally out of the car, we stumbled through the rainy dark into a brightly lit, crowded corridor, filled with bare shoulders and the musty smell of rented ostrich feathers. More hours of inching, this time through seeming miles of slightly overfed human flesh . . .

Finally, the end of the road; a magnificent flunkey arranges our trains, another bawls out: 'The Lady Redesdale. The Honourable Mrs Peter Rodd. The Honourable Jessica Mitford.' We are in the presence of what appear to be two large, stuffed figures, nodding and smiling down from their thrones like wound-up toys. One more river to cross: the curtsies, one to each of the stuffed figures, then back away without stumbling until one is out of the Presence.[4]

The coming-out of a daughter had to be celebrated in style. Lord Grantley wished to mark the occasion of his daughter's coming out, but lacked suitable London premises. 'Since our house was not large enough to entertain the crowds appropriate to this auspicious and important event, the Mountbattens very kindly gave the party for the 800 guests in their penthouse flat at the top of Brook House.'[5] Jessica Mitford recalls the constant dances, up to three of them every night, five nights a week.

World War II, and the period of austerity that followed it, cramped the style of the Season. Sporting events continued unabated, but the scale of private entertaining was reduced. By this time few of the great Mayfair mansions remained in private hands. In 1958 the Queen discontinued presentations, and the monarch was supplanted by an iced cake, the object of débutantes' curtsies at Queen Charlotte's Ball. By the 1960s there was a revival of the Season, with vast numbers of balls, dances and cocktail parties, as proud mothers vied with each other in thrusting their nubile offspring into society. Girls acquired the domestic skills – cooking, sewing, darning – in the country, and learned about deportment and flower-arranging at a finishing school in Britain or Switzerland. (The last British finishing school, the Eastbourne College of Food and Fashion, announced it was finished itself in 1996.) Then the girls came up to London for a summer of parties, culminating, with luck, in engagement, wedding and a return to the country with its familiar ambience of horses, dogs, wellington boots, Barbour jackets, church on Sunday and children.

The whole circus of the London Season was masterminded by the elusive Peter Townend, who as 'social consultant' to *Tatler* knew everybody who counted. He would invite socially acceptable families to participate and would cast a stern eye over guest lists to ensure that presentable and rich young men were on it and rakes and ne'er-do-wells were off it. If a hostess needed to boost her guest list with some eligible youths, Townend could supply names and addresses.

The royal family were quick to disengage themselves from the old-fashioned and pointless ceremonial of presentation at Court, but retained close connections with those events that interested them. It was good public relations: allowing the rich and aristocratic to mingle with them on a few afternoons each summer, and allowing the hoi-polloi to glimpse them from a considerable distance. The Season shows the royal family at play.

Royal Ascot was the first of the events that they honoured with their presence, as long ago as 1711, when Queen Anne would turn up in her carriage, just as the present Queen drives down the course in her pram-like landau, with other members of her family in train. The Queen favours Ascot, the Derby and Badminton; the Duke of Edinburgh patronizes boating at Cowes, polo and horse-driving trials at Windsor. The sovereign also shows herself to her people (or some of them) at Buckingham Palace garden parties, which were first held in 1868. These intimate gatherings are a way of rewarding some eight thousand guests for services rendered. People not accustomed to formal dress hire morning coats for the day and wander about the gardens of Buckingham Palace in considerable discomfort looking, with scant chance of success, for somebody they might know. They are unlikely to be stopped for a chat by the Queen, who takes tea in her own tent and is presented to a mere handful of the guests.

You stand a better chance of getting close to the Queen at Royal Ascot. To do so you must gain admission to the Royal Enclosure, which is slightly less exclusive than it may sound, since about seven thousand people are allowed in. Men must wear morning dress with a top hat; women may not wear trousers or short skirts, but in every other respect can be as extravagant as they like. As a class indicator, the dress code is hailed as an equalizing force by William Hartston: 'Having a proper dress code eliminates class distinctions . . . There is nothing to distinguish royalty from commoners and we can all relax and enjoy ourselves',[6] and as snobbery by Philip Howard: 'All such uniforms aim to declare: "We are members of an exclusive society." '[7]

Admission is by no means restricted to the landed élite, and an article in *The Times* laments the social decline of Ascot. Royal Ascot, it proclaimed, 'certainly enjoys in a peculiar manner royal patronage, and our aristocracy flock to it pretty much as they did a quarter of a century ago; but it has long lost all claims to exclusiveness.' Well, there you have it, and that was in the 1860s.[8] Those hoping to gain admission to the Royal Enclosure must contact the Ascot Office at St James's Palace, backing their application with the signature of a regular visitor to the enclosure. It is gratifying to note that, despite the strictness with which applications are vetted, it is still possible for some raffish and far from aristocratic people to bluff their way in. Some pillars of society can no longer endure the invasion of the Royal Enclosure by the hoi-polloi and forgo Ascot, patronizing instead the less colourful but more intimate paddocks of Goodwood.

Today the formal débutantes' balls and coming-out parties are perceived as outmoded, and have been largely replaced by drinks parties and other less formal, and less expensive, entertainments. The Season has ceased to be much of a marriage market, since young people have innumerable other ways of expanding their social and sexual acquaintance. Nor are the major balls – the Rose Ball, the Royal Caledonian and Queen Charlotte's Ball – particularly exclusive. You pays your money, and you gets to go. It's a sign of atrophy that in 1997 Queen Charlotte's Ball was cancelled for lack of a sponsor.

If the formal partying of the Season is less glamorous and extravagant than it used to be, the appeal of the sporting events has not diminished at all. Royal Ascot is still wildly popular as the best place in England to show off, and you can look just as foolish at Henley, despite some stuffy dress codes in the Stewards' Enclosure. Women in slacks or very short skirts will be barred, but men are permitted to wear revolting striped blazers. The Stewards' Enclosure is for members only, and there is a six-thousand-long waiting list for membership. Access to Wimbledon is controlled by money rather than status. Many of the best seats are made available to debenture holders, who must pay about £20,000 to acquire a five-year lease on a Centre Court seat for the entire tournament. Other chic sporting events of the Season include Cowes Week (now renamed, in honour of money, Skandia Life Cowes Week), the Badminton Horse Trials and Cartier International Polo Day at Windsor. Polo teams devour money, and each is sustained by the largesse of a patron who funds the other members of his team, often flown over especially from South America for the Season. Some claim Season status for lesser events such as the Open Golf Championship and the Varsity rugby match at Twickenham.

Since money rather than status is now all that is required to gain admission to some of the most prestigious events of the Season, the events themselves are less snobbish but more vulgar. At sporting events such as Wimbledon and Twickenham, the best seats are hived off by corporate hospitality hucksters. At Wimbledon you can enjoy the galling sight of countless empty seats on Centre and Number One Courts, while their supposed occupants are guzzling champagne in hospitality tents and, at best, watching the match on television. I once partook of corporate hospitality at the Grand National. It was very impressive: special train, vast quantities to drink, large lunch in a tent the size of Monaco, post-prandial cigars of modest quality, and excellent seats from which to watch the races, if you were still capable of doing anything at all.

'Corporate members' also mop up many of the best seats at Glyndebourne. The riverside lawns at Henley are crowded with their tents. All this means good money for the organizers and caterers, and lashings of good will for the hosts from grateful guests. Although the corporate presence does little to add to the sporting atmosphere, it won't do to be too dismissive of it. The great majority of those attending Royal Ascot or Henley aren't too interested in the races either. What they relish is the day out, the conviviality, the licence to dress up and get drunk and, in certain circles, to wear the badge that indicates that, as one of the Elect, you have access to the most exclusive enclosures. At Henley you need to know which side of the river to be on: the Berks side (bad: hospitality tents) or the Bucks side (good: Stewards' Enclosure, Leander Club and its distinctive prep-school pink caps). Henley offers a field day for snobbery.

The banalization of the Season seemed complete when the *Sunday Times* ran a 'Win tickets for the Season' contest in 1996 with the tempting slogan 'Join the VIPs at events including Royal Ascot'. The contest was organized 'in association with Rado [watches] and Events

International Ltd, one of the UK's leading hospitality companies'. The first prize included two tickets to Royal Ascot, lunch and drinks included; and two tickets to the Three Tenors concert at Wembley, a new entrant to the select band of Season events. (Godfrey Smith, in his book on the Season, admits the Royal Academy Summer Exhibition, Oxford Commem Balls, the last night of the Proms and New Year's Eve at the Ritz as Season events. Soon the last Bakerloo Line train on Saturday night will qualify.)

The lament that the Season is not what it used to be has been heard for decades. Back in the 1930s the Duke of Manchester moaned:

> There is no society at present . . . There is a twofold reason for this: firstly, there are only a few people nowadays who have any pretensions to be labelled 'society'; and secondly, those that have a claim to the title have not money enough to keep up their estates and open their houses . . . Entertaining as it was understood and carried out in Edwardian days simply does not exist at all today.[9]

In the good old days, reports the duke, hostesses knew all their guests personally, but now parties were dominated by gatecrashers. Invite three hundred and you'll end up with, and end up paying for, eight hundred. In the good old days, 'it was considered a terrible offence for a man to be drunk in the presence of a lady . . . The method of his punishment had something mediaeval about it. The usual custom was to set up what was called a Court of Honour composed of personal men friends of the "prisoner" and presided over by one of their number as judge.'[10] Sentence was pronounced on one such miscreant: 'There was no dissentient voice from the sentence which was presently pronounced by the "judge": "Go out to the Boer War, and see to it that you do not return! If you cannot live like a gentleman, at least die like one!"' The youth obliged, and was 'killed in action'.[11]

If that was 'society', then I don't think we have much cause to mourn its passing. The change the old duke recorded was from an élite operating (in theory) a strict code of conduct to a more fluid and irreverent system invaded by the more debauched standards of the 1920s and 1930s. The change now taking place is one where every occasion is exploited for its public-relations value, where individual generosity is replaced by corporate hospitality, where sponsorship sinks its teeth and its logo into every event.

Take the 'Bollinger Babe' phenomenon, a coterie of well-heeled young women such as journalists Tamara Beckwith and Tara Palmer-Tomkinson. La Beckwith is very rich, la Palmer-Tomkinson well connected in royal and aristocratic circles. They, and the handful of other young women with whom they compete for celebrity, are party animals, the constant ornaments of any Season gathering. Nothing wrong with that, except that they form part of a network that is largely commercial. Because they are 'celebrities', their images are reproduced in almost every issue of *Vogue* or *Tatler*, as well as countless other magazines and newspapers. This makes them very useful to those whose job it is to peddle merchandise such as champagne, jewellery or clothing. The young women are aptly known as the Milk Maids for their capacity to milk every occasion for the maximum publicity value. *Tatler* dubbed them the It girls, which spawned another series of articles on the significance of the term. (Answer: none.)

These women, or 'products', give good copy. Tamara Beckwith's grungy past – expelled from Cheltenham Ladies' College, single mother at sixteen, arrested for cocaine possession – and penchant for affairs with unsuitable men keeps features editors on heat. Tara Palmer-Tomkinson has her own, very boring, column in the *Sunday Times*, where she tells readers about all the parties she has attended that week and the clothes she has worn. A highlight of one column was: 'I also spotted a lot of Shanghai Tang handbags. Does everyone except me shop in Hong Kong these days?'

A standard theme of the Tara column or the Tamara interview is the unendurable burden of celebrity. Tara:

> The main 'It' quality, it seems to me, has nothing to do with allure or glamour – it is being able to endure everyone else making fun of you all the time . . . Going to parties can be hard work – mostly because so many of the people I meet are so boring. I go to up to three events a night . . . Clothes can be difficult too. People turn up their noses if you wear the same thing twice . . . I need to escape from all the attention – the paparazzi make life very difficult sometimes.[12]

Of course there are commercial strings attached to being on the celebrity circuit. It was surely no coincidence that in the same column quoted above Miss Palmer-Tomkinson referred to 'Cartier, the up-market jewellery company'. She has a contract with Ray-Ban, whose glasses she often sports whenever a photographer comes near. And who lends or gives her the designer frocks so carefully named in every article? Pretty and socially ambitious young women have always made the rounds of the Season but the Milk Maids have turned it into a lucrative profession.

In one particularly repellent column for the *Sunday Times*, Miss Palmer-Tomkinson describes her birthday party, held in some Fulham trattoria. She lists the wonderful presents she received, and then berates some of the male guests who left without paying their share of the bill. Curious party: you invite guests, you accept their presents, and then bill them for the meal. I don't know what the Duke of Manchester would have had to say.

An enormous party, hosted by the Krug family in the gloomy Dorchester ballroom on 29 May 1996, was, according to the newspapers, the opening event of the 1996 Season. As an ornament of the Season, I was invited. There were celebrities there in droves. Indeed, a complete list of celebrities was available from the PR agency that organized the bash: this 'Celebrity Attendance Update Release' was sent out to journalists. I didn't have this list, but could tell there were celebrities all around me because roving photographers and their light equipment, orchestrated by PRs with clipboards, pinpointed certain key individuals. Among the celebrities I recognized was a television doctor, a restaurant critic who doesn't drink alcohol, Janet Street-Porter and the lovely Koo Stark, who smiled at me, presumably thinking I was somebody else, or having a memory acute enough to recall the one occasion we dined together ten years ago.

I approached two women standing on their own. They were researchers for Andrew Neil's television show. They wanted to know whether Krug's Grande Cuvée, with which our glasses were constantly refilled, was worth £70 a bottle.

Krug never advertise, and spend their promotional budget on parties. I am sure they know what they are doing, and the strategy must be highly effective in boosting the image of their champagne. Some of the guests, Rémi Krug told me, were individuals who had loved and bought their champagne for years, but the majority were there because of their supposed celebrity status, which could be exploited by the Krug publicity machine. It was not for nothing that the highly sociable Rémi was at the door, ready to be photographed with one arm round any pretty woman who ventured in, the other brandishing a glass of Grande Cuvée.

It was a good party, if you like that sort of thing, but it showed how completely the Season has been transformed into a vehicle for the public relations industry. A handy reference card distributed by Veuve Clicquot lists the events of the Season, which in 1996 implausibly included the Wexford Opera Festival, the Olympic Games and the Arc de Triomphe horse race at Longchamp, all rather far from London – and, indeed, England. If the Arc de Triomphe has the merit of being fashionable, it is hard to say the same for another event also listed by Veuve Clicquot: the Last Night of the Proms. In future years, I predict, Harrods' Sale will be flagged as a highlight of the Season.

The Season has become meaningless. Where it retains social cachet – Royal Ascot, Goodwood, Henley, a few glitzy balls – it is no longer especially exclusive and is vulgarized by the heavy hand of the sponsor and the predictable generosity of corporate bigwigs. It is best regarded as London *en fête*, and no more than that.

SEVENTEEN

Two Villages

That hand that formd thee & lent pride its day
Took equal means to fashion humbler clay
John Clare, 'The Parish', 1827

Combescote lies in the heart of Gloucestershire; Wetherly in the far north-west of England, in rural Cumbria. Both names are inventions, but the villages and their equally pseudonymous inhabitants are real.

Combescote I have known for some thirty years. At one end of the social scale in the 1960s were the old maids, villagers since birth, with their strong, melodious Gloucestershire accents; at the other the families with, it appeared, private incomes living in the spacious and picturesque old stone houses in the centre of the village. A middle-aged painter lived with his tyrannical mother in one such house. He was homosexual, usually drunk and extremely good company. Alcohol, usually gin, was never in short supply in the houses of the village, and although many disapproved of the rich but raffish members of the community, there were enough of them to form a convivial society. Life in Combescote and its environs seemed to be a constant round of drinks parties and dinners.

Today that has all but vanished. Combescote remains prosperous, but those private incomes must have dwindled. The homosexual painter moved to Mexico and found true love; another hedonist homosexual, happily married to a very beautiful and very rich South African woman who shared his passion for party-giving and drinking to excess, retired to the Mediterranean, where dissipation was unchecked and the living was cheaper.

A stroll through the churchyard at Combescote tells you all you need to know about the village. Two centuries ago it was very prosperous;

wool and the mills brought in the money. In death the local industrialists slumbered in handsome tombs, intricately carved and grandly inscribed. Their houses still stand in the village and their legacies established charitable institutions, some of which survive. None of their descendants still lives in the village.

Combescote is not far from the larger towns of the county, so it has become a village of commuters. It already was thirty years ago, but there are more of them, and even a few villagers who commute to London. None the less the village supports a range of leisure activities: cricket, rugby, tennis, amateur dramatics (140 members), ballroom dancing and a horticultural club – that's just a selection. The old maids who serviced the village – as cleaners, babysitters, childminders – are dead now, and the noticeboard at the post office is plastered with ads from those seeking cleaners and domestic help; and there's a flat to let in Menorca.

Mrs Pershore remembers the village from the 1930s, when she was a child. 'Before the First World War there was a quarry nearby, and a couple of pin mills where hairpins were made. Some people in the village were outworkers who stuck the pins on to cards at home. There were building firms here, quite a lot of farms with labourers living in the village, and other villagers who were in service. The valleys around us were filled with small industries – weaving, dyeing, cloth-making. Combescote was an economic unit. But that's over and done with. Now it's just a place to live.

'My family started as newsagents here in 1932. We took six copies of *The Times* for the top professionals and the squire. In those days Combescote had its own gasworks, its own bank, five pubs, six churches. One of the local families tried to bring the railway line here, but it never happened, and that's why the village never developed and over the years the farms were sold off to outsiders.

'Today many of the villagers are elderly, like me, but we're lively enough. It's true that Combescote has plenty of retired people living here – it's a pretty village, isn't it? – but they have money and energy, which is why we have so many organized activities here.'

The vicar received me in a corner of the church where there was a memorial tablet to the Combescote men who had died in the two world wars. Many of the surnames were the same. 'This reflects a time when Combescote was a working village with a large population of local families. The real changes took place here after the Second World War. Before then the tiny two-up, two-down cottages in the village were filled with families of as many as ten people. But after the war the insurance companies and bank headquarters and civil service agencies moved into the county towns. They were hiring a lot of professional people, so new housing estates were built on the edge of the village. There were some council houses too, but of course most of those have been sold off and are no longer accessible to young people or those needing inexpensive housing. Those people have to look elsewhere. Property prices in Combescote have driven out many of the local people.

'This is now a commuter village, and everyone has one or two cars. Combescote is populated by people who have moved here because of job opportunities, people who have taken early retirement and also a band of young professionals, such as solicitors, who work in the nearby towns.

'I regret to say that the church is no longer a social focus. And nobody comes to church here just because it is socially acceptable. But that's probably true everywhere. The popular services attract all ages, all strata. There was a Nonconformist tradition in the village but that has largely gone. The Methodist chapel is now an estate agent's, the Baptist chapel is now an antiques centre, and the Baptists now team up with the Congregationalists, and even so they are a dwindling band. There are some Quakers, and a Catholic church, but that only came here about fifty years ago as the result of benefactions from wealthy old ladies who were newcomers to Combescote.

'The whole stratum of working-class people who provided domestic help in the past has gone. Now people drive here from other villages or towns to provide cleaning and cooking. The proportion of elderly people who were born in or near Combescote is now minute.

'So it's undeniable,' continued the vicar, 'that the village as a whole no longer forms a community. The big houses, except Combescote Hall, are no longer passed from generation to generation. There's no squirearchy here, nor any sense of a social hierarchy. New people keep coming to the village and creating their own social circles. They divide into groups – the amateur dramatic club, the horticultural society, the bridge groups, bowls for the elderly – but these are peer groups. It doesn't really add up to a sense of community. Ironically, the local conservation society is founded and run by newcomers. They've bought in to the village and now want to prevent others from doing so. They oppose providing car parks for visitors and so forth, and I suspect they want to turn Combescote into a chocolate-box village. They are motivated by the wish to preserve the value of their properties. Meanwhile the local shops are in decline, as most people find it more convenient to go into one of the bigger towns where there are supermarkets.

'There is no longer much rural life here. There are only one or two farms, and none has been in the same hands for more than fifty years. People keep horses, but this isn't hunting country. Crafts are disappearing, except for a few stonemasons. The rural working class represented by many of the names on the memorial tablets here has vanished. It was always what you might call the "respectable" working class, and there was never much poverty. We don't have a culture of deference here, though it probably survives in other parts of the country.'

The publican – of the five pubs Mrs Pershore remembers, and the two or three I recall, only one still exists – takes a less gloomy view. He doesn't discern any lack of social cohesion in the village, but then his pub is probably the one place in Combescote where it is most likely to be experienced. As far as he can tell, indigenous people and newcomers mix well. Any barrier between public bar and lounge in his pub vanished long ago, and there are still a few labourers and masons who live near by and patronize the pub.

'Resentment of outsiders? I don't see it myself. After all, they use the local shops and services and trades and help the village to survive. From what people tell me, while it's true that many drive into the towns where the supermarkets are, there are villagers who make a conscious effort to support local shops and services. But it's true that the grocer is nearing retirement, and it's hard to imagine who will want to take over the business. Pubs have declined because people do more entertaining at home. The only reason I survive is that I provide bar food, which brings people in. Once the commuters are back from work and with their families, they're not going to walk into the village centre just to have a pint.'

The old families who lived in the Tudor and eighteenth-century stone houses around the churchyard have long gone, but there has been continuity at Combescote Hall. It's a Georgian house set in a substantial park. It was built by the ancestors of the present Lord Gleave, who inherited the estate, much diminished since the days of its founders, twenty years ago, when he was fifty.

'My ancestors were very much the local squires,' he told me, as we sat in the capacious library, 'and the property was very large, and the house required a large staff to maintain it. But after the 1880s it went into decline, and chunks were sold off to keep the estate solvent. By the time I inherited it was down to about two hundred and fifty acres, which is not a great deal in this kind of hill country. I never had a private income, and although I knew I was the heir to Combescote, I had to earn my own living until I came into the property. When I eventually did inherit, I couldn't afford to live in the house, so we let it. That proved disastrous, but I've managed to get it back from the tenants. Since then, frankly, we've been living a hand-to-mouth existence here, but we're pleased that the Hall is once again a home. I have to run it as a business, so we let it out for wedding receptions most weekends, which means we have to evacuate the house for a couple of days each week.

'All the generations before me lived off their capital. I'm the first generation of Gleaves to go out and earn a living. We have no servants, other than a cleaning lady. I'm pretty well resigned to the fact that the Hall may not stay in the family through the next generation. I think our family has had its day, and after I go new money will take over the house. But that's exactly what happened all the time in the eighteenth century, so I'm not really complaining.

'I'm not sentimental about the Hall. I didn't grow up here, and neither did my sons. But still, I take some pride in the fact that I have recreated the Hall as a family home.'

I asked Lord Gleave whether he had any squire-like role in the life of the village.

'There's a spin-off of respect, but it's only on the surface. I don't have much contact with the village people. In fact, there doesn't seem to be much of a village community. House prices are very steep, so there aren't many young people. Shops are closing. My forebears were JPs and that sort of thing, but there is no longer that kind of forum apart from some charitable ventures. I'm not in charge of any social group. I don't ride, I'm not part of any county set, I'm simply not rich enough to support that style of life and I never grew up with county types as a child. The previous owners, who were sisters, would visit people in the village and bring them small gifts. They had this sense of obligation. Of course, I don't do that kind of thing. On the other hand, often the people they were visiting were their tenants. My ancestors also founded the village school, and a home for the mentally handicapped. They were do-gooders, I suppose. I can't play that role, in part because I'm also a businessman and I don't have time.

'There's no culture of deference in Combescote. Many people call me by my Christian name, which they wouldn't have dared to do to my grandfather. Some people call me "sir" but that may be because I'm quite old or because they don't know what else to call me. There's one old chap who insists on calling me "my lord" but thank God he's the only one.'

I asked Lord Gleave whether he believed landed families contribute to the social cohesion of the nation. 'Would we be worse off without you?'

'I think people do like the fact that the Hall is lived in, and a home. I show groups round and they are genuinely curious and interested, and they may well take a vicarious pleasure from meeting the owner, though as you can see I am not a grandee. But although I would appreciate it if, for example, repairs on this house were VAT-exempt, I accept that there is no reason for the British government to save historic houses such as this as family homes. I also find it very difficult to justify the hereditary principle in government, so I hardly ever go to the House of Lords.'

Indeed Lord Gleave, a shy and modest man, seems slightly embarrassed by the role he is expected to play. He seems to perceive himself not as an aristocratic custodian of traditional landed values, but as a middle-class businessman thrust by the hazard of heredity into a squire-like role that is no longer required in Combescote. In the next century, Combescote, once so clearly definable within the local economy and unmistakably a proud and prosperous Cotswold village, will have turned into a comfortable commuters' outpost indistinguishable from hundreds of others.

Wetherly is also a hill town but set in remoter countryside than Combescote. It's grander too. There's a courthouse in the village centre, and a much renovated castle on the heights above the village. As at Combescote, a lord lived near by, but the family, burdened with death duties, sold off the castle nearly forty years ago. The lord still owns a few farms in the locality, and is considered a benign landlord. The castle is now open to the public as a local tourist attraction. Its grounds slope down to the banks of the pretty river that traverses Wetherly. Beyond the village are some small estates owned by untitled gentry, and prosperous large farms.

Joan arrived here from the Black Country ten years ago and with her husband runs the local fish-and-chip shop. 'I expect I'll be considered an outsider for at least another ten years. We put ourselves about, to coffee mornings and other local events, but the only other people I tended to meet were other incomers, like us. They are mostly commercial or retired people. I find that the locals keep to themselves. It's the farmers who are the big families around here. Some are talkative enough, others seem possessive about what they call "our spot". They're not what you think of as gentlemen farmers. In fact, they tend to dress in rags and go on about how poor they are, but they have plenty of money. Still, I don't find many social boundaries between the locals who have always lived here. They mix well among themselves, whether they're rich or poor. But essentially it's a closed community.'

The village attracts tourists in summer, especially when the colourful annual fair is in progress, and a number of arts and crafts businesses such as potteries have been set up in recent years. Indeed, the village is growing in population. On the outskirts are a cheese factory, furniture workshops and other small industries, but there have been many lay-offs. As a market town, it has to offer certain services. The village post office and general store in Combescote will almost certainly close within the decade; that's not going to happen in Wetherly.

There's the same variety of social life as at Combescote, with many sports associations and a wider selection of churches. The big cities, with their lure of employment and opportunity, are far away, so young people without jobs, of whom there are many, tend to stay put. Wetherly is reasonably prosperous but there is a layer of the unemployed, especially in the council estates. Joan is conscious of crime, mostly opportunistic crime perpetrated by small gangs. There's some drug use, pilfering of church boxes and reports of under-age sex, but nothing too alarming. She regrets these developments, but acknowledges that there isn't much for the kids to do of an evening in Wetherly.

'Life here can be very isolated,' says Sam, a local planning officer. 'Especially on the hill farms. There the son may earn a little beer money by helping out, but he's not earning a proper wage. Some of these farm lads can escape through education or moving to a larger city. But for others there is little to do but sit in the pubs and indulge in a little drug-dealing or petty crime. If you live on a farm, you need a car to get about easily, and the younger people usually can't afford that. You'll have heard about our many sporting clubs and cultural activities, but they are only accessible to those with cars, which excludes many of the farm lads.'

It was not so long ago that, according to Sam, a culture of deference flourished around here. 'It still continues among some older folk. Some landowners will try to throw their weight around. A landowning earl near here used to generate resentment by trying to exercise some ancient rights over his lands, which got people's backs up. Some landowners get respect, others earn justified resentment.'

A local schoolteacher, Al Murray, noted that the upper-middle-class families would invariably send their children to minor public schools, and everyone else would use the local comprehensive. 'My own father's family were teachers and shipwrights, but my mother was from a family of colliery accountants. So she was considered white-collar. When we moved to a mining community in Durham, it was very much a case of us and them. So as a schoolboy, I acquired a broad local accent as a means of defence.

'I'm afraid that education is not always taken seriously in rural areas such as this. For instance, some children don't come to school at hay-making time. Unfortunately many of those children who would in the past have stayed on the land now find that there is no work on the farms and they have inadequate education for anything else, so they end up on the dole.

'I agree with Sam. The incidence of rural poverty isn't helped by the lack of transport facilities. Those affected tend to be families with lots of children, young people on the dole, and the elderly. And Joan is right when she remarks on the defensiveness of many of the local farmers. But it's a territorial response, rather than a class-based reaction. I also have a feeling that Cumbrians use this distrust of incomers as an excuse not to show initiative.'

Malcolm is a farmer's son, but has chosen a career as a photographer while his brothers continue to work on the family farm. 'I don't think class is much of an issue among us, but it probably was for my parents' generation. My mother came from a rich Newcastle family, my father from a family of electricians. They were evacuated here during the war, and ended up in agricultural college. They took up farming and have been quite successful. There are two operations: dairy and beef, so each brother has his own business. My father employed local people, and that helped integrate them into the community.

'We were all privately educated, mostly because the local schools were not particularly good. I'd say my parents were liberals, and had common interests, such as progressive farming methods, with their circle of friends, who were mostly with them at college. But they're not socially conscious. We never had much to do with the big landowning families.

'It's true that there are people around here who are hard-up. Not necessarily the agricultural workers, who have a strong union and can earn a reasonable living. It's people like shop assistants and waitresses who earn a pittance. So there is almost certainly some poverty here. People stay around here not because they can enrich themselves but because it's a good environment in which to live.'

Nell observes the Wetherly community from an unusual perspective. A university-educated middle-class woman, she had married a local gamekeeper. I visited their remote but children-packed house in the hills some twenty years ago and was enchanted by their way of life, though it was not one I would have chosen to share. But, as Nell recalled, it was not all sunshine and laughing children.

'Arthur was employed by two bachelors, one a retired naval officer. It was a feudal set-up. The local landowners invited each other to shoot on their estates. As the gamekeeper's wife, I was treated as goods and chattels, and used as unpaid labour. I had to prepare lunch for the guests, for which I was tipped one pound. The beaters received five pounds for the day. Remember this was only fifteen or twenty years ago. By the time Arthur died, I had increased my tip to about three pounds, for which I cooked for six guests in the living room and sixteen beaters crammed into the kitchen. I had to deliver food, light the fires, wash the dishes, as well as cook.

'Our employers respected Arthur because he wasn't subservient, and we had some good conversations, especially about botany. They had a fine collection of prints, which was something I knew a fair amount about. One of the brothers invited me to inspect them, which I did, but the other brother was never told about it. It was like a dirty secret. The real problem was that they had no imagination. They couldn't conceive that the wage they paid Arthur was insufficient, and that I in effect subsidized their existence.

'Today the shoots are more commercialized, so these feudal relations have changed. The old gentry was trained to shoot, but commercial shoots don't require those who go on them to be good shots. What counts is the size of the bag, rather than how it's obtained.'

There are successful farmers around Wetherly, says Nell, but also many that do not fare particularly well. 'Many of them have to diversify, by offering bed and breakfast and other sidelines. It also gives the wives something to do. Womenfolk have to be around the farm to help out when needed, and B-and-B doesn't prevent them from doing that. Still, that is all changing. Contractors do more and more of the farming jobs, and they bring their own staff.'

Nell introduced me to a burly man of advanced years. Will Broad looked like a sailor, but, like Nell's late husband, he had been a gamekeeper. For Will, class was very much alive.

'I had a socialist upbringing in a mining village. But my dad never wanted me to go down the mines. He said he'd break my legs if I ever did that. He wanted me to better myself. So I was apprenticed and qualified as an engineer. I got a job, got married, but then decided to be a gamekeeper as I like shooting and dogs. I was a union man, a shop steward, so when I left for the country my mates were shocked because I would be working for a rich man. But I always felt I was working for myself.

'I certainly experienced the class system at first hand when I was working thirty years ago. It was the boss's guests who were the worst. They didn't so much patronize me as paralyse me. They considered people like me of no consequence, with no right to an opinion. Basically, they thought of me as a peasant. That confirmed to me that there really was a class system in this country.

'I had two children, and my boss Mr Burns had three, who were younger than mine. I was told that I had to address the Burns boys as "Mister", but the boys were to call me "Broad". I refused to accept this. Then the squeeze went on. As an under-gamekeeper I was living on a bare agricultural wage. Most employers supplemented this with little extras, such as money to feed the dogs, help with transport, that kind of thing. I never got a thing. They were trying to squeeze me out, and one day Burns asked me to leave. I did leave, and then he blackballed me when I applied for another job.

'I worked for Burns for nine years, and never had a holiday. Whenever I asked for one, I was told, "You can have a holiday if you find someone who can look after the pheasants while you're away."

'In those days estate workers had a hierarchy. The head keeper was in the upper bracket. Servants tended to conform, but reluctantly. Today that has changed because many of the big estates have gone, and many that survive are owned by shooting and fishing syndicates. Syndicate keepers are another breed. They have pension funds and petrol allowances and housing and a vehicle.

'I'm still a man of the left, as I've never forgotten having my nose ground by the upper classes. I hadn't been brought up to "service", unlike the head keeper and his father before him. So I found it hard to take that kind of shit from my employers. All the more so because I was a man with professional qualifications.

'I've lived in Wetherly now for twenty-two years. Let me tell you this. As a town, it is quietly going to sleep.'

EIGHTEEN

Education: Diversity and Inequality

My father, a country clergyman, and my mother were being entertained in the early thirties by a local landowner of long and impeccable
ancestry. The hostess politely asked my mother where her children
were at school. On being informed that my eldest brother was in his
last year at Eton she paused in evident perplexity.
   'Eton?' she said. 'Not . . . not *our* Eton?'

Richard Ollard, *An English Education*, 1982

The crumbling British class system is sustained by the unequal way in
which we educate our children. Instead of working hard to ensure that
all children get the best education of which they are capable – a patriotic
and apolitical goal – the primary educational strategy of recent
governments has been to introduce ever more baroque elements of
stratification. League tables have become the principal measure of
educational quality. They sometimes compare like with like, but often
like with unlike; innumerable variables are left out of consideration, and
the principal measurement of success is performance in examinations.
In the 1960s a silly league table called the Norrington Table began to
rank the colleges of Oxford and Cambridge, using some complicated
formula based on examination results. What was revealing was how the
results varied from year to year. If, say, Emmanuel was rubbish in 1962,
how come it did so well in 1963, and nosedived again in 1964? Of course
very few people took Norrington seriously. It was a game, an excuse for
Balliol or Magdalen to be cock of the walk for a year.

Contemporary league tables set school against school, which is
hardly what education should be about. Not merely because an
assessment based on examination results alone is incomplete, but

because it identifies a few schools as 'the best' and others as 'the worst'. A comprehensive school I know well does poorly in the league tables. Given that it takes in and educates hundreds of students from impoverished backgrounds and minorities whose first lanaguage is not English, my impression was that it performed remarkably well. Its poor performance in league tables derives from the fact that many of the pupils either lack ability or receive very little parental support and encouragement. But because a student is less academically gifted does not mean that he or she should be deprived of a good education, or at least an education that stretches such pupils to the limits of their talents.

League tables do, however, document the great discrepancy in performance between public and state schools. The former, not surprisingly, perform better. State schools are deprived of resources and often demoralized; begging bowls are routinely dispatched to parents to help fund a library purchase or building extension. Public schools are sustained by fees which will purchase facilities beyond the dreams of most state schools, and can afford enough teachers to keep class sizes low.

The publication of league tables is supposed to facilitate 'parental choice'. For most parents there is no choice. They cannot afford up to £100,000 to put each child through private education; they cannot move to a distant suburb where the state education may be of high quality. The scandal is not merely that 7 per cent of children are being privately educated, but that state education is being increasingly stigmatized.

Public schools are a relatively modern creation. Before the early nineteenth century the upper classes employed personal tutors or sent their sons to a handful of venerable foundations such as Winchester and Eton. Other children attended local grammar schools. The expansion of the mercantile and professional classes placed pressure on existing schools, so new schools, most famously Rugby, were founded to accommodate the upper middle classes. Seventy-seven public schools were founded between 1840 and 1900. They did little more than provide a sound education firmly grounded in the classics. In 1884 Eton employed twenty-eight classics masters, six mathematics masters, one historian and not a single teacher of modern languages or science.[1]

The public schools also instilled a code of values that was essentially aristocratic, plus a heavy dose of vigorous Christianity. A dual process took place: the *embourgeoisement* of the aristocracy, and the imbuing of aristocratic values in the professional middle classes. It may have been inadvertent, but this fuzzing of the boundaries between two social classes surely helped to maintain political stability in Victorian England. The revolutions of 1848 that criss-crossed Europe and the Paris Commune of 1871 had no British equivalents other than Chartism, which failed.

The public schools soon developed a marked individual character, often defined by their intake. Wellington attracted the sons of officers, Marlborough the sons of clergymen. They often returned these young men to the careers or professions from which they had sprung. Others entered the burgeoning colonial and civil services, and a substantial proportion became businessmen and lawyers. Gladstone's ministers had opened the civil service and the Army to entrants chosen by competitive examination. Background was no longer sufficient; ability was required too.

The very least that parents would expect from their newly educated sons was that they would exhibit good breeding and other gentlemanly virtues. 'The end-product', explain two social historians, 'was to be an homogenized gentleman by education, whose background was not detectable in his accent, behaviour, or culture, and who was thus clearly distinct from the vulgar cotton-spinner industrialists.'[2] The mere fact of having endured a public-school regime, however inadequate educationally, was sufficient to sustain a claim that the graduate was a gentleman, whatever his social background.

The gentlemanly attributes included classical learning, leadership qualities, good manners, athletic distinction and a sense of fair play. Intellectual ability, according to Dr Thomas Arnold of Rugby, the most influential of all the public-school ideologues, counted for less than gentlemanly conduct and religious and moral principles. Thus the upper middle class appropriated aristocratic values, allowing the *nouveaux riches* and the aristocracy to mix and interact in a remarkably effective way.

The public-school ethos is more complex than the acquisition and transmission of a gentlemanly code of behaviour. It also expressed itself in a special sense of relationship (or non-relationship) to the rest of society. The historian M. L. Bush seems closest to the mark when he writes:

The public schools imposed upon middle class and aristocrat alike a compound of ideals with aristocratic roots: a sense of leadership and of public responsibility, the belief that leaders should not be specialists, a strong aversion to trade which was seen as self-seeking, socially humiliating and materialistic, a supercilious attitude towards the rest of society, a firm faith in the efficacy of continuity and tradition and the conviction that social evaluation should be determined not simply by performance but also by family or school background . . . Thus, in the age of industrialisation, the public schools upheld aristocracy by mass-producing gentlemen.[3]

Because this attempt at social engineering was so successful, education itself soon acquired a paramount importance. It had nothing to do with learning, of course. But the question 'Which school were you at?', which must still be asked more frequently in Britain than anywhere else in the world, is the quickest way to place an individual socially. From the single-word reply much can be deduced by those who still believe these things matter.

Since the new model public schools were a middle-class creation, the aristocracy continued to favour schools such as Eton and Harrow. Thus a public-school education might successfully implant a youth in the ranks of the clergy, civil service or Army, but it would not necessarily bring him into contact with the sons of the aristocracy. On arrival at, say, Malvern, he might be slightly disappointed to discover that most of his co-students shared the same wealthy middle-class background. No matter, because schools such as Malvern that advertised themselves as 'places of education for the sons of gentlemen' more or less guaranteed that the end product would be a gentleman too. Whatever your social origins, you would emerge socially on a par with your fellow students.[4]

Even apologists for public-school education, such as the Victorian philologist Rev. T. L. Papillon in *The Public Schools and Citizenship*, conceded that the scholastic accomplishments of many graduates were often meagre:

Many a lad who leaves an English public school disgracefully ignorant of the rudiments of useful knowledge, who can speak no language but his own, and writes that imperfectly, to whom the noble literature of his country and the stirring history of his forefathers are almost a sealed book, and who has devoted a great part of his time and nearly all his thoughts to athletic sports, yet brings away with him something beyond all price, a manly, straightforward character, a scorn of lying and meanness, habits of obedience and command, and fearless courage. Thus equipped, he goes out into the world, and bears a man's part in subduing the earth, ruling its wild folk, and building up the Empire; doing many things so well that it seems a thousand pities that he was not trained to do them better.[5]

Although there were undoubtedly pockets of intellectual brilliance at the best public schools, their atmosphere was predominantly philistine. In his defence of public schools, Bernard Darwin hardly mentions education: public schools, he wrote in 1931,

> merely emphasize the qualities of the Englishman of whatever class, refining and improving them perhaps in the process . . . To play fair, to try to be a good loser and, which is sometimes even more difficult, a good winner; these are wholly admirable things which the public schools do much to teach, though they are apt, through their too enthusiastic advocates, to arrogate to themselves a monopoly in this respect.[6]

A rich Thai woman recently explained to me that she sent her sons to English public schools because there they were taught 'discipline, manners and how to be a gentleman'. Victorian values, she hopes, live on.

The primary goals of the public schools were to create gentlemen and build character, goals aided by a rigorous Christian framework and by instilling athletic prowess. The result was an effective blending of the aristocratic ethos with the dynamism of the upwardly mobile middle class. Learning was, essentially, a means to an end, as the historian Harold Perkin has pointed out: 'The whole system came to be aimed not at socializing a leisured class for a life of cultured idleness and aristocratic field sports . . . but at forming an active, responsible, physically fit, self-disciplined elite of professional men and administrators for public service in church and state, the empire and the liberal professions.'[7]

Organized games inculcated team spirit. Chasing an oval leather ball up and down a muddy field had as much to do with team loyalty as with athletic development. 'Houses' within each school also encouraged competitiveness and team loyalty. Individual caprices, it was implied, needed to be suppressed in the interests of the community. Games also inure players to hard knocks, which is why public schools always favoured games that are physically demanding, such as rugby.

At the same time the ethos of the public school was rigidly hierarchical. An almost military system of monitors, sub-prefects and prefects encouraged pupils to discipline their juniors, and instilled respect for authority and skills in leadership. The nineteenth-century French critic Hippolyte Taine found the whole system baffling:

> By and large, a school conducted on such lines is a sort of primitive society in which force reigns almost unchecked, the more so in that the oppressed make it a point of honour never to denounce their oppressors. The masters intervene as little as possible: they are not, as they are in France, the standing representatives of humanity and justice.[8]

A century later nothing had changed, at any rate not at Eton. Quentin Crewe recalls: 'Discipline within each house was maintained by an autonomous clique of senior boys, who had the right of corporal punishment. There was no appeal from their decisions.'[9]

Meaningless privileges kept the troops in line. At Rugby only boys of a certain seniority were allowed to walk outdoors with their hands in their pockets; at Harrow only senior pupils could walk more than two abreast outdoors.[10] Crewe, again:

> The rules which governed behaviour outside the house were even sillier than those inside . . . Whatever the weather, we had to turn up the collars of our overcoats. We were forbidden to roll our umbrellas, neatly, but must carry them unfurled, flapping like wounded rooks. These rules were made by a self-elected society of older boys, usually good at games, who wielded extraordinary powers over the whole school . . . The privileges they arrogated to themselves amounted, together with a few extravagances of dress and the right to sit on a particular wall, to little more than those things that they denied to us.[11]

Promoting other ranks to officers, as it were, within the student body was a way of rewarding conformity and validating 'leadership qualities'.

There was rarely any correlation between academic ability and high rank within the prefecture.

At my own school, Haberdashers, I attained the dizzying height of sub-prefect. My responsibilities included monitoring lunch queues and checking that little boys weren't wearing shoes of the wrong colour. Naturally, I usually had better things to do with my time. Similarly, I would rather study or read than play rugby on chilly winter afternoons. I was spotted leaving the school early on a games afternoon and hauled before the master in charge of discipline. He threatened to strip me of my sub-prefectship. To which I replied that I would be delighted. Returned to the ranks, I would no longer have to waste my lunch hours watching scrappy twelve-year-olds punching each other in queues.

Although the complex social world of the public school achieved a partial fusion between classes that promoted social and political stability, it did nothing to lessen the barrier between the wealthy middle class and the rest of the middle and working classes who could not afford a public-school education. Many schools have supported a system of scholarships to benefit gifted poorer aspirants, today supplemented by the Assisted Places Scheme. However, until fairly recently the Common Entrance examinations required a knowledge of Latin, which was only studied at fee-paying preparatory schools. Thus there was no way in which a working-class or lower-middle-class child, educated at a state primary school, could gain admission to a public school. Even today the examination, which opens the door to public schools, is taken over-whelmingly by children at fee-paying preparatory schools.

An Eton housemaster recalled for me the mysterious ways in which boys were once admitted to the school until the 1970s: 'The parents would write at the birth of their son to a housemaster. Housemasters would compile lists, guaranteeing places to most – subject of course to passing Common Entrance – and offering provisional places to a few other boys. Inevitably some of the boys with firm places would drop off the list – emigration, choosing another school, premature death – so most of the provisionals would end up being accepted. There was also a general list of those not accepted for housemasters' lists. If a house-master had an unexpected vacancy, he could look at the general list and take his pick. But this was a very uncertain way of gaining entry.'

The criteria by which housemasterly approval could be won were informal. 'Often the parents were known to you, or had been recommended to you by other parents. Sometimes it was just a matter of gut feeling, whether we liked the sound of the letter. Some housemasters would interview the parents, but I disliked doing so. That happens more often now, as competition is so intense. But I found it awful to have to tell parents that I didn't like them sufficiently to admit their infant son. But all this was entirely at housemasters' discretion.

'It's changed somewhat. Boys are rarely put down at birth, and the general list has expanded. It's true that the old system, by giving total power to housemasters, inevitably perpetuated an élite, especially if, as often happened, the father knew the housemaster or had attended the same house himself. Some housemasters were keen to reform the system, to make it less exclusive, but usually the parents themselves would have none of it. Housemaster lists came to an end in 1975.'

Although contemporary public schools are accessible to a wider social range of pupils – in terms of class rather than income, of course – twice as many children are enrolled in public schools today than was the case a few decades ago, when the proportion stood at 3 per cent. There was then a direct relationship between public-school education and prestigious careers. In 1944 the Fleming Commission calculated that three-quarters of top civil servants, bishops, judges and bank directors had been educated at public schools. This proportion hardly altered over the next decade or so.[12]

What this meant of course was that class differences at birth were sustained all the way through the educational process to career choice and employment. This is so in many countries – children born into the French *haute bourgeoisie* will tend to receive the best education and to figure disproportionately among those holding the best jobs – but only in Britain is this process so flagrantly aided and abetted by the educational system. In 1962 Anthony Crosland wrote: 'It is no accident that Britain, the only advanced country with a national private elite system of education, should also be the most class-ridden country.'[13]

In France, moreover, admission to the top schools is determined by competitive examination, not by the parents' ability to pay fees. A. H. Halsey and others have looked at the school-leaving age in Britain from the 1920s through to the 1960s and have come to a discouraging conclusion:

The class differences were the same in the 1960s as they had been in the 1920s despite a relatively favourable demography, economic growth, and rising educational investment. Moreover, a class inequality with respect to the quality of education provided at all stages of schooling has persisted over and above the class differences in educational survival.[14]

The introduction of comprehensive education has, if anything, exacerbated the situation. Most countries operate an educational system akin to our comprehensive system. There are undoubtedly variations in approach to streaming, the provision of schools for children with special abilities or special needs, and so forth. None the less it is not a particularly demonic piece of social engineering to provide the same fundamental educational structure for all children. Certainly there was little social justice in the iniquitous system of the Eleven Plus, which, at the immature age of eleven, separated children supposedly only capable of a technical education from those likely to benefit from a more academic approach. Everybody knew that secondary modern schools, which usually threw pupils out at fifteen or sixteen, were educational dustbins. It was very rare for a student to succeed in switching from a secondary modern to a grammar school. I myself performed poorly at the Eleven Plus, failing to secure a place at the school of my choice. I could have gone to a local grammar school of no distinction. My subsequent success in the entrance examinations for three top London schools suggested that my poor showing in the Eleven Plus was aberrational. My parents could afford, just, to send me to a direct-grant school; there must have been thousands of children who also performed below their best at Eleven Plus and had no such second chance.

However, parents with children in the very best sectors of state education, the outstanding grammar schools, were worried by the introduction of comprehensive education. By the mid-1970s many well-to-do parents were pulling their children out of the state system in favour of fee-paying schools. Public schools cleverly relabelled themselves 'independent schools', thus distancing themselves from the arcane traditions of fagging, thrashing, chapel and games. Whereas the rich entrepreneur from a working-class background may have baulked at sending young Kevin to a 'public school', he now need have no qualms about dispatching him to 'an independent school'.

The explanations for the expansion of the fee-paying school are multiple. For some parents the motivation was educational; the disappearance of the direct-grant school and most grammar schools has meant the choice between comprehensive and independent education has become more stark than before. What is also likely, however, is that many parents perceive, as their nineteenth-century counterparts did before them, that a public school will confer social advantages on their offspring. These may take the form of giving them an inside track when it comes to sixth-form education and university entrance, or may be a calculation that their child will profit from meeting children from a higher social background. Equally, the deterioration in many urban schools, reflected in a perceived fall in educational standards and in occasional but well-publicized lapses in discipline, has led many parents to view the state system with dismay. I know many professional couples, all committed Labour supporters, who cannot contemplate sending their children to the dreadful schools in their catchment areas, and who therefore send them to fee-paying schools.

Fee-paying education by definition is intended to confer advantage on those who use it. Jeremy Paxman's research provides grim reading for those of us who believe educational opportunity should be equally available to our children:

> Over forty years after the legislation which opened secondary education to all, the public schools account for 7 out of 9 of the army's top generals, two-thirds of the external directors of the Bank of England, 33 of the 39 top English judges, all the ambassadors in the 15 most important overseas missions, 78 of the Queen's 84 lord lieutenants and the majority of the bishops in the Church of England. Even the bold, thrusting entrepreneurs who have become such folk heroes have failed to cast aside old money: of the 200 richest people in Britain, 35 were educated at a single school, Eton.[15]

Of the thirty-nine prime ministers who served between 1721 and 1927, sixteen were Old Etonians. In the new parliaments of 1931 and 1935, 104 members were Old Etonians.[16] In 1959 one-fifth of all Conservative MPs had attended Eton. The same proportion of government ministers from all parties serving between 1900 and 1985 had also been to Eton, four times as many as had been to Harrow, the runner-up.[17] But this pre-eminence is in decline. Anthony Sampson noted with exasperated astonishment that in 1982 the two top people at the BBC, the chairmen of all five high-street banks, the Home

Secretary, the Chancellor of the Exchequer, the editor of *The Times* and the heads of both the civil and foreign services were all products of Eton and Winchester.[18] Fifteen years later that is no longer the case and never likely to be so again.

The objection to public-school education is not merely that it confers privilege on those who can purchase it. It is also that public-school bonding still prevails in corners of the professional world. This goes back a long way: there were Old Etonian dinners in the City of London during the reign of Queen Anne.[19] Mark Bence-Jones remarks with typical complacency: 'Once someone is an Etonian, his fellow Etonians will accept and protect him, regardless of who he was before he entered the school. It is only to outsiders that the institution might appear to be exclusive and snobbish.'[20]

Vestiges of the public-school ethos persist: the instinctive recognition of good and bad form, the niceties of the dress code, staff dining rooms for executives (often two or three for different grades) and canteens for the workers, and the insistence on loyalty as the supreme virtue (embodied in the Official Secrets Act). Etonians are quite open about their tribal solidarity. Knowing that, whatever your personal shortcomings, your predecessors have been running the country for three centuries does engender a certain confidence. The sports commentator Brian Johnston noted: 'I always call it the best trades union in Great Britain because in my life, where I go round all over the place, there is always some OE somewhere.'[21]

The literary critic G. M. Fraser once gave an impassioned assessment of the nudges and winks of public schooldom:

> It is all there – as it always is, in a tone of voice, a look, a particular kind of accent, a way of laughing, a use of certain phrases, or even just a vague, unspoken sense of something exclusive. Everyone in Britain knows and recognizes it; sometimes it is nearly invisible, but it is always real. It is the difference between the boy, or man, who was at a public school, and the rest.[22]

Fraser was writing twenty years ago, and the phenomenon has diminished; in most careers and professions nobody greatly cares any longer where you went to school. Moreover, the code – the accent, the turn of phrase, the laughter, the confidence – is less prized. Those in possession of it may choose not to wield it. An Old Etonian busily making a killing as a record producer will not find a pukka accent a particular asset. Here and there the code remains significant: among the smarter army regiments or estate agents, within the Foreign Office or the salons of auction houses and the boardrooms of the more old-fashioned wine importers. The assault on the more stuffy upper-middle-class institutions undertaken by their scourge, Margaret Thatcher, has marginalized these survivals.

The publisher Anthony Blond recalled:

> What is remarkable about Eton (and it's why Etonians are such good politicians) is that you are trained in every nuance of social and political climbing, and a young Etonian understands very quickly the art of how to influence people, and how to be helped by people, and that is why they are brilliant politicians, diplomats, ambassadors, employers, generals. There is a certain way in which even a young Etonian would expect doors to be opened for him, literally and metaphorically. A sort of assumption of superiority, I think.[23]

The great change that has occurred is that independent schools are, with few exceptions, no longer concerned with imparting Christian values or a gentlemanly code. The upwardly mobile middle-class parents who send their children to these schools want, above all, a superior education, not because they necessarily value intellectual training as such but because everybody recognizes that, in an increasingly competitive world, education confers essential skills and qualifications. A couple of decades ago family background alone would usually ensure admission to some of the smarter schools such as Eton. That is no longer the case. You may be a lordling, but if you can't add up or spell your name, the school won't accept you. Independent schools, and the preparatory schools that were tributaries feeding them, had to maintain high academic standards. That is admirable, but ironically it has merely widened the gap between the private and public sectors. The very excellence of many fee-paying schools will, as a side effect, perpetuate class distinctions. The current controversy about declining examination standards can only pile on more pressure. I cannot assess whether or not it is easier to obtain a GCSE or A-level grade today than it was five or ten years ago. But the perception that it may be so will, in effect, devalue that currency and favour those schools with the facilities to push pupils to ever more statistically impressive examination results.

It was in 1971 that David Martin and Colin Crouch wrote:

> Social mobility through education in Britain has been described as a sponsored (as opposed to contest) system, whereby the existing elite coopts members of other classes who manage to acquire *its* social norms and life styles. This is reinforced by the belief of many working-class parents that education, particularly its higher levels, is the preserve of other classes.[24]

It is a measure of how things have changed that this last statement is no longer true. The upwardly mobile working classes are fully aware of the utility of education, and in this respect are indistinguishable from the professional middle classes.

Since it cannot be denied that the independent sector sells advantage to those who can afford it, that it confers social cachet, that it drains good teachers and students from the state sector and that it reinforces the class structure by dividing the nation, the question arises: What can or should be done about it? The obvious difficulty is that in a free society it is not acceptable to deny people a purchased education if that is how they wish to spend their money. Even Tony Benn, never one to give up on a socialist agenda, told me: 'I'm in favour of a comprehensive system but you cannot make it illegal for somebody to educate somebody for money. You can't go round and close schools. What I think you can say is that if any state money goes into a school then there must be a non-selective entry. And that's quite a different thing. The idea that you abolish public schools is not sustainable, and anyway ninety per cent of people in this country go to comprehensive schools.'

Even those tempted to 'abolish' fee-paying schools have to admit that their educational standards – especially among former direct-grant schools – are probably higher than ever before (even though there are also a number of independent schools that offer fewer A-level options and perform less well in examinations than comprehensives within the same catchment area). The former headmaster of Westminster, John Rae, highlighted this dilemma some years ago: 'The basic problem is social justice – yet you need injustice to achieve long-term ends. The biggest damage we do is to perpetuate a class division. But it may be the price we have to pay for excellence.'[25] The counter-argument could be offered that if state schools were of a more consistent and higher standard then there would be less incentive for families to spend small fortunes on private education.

Abolition has been proposed in the past. R. H. Tawney intoned in 1931:

> The English educational system will never be one worthy of a civilized society until the children of all classes in the nation attend the same schools . . . The idea that differences of educational opportunity among children should depend upon differences of wealth among parents is a barbarity . . .
>
> A special system of schools, reserved for children whose parents have larger bank accounts than their neighbours, exists in no other country on the same scale as in England. It is at once an educational monstrosity and a grave national misfortune. It is educationally vicious, since to mix with companions from homes of different types is an important part of the education of the young. It is socially disastrous, for it does more than any other single cause, except capitalism itself, to perpetuate the division of the nation into classes of which one is almost unintelligible to the other.[26]

Others criticized the system as a conspiracy on the part of a self-perpetuating élite. Two precocious radicals, Giles and Esmond Romilly, wrote a book jointly about their public-school education in the 1930s. Giles's contribution included the following blunt declarations:

> In criticising the public schools, it is essential to bear in mind the part they play in relation to capitalist society, to see how all their teaching, the emphasis on games, for instance, is conditioned by the economic motives of the middle class. The aim is to produce a being so indoctrinated as to be fitted to maintain their ascendancy . . . In my opinion public schoolmasters as a class are deficient and dangerous, and should be at once removed to some place where they can never pervert anybody again, perhaps to the society of each other. The old sadists, the smarmy hypocrites in chapel, the hearty incompetents, the bogus aristocrats, they should all go.[27]

In 1959 the historian Hugh Thomas (now a Conservative life peer) penned the following battle cry:

It is in childhood that the men who make the present Establishment are trained; and . . . therefore we shall not be free of the Establishment frame of mind, permeating all aspects of life and society, and constantly re-appearing even when apparently uprooted, until the public schools are completely swept away, at whatever cost to the temporary peace of the country.[28]

Attempts at reform have always foundered. The Labour Party, returning to power in 1964, had promised in its manifesto to 'set up an educational trust to advise on the best way of integrating the public schools into the state system of education'. That was clearly a fudge. The 1970 manifesto frowned at the idea of 'educational and social inequalities'. The 1974 manifesto merely pledged to withdraw tax relief and charitable status from public schools, but this was never done. This failure to make any significant alteration in the status of independent education reflected the obvious difficulty mentioned by Benn: abolition is inconsistent with a defence of individual liberty.

A handful of politicians on the left still argue for abolition. Dennis Skinner MP told me: 'I'd get rid of the public schools . . . There are a lot of people who send kids to private schools because they don't want them to be with certain groups of other kids. Some of it is racist.' When I pointed out that fee-paying schools were perceived, even by some working-class people, as a means of 'bettering oneself', he responded: 'That's not true of the vast majority of the people from where I come from. I represent villages, not the inner city.'

A schoolteacher with long experience in East Anglia and the Home Counties came close to favouring abolition of private education. 'I would argue quite simply that neither class nor money should give people access to good education, which I see as a right that should be accessible to all. As a teacher, my objection to the private system is not only that it creates privilege but that it undermines state education, if only because people with power and privilege don't care about it. Inevitably, independent schools cream off many of the best teachers, who can't help being attracted to the prospect of shorter terms, better pay, smaller classes and better resources and surroundings.

'I also resent the fact that independent schools are absolved from participation in the national curriculum and the testing that goes with it. If the curriculum and regular testing are deemed necessary for the state sector, the same should apply to the private sector too.'

She was unmoved by the argument that abolition of the private sector would lead to the disappearance of some of Britain's finest schools. 'In my view,' she replied, 'their very excellence is a greater argument for their abolition as private institutions accessible only to a privileged few.'

George Walden, when still a Conservative MP, posed the question to left-wing abolitionists: 'How do you propose to rid the country of the kind of segregation in education you so loudly deplore, given that abolition is a myth, that no private school worth its salt is going to cross the line to become a comprehensive, and that the notion that state schools can rival private schools in quality provided they are given similar resources is intellectual escapism?'[29]

His own solution suggested he had some sympathy for the left-wing distaste for private education:

> If private schools disappeared by magic, the result would be a cultural revolution in state education, instigated and sustained by the upper middle classes. For the first time in memory, there would be serious thinking, at all levels of society, followed by determined action. At once there would be more money, smaller classes, fewer crumbling buildings, and nurseries for all . . .
>
> The problem is not how to do away with the best schools in the country, but how to open them up to the best pupils, to make them part of the national educational endeavour, and to involve the most articulate and influential people in society in the educational well-being of the remaining 93%.[30]

His solution was to propose a new sector to be known as the 'open sector'.

> Admission of pupils to this sector would be by aptitude, potential, and examination . . . Given their costs, and the probability of a largish number of places being won by pupils of the 'fee-paying classes', it would be necessary to charge a range of fees . . . There would be no comparison with the assisted places scheme, where pupils have to show they are poor enough to be awarded a place. Here, every qualified pupil would be entitled to entry as of right, not of charity. The APS would be abolished, the savings going towards the cost of the open sector.[31]

It is not clear that Walden's prescription would significantly diminish social divisiveness; he could also be criticized for his preoccupation with the 'best pupils' rather than with overall national educational standards. It is inconceivable that his ideas will be taken up by the Conservative Party, and, although they may appeal to some in the Labour Party, they are unlikely to win the approval of ideologues. In any case, the Labour Party has, since the introduction of comprehensive education, been less than bold in matters of educational reform.

During the 1970s, the Labour government directed its reformist zeal not at public schools but at a softer target: direct-grant schools, which had been created in 1902. Such schools were obliged to make 25 per cent of their places available to children from state primary schools. Consequently they contained children of considerable ability but of a much broader social mix than would have been encountered in public schools. My own school, Haberdashers, was a direct-grant institution when I attended it in the 1960s, and there were plenty of working-class boys mixed in with the rest of us. It certainly prevented Haberdashers from being an upper-middle-class enclave, even though there was from time to time considerable class tension, with some working-class boys taunting the more intellectually inclined middle-class boys, especially if they were Jewish or Asian. No doubt some of us on the receiving end must have been somewhat obnoxious, flaunting our copies of *Ulysses*. Most direct-grant schools maintained very high educational standards, which was precisely why they offered a threat to the comprehensive system. Many public schools were filled with dim boys from wealthy backgrounds, but the direct-grant schools were far more dynamic and deprived the comprehensive schools of some exceptionally able students. So in 1975 the Labour government offered the direct-grant schools two options: to become comprehensives or fee-paying. Almost all of them opted for the latter, with the bizarre consequence of a Labour government presiding over the largest creation of independent schools in a single year.[32]

Four years later power returned to the Conservative Party, which gradually readopted the principle of selection. It was a bit of a con. The impression given was that 'selection' would expand parental choice, but in practice the 'selection' was exercised by the schools more than by the parents. Some schools were reluctant to impose selection, presumably on the grounds that it would undermine the principle of equal educational opportunity. Predictably, many Labour politicians were opposed to selection. Less predictably, others welcomed it.

The research director of the Fabian society, Stephen Pollard, wrote in 1996:

> Grammar schools were once regarded by the left as the pinnacle of socialism: opening up opportunity on the basis of ability and stretching all children to realise their potential. Yet today selection is the greatest taboo of the left . . . For too long the left has been in the grip of an ideology which believes that the primary purpose of a school is social engineering – that only by forcing all children, irrespective of their individual abilities, to be educated together can a truly equal society be created.[33]

Although this is an unusual line for a Labour intellectual to pursue, Pollard does illuminate the uncomfortable fact that Labour is trying to bow in all directions at once. It favours comprehensive education – but is resigned to grant-maintained schools, a stance at odds with the comprehensive principle and savouring a shift in control from local authorities to central government. It could also be argued that the success of grant-maintained schools is inevitably at the expense of other schools within the state sector. Labour opposes selection but with diminishing fervour, and has no plans to tamper with private education.

As grant-maintained and selective schools multiply, and the British education system becomes ever more stratified, there are a few dissenting voices. George Walden, again:

> In education there are two kingdoms, and the twain do not meet. Bridging the divide without lowering standards would be widely popular. Encouraging private schools, specially the 120 former direct grant grammar schools, to opt into the state sector, to create an internal educational market open to all, should be Tory policy.
>
> Which is not to say that the prime minister should echo Labour on a 'classless society'. Classlessness is a class concept: a guilty reaction to the sins of the past. That is how we got the guilt-stricken Shirley Williams and her comprehensive schools. It is nobody's ideal to be like everybody else. The Tory aim should be a dynamic society of maximum diversity and distinction, based on maximum opportunity for all.[34]

Walden's distaste for the comprehensive ideal is shared by Canon Peter Pilkington, the former High Master of St Paul's: 'Britain is the only country in Europe that has adopted a comprehensive system. A principle of selection has been retained in the French *lycée* and the German *Gymnasium*. The Germans have a tripartite system, and both the Germans and the French have improved their technical and vocational education. The reforms which gave us the comprehensive system were based not so much on educational improvement as egalitarian theory. The system is based on an academic model that isn't suitable to all students. It offers education by estate agent. If you live in the wrong part of the country or the inner cities and can't afford a fee- paying school, you're doomed.

'The problem has always been that the right is not interested in education and unwilling to spend money on it, and the left is more interested in ideology than good education. So the only way to solve the problem is to alter the structure. The French system obliges students to choose at sixteen between academic and professional/technical baccalaureats. The Labour Party still argues that class is so ingrained that we cannot accept something similar to the French model. Therefore the comprehensive system must be retained. I can accept that many secondary modern schools were inadequate. As vocational schools they were poorly funded and put into the worst buildings. But in order to get rid of the secondary moderns was it necessary to create the comprehensive school, thus throwing out the baby with the bathwater? Secondary moderns could have been developed into good technical colleges, but never were. Britain still lacks the kind of prestigious vocational qualification available in France and Germany.

'Class is undoubtedly a factor in British education. We have greater mobility than ever before in terms of class identity, but we are still obsessed by it and allow it to govern our educational system.'

Lord Pilkington looks back regretfully to periods such as the 1950s, when the public schools catered to a far smaller proportion of the population and were counterbalanced by the many excellent grammar schools that achieved comparable academic results. Not that the expansion of the private sector has much, in his eyes, to do with the quality of education it offers: 'It's true that the independent sector now educates 7 per cent of the school population. But that doesn't mean they are necessarily well educated. About half the independent schools are totally useless.'

*

When it comes to university education, Oxford and Cambridge retain, even today, a cachet that other universities lack. Institutions such as Imperial College and universities such as Edinburgh and Manchester may, in specific faculties, provide educational standards every bit as high as those offered by Oxbridge; none the less Oxbridge still draws an élite and educates an élite, although less so than in the past. In the nineteenth century the classical education provided by the ancient colleges was regarded as the perfect training for those who would be spending their professional lives in the civil or diplomatic service, in politics or the learned professions.

They were certainly not aristocratic institutions, although individual colleges such as Christ Church in Oxford, and Trinity and Magdalene in Cambridge, always recruited heavily from the most prestigious public schools. However, there were other colleges where the public-school and upper-class contingents were far smaller. Even in the early years of the twentieth century the vast majority of those attending the Sidney Sussex College, Cambridge, were the sons of the professional middle classes.[35]

The power of the individual admissions tutor clearly affected the composition of the student body. At Trinity one tutor made little secret of his preference for public-school boys; another, however, provided a counterbalance by confessing he was more swayed by good looks than by schooling. No doubt skilled careers officers at many schools soon learned which tutors were likely to be sympathetic to their applicants. Today one hears anecdotal evidence of inverse snobbery, in which boys from leading public schools are turned down by certain colleges, in spite of impeccable academic qualifications. One story I heard re-counted the rejection of a well-qualified boy whose family had attended the same college for many generations on the grounds that 'We don't need any more of that kind of thing'.

Michael Beloff, the President of Trinity College, Oxford, has commented that 'on the one hand, old members complain that there is no guaranteed place for their offspring and suspect a bias against the products of independent schools. On the other, Labour Party spokes-men suspect a bias in favour of precisely such people.'[36] In the same article he reveals that 40 per cent of the college's latest tranche of undergraduates came from the state sector. Since 10 per cent consisted of overseas students, that leaves half of the student body coming from independent schools. Of that 40 per cent from the state sector, 'well over half were from comprehensive schools',[37] which suggests either that the comprehensives are underperforming (or underapplying) or that Trinity, Oxford, is indifferent to such a small intake.

'The admissions tutors here', a visiting fellow at a small Cambridge college told me, 'were unhappy about the fact that half of all places still go to privately educated applicants. At the college there was no bias against state education as such, and the high proportion of public-school students reflected the unwillingness of teachers and students in the state sector to apply to universities they consider élitist and unlikely to accept them – often a false perception. But I have to admit that private education gives kids fluency and confidence, qualities that ease their path into higher education. I remember how the Cambridge admissions department compiled a video to counter the idea that the university was only for toffs. It began with scenes from *Brideshead Revisited*, then switched to scenes featuring women, blacks and so forth, showing that Cambridge was full of real people. This video was sent out to schools across the country, but unfortunately during the same week that *Porterhouse Blue* was screened. So it had no effect.'

At Trinity in the 1960s there was, unquestionably, much intense snobbery. One of my neighbours in Great Court, a particularly dense Etonian, once declared that he only spoke to chaps who had been to Eton, Harrow or Winchester. So far as I could tell, he did his best to adhere to this principle. He was, of course, an idiot, and only other idiots sought his exclusive company. Although there were snobbish cliques within fashionable colleges, it remains true that the dominant principle of selection was meritocratic. Both among the student body and the fellows there was a broad social mix.

The power of Oxbridge stemmed from its prestige. Retired diplomats and politicians yearned to retire to the masters' lodges because it enabled them to maintain their influence within comfortable surroundings. Dons, and certainly heads of colleges, were obvious recruits for the Great and the Good. Governments could rely on their shared values. Whitehall civil servants, Gray's Inn barristers, Westminster politicians and masters of Balliol or Corpus Christi usually spoke the same language. Elite colleges such as All Souls deliberately fostered this close network between different branches of the Establishment. One Oxford don spoke to me disdainfully of the *folie de grandeur* of some of his colleagues, who were only too eager to dash to London to offer their expertise and time to commissions and committees.

It is not that different in the United States, although the situation is somewhat corrupted by the perpetual need of universities to raise funds. Wendy Lesser, a leading West Coast editor, writer and intellectual, remarked: 'Graduation from Ivy League and comparable universities is still a considerable aid to advancement, even though no one will openly admit it. No one cares how well or poorly you did at Harvard or Berkeley; what counts is that you went there. This handful of colleges does have a network of old boys and old girls that operates in terms of admitting people to the right companies, the right law firms. There are other colleges that are the academic equal of Ivy League – Swarthmore, Rice – but they have no status, no clout. The important thing to remember is that alumni are always favoured. It's something that's been used during the affirmative action debate. Proponents point out that if two equal candidates present themselves to a distinguished university, the child of the alumnus will invariably have an edge. This is linked to fund-raising. It's essential to coddle the alumni, who are a source of funds, even if only on their deathbeds, and what better way than by admitting their children?'

Thus certain universities are prized as much for giving graduates a master key as for their educational distinction. If social and professional advancement strongly influence the choice of university in the United States, secondary education is less significant. There are smart secondary schools such as Groton, but little tradition of boarding-school education in America. True, in cities where state education is dire and dangerous, expensive and prestigious day schools cater to the professional middle classes. Moreover, American high schools offer a less exacting academic education than their European counterparts, as it is expected that universities, with their four-year degree programmes, will provide the additional training that in Europe is undertaken by the school system.

'Nevertheless,' says Lesser, 'what is different in Britain is that the choice of secondary school is a class choice, and a difficult and wrenching one, because of the wide gap between the private and state sectors.'

There is nothing in the policies of the major political parties to suggest that this is likely to change.

NINETEEN

Snobbery: Lackeys and Parasites

So Evelyn Waugh is in his coffin. Died of snobbery. Did not wish to be considered a man of letters; it did not satisfy him to be thought a master of letters; it did not satisfy him to be thought a master of English prose. He wanted to be a duke.

Cecil Beaton, *Diaries: The Parting Years*, 11 April 1966

There are two kinds of snob: those who look up and those who look down. Snobbery is like Medusa's head: too close a contemplation of its nuances and you become fatally infected. By dwelling too lovingly on class distinctions, you turn into a snob yourself.

Thackeray it was who developed the concept. In 1829 he edited an undergraduate magazine called *The Snob*, in which an ancient term for a cobbler was used to designate the ill-bred town dwellers, as opposed to the refined, well-bred undergraduates. When in 1848 he wrote *The Book of Snobs*, the term was used disparagingly of those who look down on others for their vulgarity or cosy up to social superiors. Such people he cheerfully labelled 'crawling, truckling lackeys and parasites'.

Snobbery in Thackeray's sense was a matter of attitude, an expression of class anxiety. Class consciousness has been a constant of British society for as long as anyone can remember. Recall Sir Walter Elliot in *Persuasion*, a man 'who, for his own amusement, never took up any book but the Baronetage . . . He considered the blessing of beauty as inferior only to the blessing of a baronetcy.'

Nor was class consciousness less pronounced lower down the social scale. To take another fictional example, consider Mrs Cadwallader in George Eliot's *Middlemarch*: she

believed as unquestionably in birth and no-birth as she did in game and vermin. She would never have disowned any one on the ground of poverty: a De Bracy reduced to take his dinner in a basin would have seemed to her an example of pathos worth exaggerating, and I fear his aristocratic vices would not have horrified her. But her feeling towards the vulgar rich was a sort of religious hatred: they had probably made all their money out of high retail prices, and Mrs Cadwallader detested high prices for everything that was not paid in kind at the Rectory: such people were no part of God's design in making the world; and their accent was an affliction to the ears.

In Hardy's *Return of the Native*, Thomasin Yeobright replies to Diggory Venn's offer of marriage in social terms: 'Another reason is my aunt. She would not, I know, agree to it, even if I wished to have you. She likes you very well, but she will want me to look a little higher than a small dairy-farmer, and marry a professional man.'

Snobbery is the occasion for sadness as well as disapproval, for it encloses the world and makes it a smaller place. The conscious layering of society into social bands separated by walls of deference, fear and aloofness impoverishes those who value such exclusions.

Jessica Mitford expressed impatience at this kind of restriction in recalling how as a child she wanted to ask some friends for tea. Her mother was aghast, responding:

'Oh no, darling, of course not. If you have them to tea they'll invite you to tea with them, and you wouldn't be able to go. You see, I don't know any of their mothers.'

No use arguing, or pressing for a reason. This sort of discussion always produced a cold, grim anger in the Grown-Ups . . .

It was also a complicated matter. My parents would have been not so much shocked, as blankly uncomprehending, if anyone had accused them of 'being snobbish'. Snobbishness was, surely, by definition a purely middle-class attribute, finding expression in an unhealthy desire to rise above one's station, to ease oneself in where one wasn't wanted, and in turn to look down superciliously at those below one in the social scale. My parents would not have dreamed of looking down on anyone; they preferred to look straight ahead, caring not at all if this tended to limit their vision. Neither were they social climbers, for they rather disliked really 'smart' society.

The Lower Orders were much less of a problem than the middle-class . . . In my parents' view of history, upper class, middle class and working class were destined to travel for ever harmoniously down the ages on parallel tracks which could never meet or cross.[1]

Children, of course, tend to be the most acute social observers, detecting the most subtle of nuances. The journalist Peregrine Worsthorne recalls his schooldays:

Stowe was not a grand school. It was mostly made up of the sons of professional or business people, with just enough 'honourables' to make the list look respectable. In my time there was even a boy baronet. But there were also a number of very obvious non-gentlemen who were the sons of what were then called the 'nouveaux riches'. It is no good pretending that this did not matter. It mattered enormously. Class consciousness was a fact of life. I was at once aware, for example, that most of the boys in my dustbin of a House were exceedingly common; not at all the kind of people one would ever expect to meet at home. They spoke with funny voices, used brilliantine, had never learnt to ride or shoot, had home addresses in industrial cities, referred to their parents as Mum and Dad . . . I felt exceedingly ill-done-by to be among them.[2]

Worsthorne admits his feelings were snobbish, but adds: 'In self-defence I must plead that it would have been peculiar if I had felt anything else, since in those days the gap between gentry and manufacturers was still immense. And not only between gentry and manufacturers. Even the local doctor at home, or the solicitor, were never treated as equals.'[3]

If Worsthorne recovered from his childhood snobbery and fastidiousness, others did not. Harold Nicolson, married into the aristocracy, had to accommodate his leftish political stance to his conviction of social superiority. He justified his belief in aristocracy by allying it with learning rather than with wealth, which is a peculiar slant:

I have always been on the side of the under-dog, but I have also believed in the principle of aristocracy. I have hated the rich but I have loved learning, scholarship, intelligence and the humanities. Suddenly I am faced with the fact that all these lovely things are supposed to be 'class privileges'. The snobbishness of the British people (the factor upon which the aristocratic principle relied and often exploited) has suddenly turned to venom. When I find that my whole class is being assailed, I feel part of them, a feeling that I have never had before.[4]

James Lees-Milne, himself a snob of epic proportions, recalls dining at Brooks's with Nicolson in 1943: 'He complained that his enemies criticized him for being National Labour when they saw how much he enjoyed the delicacies of life. They called him inconsistent. He said, "True, I do not care for the society of the lower classes. I have no desire to live with them, or be like them. I hate them. I do want them to become like me." '[5]

Lees-Milne himself would not have been shocked by this disclosure. He fully approved of class distinctions but disclaimed any snobbery, arguing instead for the separateness of the classes:

> I feel deeply humble in the presence of manual workers because of their skill, which I am totally without, and their physical courage, which is its usual accompaniment. But I cannot be intimate with them, and I consider it cant to pretend what one does not feel. I do not on this account consider myself any more snobbish than the robin which is incapable of mating with the sparrow.[6]

I am sure the working class was very touched by Lees-Milne's humility before them. (They also had their admirers among the European nobility. The Duchess of Sermoneta in 1947 graciously recalled: 'The lower-class Austrians were delightful, with friendly smiling faces and nearly all the men very good-looking.')[7]

Transparent snobbery is no longer acceptable, which may be why a few people still parade a ferocious snobbery as an attention-seeking badge of political incorrectness. Alan Clark MP is our best-loved exponent of this attitude. His wife once famously denigrated a family he had humiliated as 'below-stairs', and Clark snubbed the self-made millionaire Michael Heseltine MP by repeating the jibe that he had bought all his own furniture (in contrast to those lucky few who inherit the family antiques). Such remarks were, of course, calculated to offend. What is odd is that the Clarks must have known that such scorn would land them in trouble because they themselves could scarcely brag of their pedigree. They were very rich and lived in a castle, but were no aristocrats, as Clark's brother Colin made clear at the time:

Al is always going on about how our family is upper-class, hunting-shooting-fishing types. It's absolutely not true. My father always made it very clear to us that we were *not* upper class. He never in any way aspired to become so, and he never forgot that we made our money from trading cotton – and not that long ago. He never felt easy mixing with dukes and members of the Royal Family. If anything, he was an aesthete. He wouldn't have dreamt of going hunting. He bought Saltwood Castle because it was a beautiful house in a lovely setting, but it was partly a bit of a joke. The thing is, Al's gone and taken it all a bit too seriously. He so desperately wants to be Establishment, to be gentry.[8]

After Jane Clark had delivered her ultra-snobbish remark about 'below-stairs' people, some newspaper columnists couldn't resist the temptation to investigate her own background. Stephen Glover established definitively that Mrs Clark was the daughter of a colonel 'whose name does not figure in any edition of Burke's Landed Gentry I can find. I can imagine that her origins are those of a nice local middle-class girl.'[9] It is a very British preoccupation, allowing oneself to work up such a lather over social origins.

Auberon Waugh has even less reluctance than Alan Clark to utter the unutterable. Typical of his proclamations is: 'All too often we have been persuaded to accept some new leader as "classless" only to discover that he is really lower-class. It is time to state quite clearly that we do not wish to be ruled by the lower classes.'[10] With Waugh one often has the impression that he feels it is time to give some unpalatable views an airing. Compelled by his profession to have views on everything, he feels obliged to whip up a little outrage from time to time to keep the readers satisfied.

It is not hard to find a pretext for snobbery, if one is determined enough. Some twenty years ago I was chatting to a rather drunk but very attractive woman at a party. She revealed that she had married into a very aristocratic family and, on learning that I was keen on antiquarian books, wondered whether we could jointly hatch a plot to remove and sell a few incunabula from the family library. When she suggested that I, as her new partner in crime, join her party for dinner, I eagerly accepted. Her party consisted of, among others, an Irish aristocrat of immense lineage. He was clearly irritated that some callow youth was being invited to tag along, and expressed it by remarking in a loud voice that my shoes looked cheap but my shirt was all right. As it happened, I told him, my shoes were hand-made but my shirt came from a department store. At the time I thought, and still think, that his rudeness was appalling. I was undeterred and spent a memorably enjoyable and drunken evening.

Only the most romantic of souls would actually wish to hail snobbery as somehow laudable. One of the few explicit defences of snobbery I have encountered is by Andrew Roberts, historian and newspaper columnist: 'Snobbery is the pole opposite of envy, because the snob actually takes pleasure from someone else's lineage, rank, wealth or status, rather than resenting them. Envy, which Churchill called "that most barren of vices", is a far greater threat to today's society.'[11]

An obsession with genealogy, especially one's own, can also become a form of snobbery. There is nothing strange about genealogy as an object of study; snobbery enters the frame only when you consider your lineage to be of interest to others. Take the novelist Anthony Powell, who is so obsessed by genealogy that 20 per cent of his first volume of memoirs is devoted to the subject. Perhaps he just takes pleasure in boring the world with information along the lines of: 'In addition to the peerage from which he took his name, Lord Talboys also held (according to the 19th century peerage doctrine) the *de jure* barony of Kyme.'[12]

Still, it has to be said that when it comes to snobbery, at least when expressed as *hauteur*, the British and Irish can't hold a candle to some Europeans. There is nothing in London to compare with the Paris Jockey Club. Not only must its members be titled but their titles must date back to pre-Revolutionary times; no descendants of Napoleonic creations need apply.

In Europe there is far more snobbery within the ranks of an aristocracy jealously clinging to distinctions that have long ceased to matter in the slightest. In France the *noblesse d'épée* still look down on the more numerous *noblesse de robe*, and German or Austrian *Landädel*, the landed élite with feudal origins, look down on more recently created nobles. It is all incredibly silly. Even Americans are not immune from social pretension: their Social Registers lay down the law on which families are acceptable in the great cities of the republic.

My Hungarian grandmother looked down on the then Prime Minister, Harold Wilson, whom she dismissed as 'common'. Arguments from other members of the family that Mr Wilson was doing far more for her pension than the toffs who had preceded him cut no ice. My grandmother, it should be pointed out, was not a countess with a lorgnette, but a supermarket cashier. Her snobbery was a form of pride, however misplaced.

If the snob who looks down is a disagreeable phenomenon, the snob who looks up offers greater amusement, especially to those on the receiving end. It is flattering to be regarded with awe, and the act of shrugging it off with embarrassment is sometimes tinged with gratification that it is happening at all. In her diaries, Lady Cynthia Asquith records a stay at a hotel in Brighton: 'The gentility of this establishment, the commercial hotel, beggars all description, and the landlady is the queen of snobs. I hear her talking about "her ladyship" with bated breath, and issuing stern injunctions to the poor parlourmaid to be sure and help me first, and to mind and open the door for me, and so on.'[13]

This kind of snobbery is allied to social climbing. Association with one's superiors is supposed to have an adhesive effect; nebulous aristocratic virtues may, it is hoped, rub off and cast their aura around your person. Despite Cynthia Asquith's faint disdain, the upper classes don't necessarily reject or despise the social climbers. After all, to have upwardly mobile spaniels trotting at your heels validates your own social value. Furthermore, the upper classes will always have the last word on those who try to clamber into their midst. As an upper-class friend of mine cheerfully put it, 'By showing that you want to belong to a particular class, you rule yourself out.'

A worship of the socially superior also allows you to feel superior to those inhabiting classes lower than your own. As the social historian and novelist Andrew Sinclair remarks:

The demarcations of snobbery below the line have much to do with the admirations of snobbery above the line ... If one feels oneself superior to many, it is easier to accept a few men's superiority in their turn. It is only the position at the bottom of the ladder that makes a man want to throw it all down. Otherwise there is the hope of social climbing, the search after status.[14]

The truly devoted and skilled social climber deserves some respect. For the likes of Marcel Proust and 'Chips' Channon, it bore fruit, in artistic terms for the former and in social and political terms for the latter. The future Lord Curzon, as an undergraduate, was regarded with suspicion because of his habit of cultivating aristocratic students. Curzon did not deny the charge, and observed, with some pomposity: 'Anyone who tries to get hold of young men of rank or wealth must expect to be accused of snobbishness, but one must remember how important it is to influence towards good those who are going to have an influence over hundreds or thousands of other lives.'[15]

Nor is there anything new about social climbing. Michael De La Noy notes that it was rampant in Tudor times:

> Social climbing, snobbism and pretension, inevitable concomitants of any honours system, have flourished through the centuries. But the Tudors even went so far as to forge medieval seals and deeds, effigies and coats of arms, and the tracing of their ancestors became a national pastime. By 1577 the Earl of Essex had satisfied himself that he could legitimately lay claim to 55 quarterings, only to be outdone by the Grenville family, who collected a total of 719.[16]

Until the early twentieth century there was more than social ambition involved in cultivating good relationships with the upper classes. The landed élite had real power: appointing clergy to livings, issuing licences and dispensing justice from the magistrate's bench. There was a fine line between a snobbish cultivation of the aristocracy and mere careerism.

Nowadays our attitude to social aspirations is more complex. Take a bizarre competition run by the *Sunday Times* in June 1996. For some time hard-up landlords have been flogging off lordships of the manor at auction. The current record price is £188,000 for Wimbledon. They are worthless in that they confer neither title nor property nor privilege on the possessor. The prize offered by the newspaper was the lordship of the manor of Cold Aston in Gloucestershire. It was won by Joan Eastwood, a Lancashire school secretary, aged sixty-seven. Mrs Eastwood was coaxed down to open the village fête and was persuaded to don ermine and coronet (as though she were now a peeress, which she wasn't) for the benefit of the *Sunday Times* photographer. The newspaper acknowledged the triviality of the whole business, but at the same time lavished two pages on the story, sending up poor Mrs Eastwood in the process. Perhaps she enjoyed her outing, but she may have felt some chagrin at having to appease the inverted snobbery of the *Sunday Times*.

*

Snobbery resides in the details. The British addiction to dress codes has transformed clothing into a class indicator. It was always thus, and by the end of the twentieth century we have scarcely grown up as a nation. My Irish acquaintance used the dress code as his way of snubbing me, as though I would be mortified at having been exposed wearing the wrong kind of shoes. There are multiple offences that can be committed by the middle classes: pre-knotted bow ties (very handy, in my experience), smart clothes that are too obviously new, naff blazers or college ties and cufflinks. The great sporting events of the Season, the Henley Regatta and Royal Ascot, insist on an irrational dress code so that the insiders can differentiate themselves from the hoi-polloi. Clothes provide pretexts for social humiliations. James Lees-Milne noted in a diary that Kenneth Clark 'dresses like a dapper footman on his half-day off'.[17] (Perhaps he did, but his books are likely to outlive Lees-Milne's.) The diarist also indulged in some truly fatuous cant when he noted on the subject of clothes: 'It is curious how today people want to abolish uniforms as though they are something to be ashamed of, or are emblematic of servility. But we are all servants, whether we are generals, bishops, cooks or Etonians.'[18]

If you fail to squash somebody on the grounds of their inappropriate dress, then the next best thing is to comment on their deplorable eating habits. Quentin Crewe, in his memoirs, recalls: 'An aunt coming for dinner said, by way of encouragement to Angie, who had made an egg mousse: "How amusing to have a luncheon dish at dinner." It was on a par with Randolph Churchill's observation that "only jumped-up people have soup for lunch".'[19]

Gardening too offers expressions of class allegiance. In his book *Yew and Non-Yew*, James Bartholomew declares, 'The garden has become one of the last bright sparks among the dying embers of British class,' and devotes the rest of his book to proving it. Apparently small green flowers, herb gardens, teak benches and York stone are all favoured by Yew gardeners, whereas petunias and pampas grass, dwarf conifers, white plastic garden furniture and concrete paving betray Non-Yew taste.

One of the legions of well-connected young men who used to work for Sotheby's shed light on some class-related habits of the workplace. 'Smart businesses start the working day late. Publishers never surface till ten, it would seem. Sotheby's starts at nine (it used to be nine-thirty), whereas Phillips' started at eight-thirty. Moreover the staff at Sotheby's are all on first-name terms, whereas there is a more hierarchical structure at Phillips'. The Sotheby's assumption is, in effect, that, however lowly your position on the ladder, you are still an officer in the same mess as the generals.'

Wine offers rich pickings for social one-upmanship. Some friends of mine were invited to dinner by the novelist V. S. Naipaul and dutifully stopped at the off-licence before arriving at his home. They handed over the bottle. The great man peered at the label, and looked up in astonishment: 'You're most kind,' he responded, 'but I'm afraid we can't possibly drink this.'

There is still a strange assumption that the working classes are incapable of enjoying wine and should stick to wholesome beer. The working classes no longer behave as they are supposed to, in this and other respects, but they are being kept in line by the guardians of social correctness. During the discussion about the class status of John Prescott MP, the *Evening Standard* doctored a photograph of Prescott and his wife, substituting a champagne bottle for a beer bottle on the table before them. Clearly the newspaper was trying to insinuate that it was inappropriate for a railwayman's son to drink champagne; it was trying to convict Mr Prescott of having ideas above his station, and thus revealed the newspaper's snobbery, not his.

When *The Times* reported that a Wine & Spirit Education Trust scholarship had been awarded to a school dinner-lady, it was the supposed inappropriateness of her profession that took pride of place in the article. She also, it was noted later in the article, worked part-time for Victoria Wine, so perhaps it wasn't entirely surprising that she had developed some knowledge about the subject. But the implication was clear: working-class folk aren't supposed to be able to tell their Sauvignon from their Viognier.

An employee of one of the stuffier wine merchants was astonished by the snobbery of its directors: 'There is a huge barrier in the company between directors and the rest – the shippers, the people who do the paperwork. We once had a few people, merchants and press, in to lunch, and there was a last-minute cancellation. I suggested to the chairman that we fill the gap by inviting the staff person who had organized the lunch and obtained the wines. He was aghast.

'The directors are very keen on their dress codes and were appalled when a wine writer came to lunch in a sweater rather than jacket and tie. They think this kind of thing is important and talk about it among themselves with grave disapproval. They tend not to have much in the way of brains, so they fall back on their common background: the public schools, the Army, their social traditions. It's a typical second-son profession, socially acceptable, I suppose, because of the nature of the product. They cling to their values, and even though most of them are by no means rich, they'd rather skip a few meals, I imagine, than turn down an invitation to go shooting.

'It's true that the clientèle has changed, and that they are dealing with entrepreneurial types with whom they have nothing in common socially. They deal with them of course, but that doesn't mean they have to like them.'

Snobbery is evident in many areas of British life, where tiny distinctions assume enormous importance for individuals. Where you live can easily give the game away. Many will recall the despair that filled the hearts of suburban Londoners banished to the 081 telephone zone when codes were changed in the 1980s. A redoubtable lady I met at a drinks party informed me, during chitchat, that 'We live in Redington Road,' and then hastily added, 'the *right* end of Redington Road.' This kind of thing is, of course, not an especially British trait. Americans are very keen to claim status by association, if only because the more meritocratic nature of American society leaves few other means of doing so. Thus any tacky housing estate on the remoter outskirts of Houston or Cincinnati is likely to be named Versailles Gardens or Ritz Lanes.

Class association certainly permeates sport. Polo and rowing are pukka, boxing and soccer are not. The expense of certain sports has the side effect of excluding people. To play tennis you need access to courts, to play golf you need access to a golf club, and some of those are notoriously choosy, even discriminatory. Cricket is ambivalent, its strong regional basis being more important than its middle-class image. Hunters insist their favourite pursuit is open to all classes, but everyone knows that the toffs ride ahead.

Names are class indicators too. Emma and Charles have very different resonances from Liam and Tracy. Social climbers know well that the names you give your children are banners fluttering with class association. The peculiar British custom of pronouncing smart names in ways unrelated to how they are spelled is a minefield not only for foreigners but to those not *au fait* with such matters. I still can't remember how to pronounce 'Dalziel' and it was years before I was put right about Cholmondeley and Beauchamp. I still don't know why Menzies is pronounced 'Mingis'. Running into a poet called Frederick Grubb at a youth hostel in the Dordogne, I was puzzled for some time when he asked me whether I cared to join him on a walk to 'Byoolee', his doggedly English pronunciation of the French town of Beaulieu.

Those who dwell too closely on these nuances are in danger of displaying the very snobbery they seek to expose. Paul Fussell, a shrewd literary critic and social historian, can't avoid a knowing and fastidious air when he writes:

> Worried a lot about their own taste and about whether it's working for or against them, members of the middle class try to arrest their natural tendency to sink downward by associating themselves, if ever so tenuously, with the imagined possessors of money, power, and taste. 'Correctness' and doing the right thing became obsessions . . . The desire to belong, and to belong by some mechanical act like purchasing something, is another sign of the middle class.[20]

Maybe, but the desire to belong is just as keen among the upper classes.

Jilly Cooper's *Class* is a wickedly sharp catalogue of class indicators, but sentences such as 'Mrs Definitely Disgusting . . . gets her children's names from the *TV Times*' leave a nasty taste in the mouth. Paul Fussell does exactly the same in his curiously obsessive journalistic study of American social mobility. Their gleeful, malicious catalogues, poking fun at the upper classes but pouring venomous scorn on everyone else, don't miss a trick when it comes to sorting out the nuances of clothing, housing, decor, cars and weddings, but the intensity of the preoccupation is clearly driven by snobbery.

Fussell can be acute, if condescending, on class and clothing. He is writing about the United States, but his observations are as true of Britain:

> When proles assemble to enjoy leisure, they seldom appear in clothing without words on it. As you move up the classes and the understatement principle begins to operate, the words gradually disappear, to be replaced, in the middle and upper-middle classes, by

mere emblems, like the Lacoste alligator. Once, ascending further, you've left all such trademarks behind, you may correctly infer that you are entering the purlieus of the upper class itself . . . By wearing a garment reading SPORTS ILLUSTRATED or GATORADE or LESTER LANIN, the prole associates himself with an enterprise the world judges successful, and thus, for the moment, he achieves some importance.[21]

It's no different from John Betjeman's famous little poem called 'How to Get On in Society', beginning 'Phone for the fish-knives, Norman'. It rattles through the ghastly middle-class euphemisms and coinages, a miniature compendium of non-U usage: 'serviettes' and 'toilet', 'comfy' and 'couch'. Here too are the circumlocutions: 'Is trifle sufficient for sweet?' and 'the girl has replenished the cruets'. It's all very deft and amusing, but it's also a parade of snobbery, allowing the reader to bask in superiority as the eyes glide past 'switched on the logs in the grate' and 'Are the requisites all in the toilet?'

The most powerful of all class indicators, and one easily deployed in the service of snobbery, is accent. Accent cuts its swathe in two ways: through zones of regionalism, and zones of class. You can't mistake Somerset or Birmingham; nor can you mistake working-class London or upper-class anywhere. Accent is often acquired just like any other aptitude. As a teenager on a skiing holiday in Switzerland, I met a couple of girls from Glasgow. I remarked how their speech seemed free of one of Britain's most distinctive accents. Of course, they said, one of the reasons they had been sent to a Swiss finishing school was to obliterate their Glaswegian accent once and for all.

It is widely believed that the Queen's English (also known, depending on the status symbol of your choice, as Oxford English or BBC English) was the nineteenth-century creation of the public-school system, that in earlier times the gentry had revelled in regional accents, that Squire Westons were the norm in rural England. However, in the sixteenth century Sir Thomas Elyot, who wrote *The Book Named the Governor* in 1531, recommended the pronunciation of every letter by the sons of the nobility (clearly implying that dropped vowels or consonants were the norm in popular speech), and in 1622 Henry Peacham in *The Compleat Gentleman* was urging his readers to acquire a 'gracefull' pronunciation as part of the accomplishments of a gentleman. This 'gracefull' accent may well have originated at Court and spread through the country via the universities and visits to aristocrats' country seats.[22]

Still, it is hard to know whether this graceful pronunciation was little more than an affectation promulgated by fashionable courtiers or whether it was widely adopted. It was not until the eighteenth century that grammar was formally codified and notions of correct and incorrect speech became current. Such codifications usually proscribe more than they recommend, and it was lower-class usage that was to be avoided at all costs. For John Walker, author of *A Critical Pronouncing Dictionary* in 1791, Cockney speech was a major offender, all the more because its practitioners were close, then as now, to centres of power and culture such as the Court and Parliament.

According to Dick Leith, the imposition of a standardized accent by public schools confirmed a trend already well established. By the early nineteenth century,

> correct pronunciation was an issue of class. And the identification of the 'best' pronunciation with a particular social class is given institutional expression by the development of the fee-paying public school system. In these schools, a pronunciation that may be described as codified grew up, or was cultivated and taught . . . In no other country in the world are pronunciation and social class so closely and clearly linked.[23]

There was universal agreement that urban proletariat accents, such as Cockney, were to be shunned, but a slight rural burr was acceptable among the squirearchy. But it was not only the sound of your speech that became a source of social anxiety: correct usage was considered extremely important. Victorian handbooks such as *Society Small Talk* and *The Vulgarities of Speech Corrected* (1826) cited the rules. However, the very grand and socially secure could always get away with infractions. Lady Grove, in *The Social Fetich* of 1907, loftily declares 'that rules of etiquette are made to be broken by those with sufficient position and personality'.[24] Indeed, the historian Harold Perkin asserts that received pronunciation (RP) was not the speech of the aristocracy, but 'the speech of a new, aspiring middle class who believed themselves to belong to a nationwide elite . . . It was not, as many believed, hallowed by tradition – few Victorians spoke like that – but a new invention, created in the reformed public schools and the southern grammar schools and now imposed on the new middle class by the BBC.'[25] Acquiring an accentless accent was little more than a smart career move for the upwardly mobile middle classes.

The effect of fashioning a form of speech free from regional accent and grammatical error was to insinuate the rather strange idea that 'pure English' or received pronunciation was somehow accentless; 'accents' were all forms of speech that did not conform to RP. 'Accent' tarnished parts of England far from London; mastery of RP put the speaker on the same level as those who wielded power and prestige. Yet speech was never as featureless as the warriors against accent would have liked; vowels were clipped to a greater or lesser degree, and there were considerable variations in speech forms and accent, even among the upper classes. Even today supposedly upper-class pronunciations such as 'orf' for 'off' and 'otel' for 'hotel' are heard from only a few lips. Those who sought to impose the iron hand of RP were never able to staunch the flow and stretch of a living language. Correct *usage*, however, was a less pliable class indicator, since it had to be codified and then drummed in. I recall the look of amused dismay on the face of a West Country friend, very keen on correct usage and RP, when her small daughter would return from school each day not only with a broad local accent but saying 'I be' instead of 'I am'. Accent and 'incorrect' usage are often the possession of the majority in regional England, not of a semi-literate minority. The little girl was acquiring the speech of her peers by day, and having it drummed out of her every evening.

Today RP and 'the Queen's English' are surely in retreat. Very few of the public-school-educated boys I encounter sport cut-glass vowels any longer. Evelyn Waugh's statement of 1955 – 'An upper class voice is always unmistakable though it may have every deviation of accent and vocabulary'[26] – is no longer true. Younger members of the royal family speak a casual middle-class style of English that is remote from the glassy precision of the Queen herself. Anyone under fifty referring to 'young gels' would receive some very odd looks. Prime ministers, from Edward Heath onwards, have struggled to impose some kind of RP over their regional tones. As recently as 1971 Nancy Mitford moaned in a letter to Raymond Mortimer: 'The B.B.C. rang up & asked what I think of Mr Heath's French accent? I longed to say it's his *English* accent which is so fearful but thought I'd be in trouble again so pleaded illness & cried off.'[27]

Few would share the stuffy regrets expressed by those chief mourners for the aristocratic way of life, Mark Bence-Jones and Hugh Montgomery-Massingberd:

> Whereas the public schoolmasters of old took pains to improve the speech of the humbler boys in their care, believing this to be part of the education they were providing . . . now masters not only do nothing about the accents of their more plebeian charges but some of them are positively gratified when boys of aristocratic background begin to talk likewise.[28]

Popular culture is rapidly transmitted by television, radio and video. New expressions, argot and coinages slide in and out of current use. The enemy, if there is one, is not, as Bence-Jones and Montgomery-Massingberd believe, regional accents but rather the argot of rap singer and Hollywood starlet, of corporate obfuscation and adspeak. Regional accents are even fashionable or desirable in some quarters, though you have to choose carefully. In 1996 certain companies offering financial services over the telephone were recruiting Scottish receptionists because their accents were thought to suggest probity and reliability. It is now perfectly acceptable for a newsreader, once the iconic standard-bearer of RP, to speak with a light West Indian lilt. Some regional accents have become almost fashionable. No one need blush when speaking with an Edinburgh or Yorkshire accent, though anyone from Birmingham is still considered to be in need of elocution lessons.

A friend of mine with a decidedly plummy accent ended up teaching in fairly tough secondary schools in the East End of London. I watched him teaching *Hamlet* to his sixth-form class and was astonished that, despite the enormous gulf in accents between teacher and charges, there appeared to be complete acceptance of his unreconstructed ruling-class speech. When I asked him about this, he explained: 'When I started teaching this class, I invited the boys to make fun of the way I spoke simply as a way of neutralizing the issue. I don't think they're too bothered by my accent because, being solidly working-class, they associate it with authority figures.'

Although it is undoubtedly true that accent and usage are far less important than they used to be, many people remain acutely self-conscious about it. I was astonished to hear the 1996 Reith Lecturer, June Aitchison, an Oxford professor of language and communication, confess in a radio interview that she employed different tones and sentence structures when buying tomatoes at a market from those she would use in the classroom or in the privacy of her home. She seemed to think this was entirely appropriate as she didn't want to appear a 'toff' when dealing with a market vendor – though she seems quite content to risk being thought patronizing and a dissembler. I hear this kind of thing around me all the time: men possessed of perfectly grammatical RP English saying, 'Cheers, mate' when buying something from the lower orders, terms they would never employ when buying a shirt in Jermyn Street.

Accent can be a weapon in the class war, but is no longer intrinsic to it. Neither social nor political nor business success is dependent any longer on how you speak. Whereas forty years ago it was considered good sport to mock regional accents, now the pukka accents sported by the likes of journalist Brian Sewell are regarded with awe and amazement as museum pieces; Mr Sewell is required to parade his accent from time to time so that audiences can be astounded by its freakishness. He even sustained a radio slot over many months based on the premise that his fastidious clenched-jaw accent and the rougher vowels and looser consonants of Robert Elms were so remote from each other, socially as well as audibly, that their conjunction would provide innocent amusement for millions. It is, perhaps, one of the few signs that a class-based society is crumbling that accent matters so much less than it once did. As a weapon of snobbery, it is just about defunct.

TWENTY

Class Dismissed

'The New York Rowdy Journal, sir,' resumed the colonel, 'is, as I expect you know, the organ of our aristocracy in this city.'
'Oh! there *is* an aristocracy here, then?' said Martin. 'Of what is it composed?'
'Of intelligence, sir,' replied the colonel; 'of intelligence and virtue. And of their necessary consequence in this republic. Dollars, sir.'
Charles Dickens, Martin Chuzzlewit, 1844

Class as social stratification will always be with us. Few, if any, societies or nations have evolved without it. As has often been pointed out, the now defunct Communist regimes, supposedly egalitarian, were thick with privilege, and a baroque system of rewards, perks and disincentives flourished in order to retain Party loyalty. It may not have been a class system as such, but it created a distinct social and economic hierarchy.

What makes Britain different from other societies is that class is institutionalized. The monarchy, the House of Lords, the aristocracy, an Established Church, a large private sector in education and an anachronistic honours system all ensure that class remains a vital component in our social consciousness. Growing economic inequality has made the gap between the highest and lowest strata greater than for many decades.

Class is of course far more fluid than it used to be. Indeed, the pace of change is remarkable. Witness the rapid evolution of the Labour Party from a class-based organization to a centrist social democratic party. Although there may still be pockets of rural England and, especially, Scotland where feudal relations between proprietors and tenants persist, we no longer expect deference from the lower orders. Accent is still a powerful class indicator, but it can no longer be assumed that the possessor of a so-called Estuary accent is a bloke from Essex. Social mobility has increased, and it is possible for British people to turn to that peculiarly American technique of reinventing oneself in class terms. Class matters, but it can be circumvented much more easily than, say, twenty years ago. Britain is evolving into a society in which status will soon count for more than class.

This is already the case in the United States. The upper class is so tiny that it is of no significance. The handful of families, mostly on the East Coast, who can trace their pedigree back to colonial times or even to Mayflower immigrants can claim, I suppose, to be a kind of aristocracy, but the whole notion goes against the American grain. Living in Boston, Massachusetts, in the 1970s, I was very much aware of the working-class Boston Irish, with their flat accents, and the upper-crust Boston Brahmins, with accents so discreet they could almost pass for English. But Boston was an extreme case. In most other cities there would be endless distinctions based on status and wealth, but class as an inherited characteristic is just about non-existent.

The American critic Wendy Lesser recognizes major differences between the concepts of class in Britain and the United States. 'In the States you don't become conscious of class the moment you open your mouth, which is the case in Britain. Accent, dress, mannerisms all convey class in a series of codes that is difficult for us to read. And there are differences that strike me as odd. In America a high-street bank manager is invariably upper-middle-class, but in Britain he's usually considered lower-middle-class.

'The word "class" in the United States is a metaphor too. We talk of people having "no class", meaning that they are tacky in some way. And we talk of a "class act". But as a metaphor, the word has to do with honour and dignity and how you treat others rather than social status.

'Coming to England frequently, I can't help noticing that deference is much more evident here than in the States. One of the invigorating things about New York is that no one feels inferior to anyone else. A cab driver or fast-food cook simply won't accept that there are social differences between you.'

Curiously, the more egalitarian nature of American society does not seem to have had any striking effect on social mobility when compared to more traditional, class-bound European societies. The so-called FJH hypothesis, first proposed in the 1970s, argued that, however an industrial society was organized, social opportunities were not significantly greater in any one of them. A Europe-wide research team in the 1980s looked at generational changes in social status, and found that even in east European countries social mobility was much the same. The children of upper-strata parents such as managers were far more likely to rise to the top than their working-class counterparts. Privileged groups, whether the Great and Good in Britain, captains of industry in America or factory bosses in former Communist countries, all sought to perpetuate themselves generationally and usually succeeded.[1]

If this is the case, then what chance does the 'classless society' have? John Major, in his now celebrated endorsement of the concept in 1990, defined it as a society 'in which people can rise to whatever level that their own abilities and good fortune may take them, from whatever their starting point'. If the FJH hypothesis is correct, John Major was on a hiding to nothing. Whether it is for lack of political will or whether the ambition was impossible to fulfil in the first place, few would dispute that Major made very little headway in achieving a classless society. There was some minor adjustment to the honours system, but his opposition to constitutional reform, notably with respect to the House of Lords, was determined. There may have been some indications of greater classlessness, such as more share ownership, but there was also evidence of widening economic inequality and a clearer division between those who could afford to use private-sector services and those dependent on the increasingly inadequate state sector. The Conservative buzzword 'choice' had little to do with equality of opportunity, since the choices on offer were restricted to those bands of people who could afford to exercise them.

For social commentators and journalists such as Greg Hadfield and Mark Skipworth, class is no longer about social position but has become a Darwinian struggle for status enhancement, which in turn will open up 'choice': 'In the end, class is really about choice. The higher up the social ladder you are, the more choices you can afford and the more you are offered; how you exercise those choices determines how much higher up the social ladder you climb. As the number of options increases, the trick is to know which are the right ones to choose.'[2]

What they have done is to adopt, wholesale, the American model of class, which is almost synonymous with status. Like Paul Fussell, they see 'class' as a game: all you need to do is master the rules. Their technique is to list class indicators – schooling, clothing, housing, cars, newspapers – and advise readers to latch on to the right ones. You can, in short, reinvent yourself socially: 'Class has for too long been regarded as a condition we all suffer from. It is, in fact, a journey that we all travel on; at different times in our lives our position changes, even if our job remains the same. Class is a process that you can participate in; you can, if you wish, transform your position to suit your own ends by changing your lifestyle, tastes and cultural habits.'[3]

I do not believe this is true. Hadfield and Skipworth see 'class' as an individual choice. But by definition that cannot be the case. They write: 'Class is now less a measure of what makes you similar to others in a group; it is a mark of what distinguishes you from other individuals . . . Class creates order out of chaos, and gives meaningful direction to the lives of individuals.'[4] If this is so, then they cannot be talking about class. They may be arguing that class has broken down to such a degree that group values no longer matter; but that is not what they appear to be saying. Instead they are urging readers to join the right group as a means of self-advancement, and showing them how to do so. Indeed, by the end of their book they seem to be welcoming class structures with open arms: 'The shared values and ambitions implied by a commonly accepted class structure provide society with coherence and stability. A "classless society" would be uncivilised anarchy; a society without class would not be a society at all.'[5]

This puts them in league with the reactionaries. Class, declares the historian Andrew Roberts, is 'a liberating and invigorating institution, unleashing positive forces that enrich British society. It is no coincidence that the time of our greatest global power and influence, the late Victorian period, was precisely the point at which the class system reached its apogee.'[6] It is not, I hope, still necessary to labour the point that the Victorian era was not the utopian age that reactionaries like to conjure up. 'The forces of differentiation and plurality', Roberts continues, 'should be encouraged against those of uniformity and drudgery, and a society in which all classes merged into one coagulated, unstructured mass would be an ugly one.'[7] Here, at his peroration, Roberts loses me. Those of us unhappy about the grip of class on Britain argue that class distinction is to be deplored because it militates *against* plurality. 'Differentiation and plurality' suggest an American model, not the British one that Roberts so ardently advocates.

The argument against class is that it stifles mobility and plurality, that it institutionalizes differences based on birth and pedigree. Class is a stranglehold. Class enforces hierarchy and seeks to elevate rank over other indicators of social worth. It erects barriers and nails them firmly into place. It glories in exclusion rather than inclusion.

In Britain class is slowly shuffling towards the exit, and few will weep as it heads out through the door. A farewell to class will, of course, not mean the end of social distinctions and stratification. It seems most likely that it will be replaced by meritocratic models or a system based on wealth and status. Growing inequality and an acceptance of a harsher economic climate that favours individualistic over community-based endeavours, offering great rewards for some and harsh abandonment for the unfortunate, may lead to greater polarization. At such a time I may even find myself sympathetic to the sentimentalists I have repeatedly deplored in this book, and look back to a time when the values and solidarities of British classes, for all their snobberies and foolishness, represented a kinder, more indulgent world. Yet I doubt it. I look forward instead to a classic British compromise, when class will merely be vestigial, defanged, quaint and irrelevant.

NOTES

Introduction

1 Bryan Gould, *Goodbye to All That*, p. 37

Chapter 1: Class, Status and Other Confusions

1 R. H. Tawney, *Equality*, p. 56
2 *Daily Mail*, 18 April 1996
3 Anthony Giddens, 'Elites in the British Class Structure', in Stanworth and Giddens, eds, *Elites and Power in British Society*, p. 14
4 *Independent on Sunday*, 5 January 1997
5 Malcolm Mckay, *The Origins of Hereditary Social Stratification*, pp. 21, 25
6 Georges Duby, *The Three Orders*, p. 1
7 Ibid., p. 104.
8 Quoted in P. N. Furbank, *Unholy Pleasure*, p. 11
9 Robert Roberts, *The Classic Slum*, p. 14
10 Tony Benn, *Against the Tide*, entry for 5 July 1973, pp. 52–3
11 Patrick Joyce, *Visions of the People*, p. 10
12 Ralf Dahrendorf, *Class and Class Conflict in Industrial Society*, pp. 148–9
13 Leonard Reissman, *Class in American Society*, pp. 8–9

14 E. P. Thompson, *The Making of the English Working Class*, pp. 9–10
15 Quoted in Theodore Koditschek, *Class Formation and Urban-Industrial Society*, pp. 6–7
16 P. N. Furbank, op. cit., p. 5
17 Ibid., p. 14
18 William M. Reddy, 'The Concept of Class', in M. L. Bush, op. cit., p. 18
19 Leonard Reissman, op. cit., p. 40
20 Margaret Scotford Archer and Salvador Giner, *Contemporary Europe: Class, Status and Power*, p. 28
21 Quoted in Robert McKenzie and Allan Silver, *Angels in Marble*, p. 26
22 *Political Quarterly*, April–June 1953, p. 139
23 Duff Cooper, *Old Men Forget*, pp. 65–6
24 *Daily Mail*, 18 April 1996
25 Julian Critchley, *Westminster Blues*, pp. 26, 50

Chapter 2: The Aristocratic Ideal

1 J. V. Beckett, *The Aristocracy in England 1660–1914*, p. 26
2 Nora Wydenbruck, *My Two Worlds*, p. 121
3 *Daily Telegraph*, 10 July 1996
4 Ernst Kohn-Bramstedt, *Aristocracy and the Middle Classes in Germany*, p. 154

5   Alexis de Tocqueville, *Journeys to England*, p. 67

6   Andrew Sinclair, *The Last of the Best*, p. 96

7   David Kelly, *The Ruling Few*, pp. 179–80

8   Cecilia Sternberg, *The Journey*, p. 70

9   Hippolyte Taine, *Notes on England*, pp. 144–5

10   Ibid., p. 167

11   Anthony M. Ludovici, *A Defence of Aristocracy*, p. 13

12   Ibid., p. 239

13   Ibid., pp. 295–6

14   Ibid., p. 367

15   Ibid., p. 414

16   Robert Lacey, *Aristocrats*, pp. 21–2

17   Sir Edward Cadogan, *Before the Deluge*, pp. 9–10

18   Paul Fussell, *Caste Marks*, pp. 72–3

19   M. L. Bush, *The European Nobility: Rich Noble, Poor Noble*, pp. 114, 123

20   Luigi Barzini, *From Caesar to the Mafia*, p. 101

21   Ernst Kohn-Bramstedt, *Aristocracy and the Middle Classes in Germany*, pp. 18–19

22   Quoted in Lawrence and Jeanne Stone, *An Open Elite? 1540–1880*, p. 300

23   M. L. Bush, op. cit., pp. 7–11, 14–17, 24

24   Patrick Montague-Smith, 'The Peerage and the Aristocracy', in Richard Buckle, ed., *U and Non-U Revisited*, p. 14

25   Richard Ollard, *An English Education*, p. 137

26   Ibid., p. 139

27   Mark Bence-Jones and Hugh Montgomery-Massingberd, *The British Aristocracy*, p. 181

28   Ibid., p. 183

29   Ibid., p. 183

30   Ibid., p. 201

Chapter 3: From Warlords to Grandees

1   Hugh Montgomery-Massingberd, *Debrett's Great British Families*, pp. 154–6, 160, 162

2   Alexis de Tocqueville, op. cit., p. 135

3   M. L. Bush, *The English Aristocracy*, pp. 17–18, 20–1; J. V. Beckett, op. cit., p. 24

4   G. E. Mingay, *English Landed Society in the Eighteenth Century*, p. 281

5   Seymour Becker, *Nobility and Privilege in Late Imperial Russia*, pp. 18–19

6   Michael De La Noy, *The Honours System*, pp. 32–5

7   Lawrence and Jeanne Stone, *An Open Elite? 1540–1880*, pp. 402–3

8   G. E. Mingay, op. cit., pp. 26–8; Lawrence and Jeanne Stone, op. cit., p. 206

9   Lawrence and Jeanne Stone, op. cit., pp. 239–40

10   M. L. Bush, op. cit., p. 44

11   M. L. Bush, *The European Nobility: Rich Noble, Poor Noble*, pp. 25–6, 85

12   J. V. Beckett, op. cit., p. 208

13   David Cannadine, *Aspects of Aristocracy*, p. 15

14   F. M. L. Thompson, *English Landed Society in the Nineteenth Century*, p. 9

15   William Cobbett, *Rural Rides*, pp. 209–10

16   Alexis de Tocqueville, op. cit., p. 59

17   J. V. Beckett, op. cit., p. 432–3

18   G. D. H. and M. Cole, eds, *The Opinions of William Cobbett*, p. 281

19   Quentin Crewe, *The Frontiers of Privilege*, pp. 20–3

20   Heather A. Clemenson, *English Country Houses and Landed Estates*, p. 21

21   J. V. Beckett, op. cit., p. 45

22 Heather A. Clemenson, op. cit., pp. 19–20
23 Lawrence and Jeanne Stone, op. cit., p. 206
24 F. M. L. Thompson, op. cit., p. 294
25 M. L. Bush, *The English Aristocracy*, pp. 68–9
26 Andrew Sinclair, *The Last of the Best*, p. 22
27 Ruth Brandon, *Dollar Princesses*, pp. 27, 33
28 David Cannadine, *Aspects of Aristocracy*, pp. 11–12

Chapter 4: Gents and Gentry

1 Mark Bence-Jones and Hugh Montgomery-Massingberd, *The British Aristocracy*, pp. 1–2
2 Ibid., p. 12
3 Quoted in Lawrence and Jeanne Stone, op. cit., p. 23
4 P. N. Furbank, op. cit., p. 97
5 K. C. Phillips, *Language and Class in Victorian England*, p. 7
6 M. L. Bush, op. cit., p. 111
7 G. E. Mingay, *English Landed Society in the Eighteenth Century*, pp. 21–2
8 William Cobbett, *Rural Rides*, entry for 21 November 1821, p. 34
9 F. M. L. Thompson, op. cit., pp. 124–5, 127
10 Quoted in F. M. L. Thompson, op. cit., pp. 187–8
11 M. L. Bush, op. cit., p. 150
12 Jessica Mitford, *Hons and Rebels*, pp. 27–8
13 Nancy Mitford, *The Letters of Nancy Mitford*, letter to Jessica Mitford, 30 March 1960, p. 381
14 Michael De La Noy, *The Honours System*, pp. 54–6
15 Lawrence and Jeanne Stone, op. cit., p. 242
16 Michael De La Noy, op. cit., p. 102

Chapter 5: The Survival of the Upper Classes

1 Harold Perkin, *The Rise of Professional Society*, pp. 71, 154
2 Harold Perkin, op. cit., p. 63
3 Lord Grantley, *Silver Spoon*, pp. 60–1
4 Ibid., p. 97
5 F. M. L. Thompson, op. cit., p. 51
6 Quentin Crewe, op. cit., p. 68
7 Heather A. Clemenson, op. cit., pp. 110–11; F. M. L. Thompson, op. cit., pp. 322–33
8 J. V. Beckett, op. cit., p. 478
9 M. L. Bush, op. cit., p. 152
10 Sean Hignett, *Brett, passim*
11 Duke of Manchester, *My Candid Recollections*, pp. 256–8
12 Duke of Bedford, *A Silver-Plated Spoon*, p. 8
13 Ibid., p. 9
14 Ibid., pp. 10–11
15 Quoted in Diana Cooper, *The Light of Common Day*, pp. 140–2
16 Harold Acton, *Memoirs of an Aesthete*, p. 54
17 Michel and Monique Pincon, *Grandes Fortunes.*
18 *Le Figaro*, 10 July 1996
19 Heather A. Clemenson, op. cit., p. 113
20 Harold Nicolson, *Diaries and Letters 1930–1939*, entry for 1 September 1939, p. 418
21 Hugh Montgomery-Massingberd, *Debrett's Great British Families*, p. 12
22 *Sunday Times*, November 1995
23 Jeremy Paxman, *Friends in High Places*, p. 45

24 Roy Perrott, *The Aristocrats*, p. 9
25 Quoted in Roy Perrott, op. cit., pp. 35, 37

28 Heather A. Clemenson, op. cit., p. 151
29 Roy Strong *et al.*, *The Destruction of the Country House*, p. 14
30 David Cannadine, op. cit., p. 243

Chapter 6: A Life in the Country

1 Lord Grantley, *Silver Spoon*, p. 17
2 Consuelo Vanderbilt Balsan, *The Glitter and the Gold*, p. 60
3 Kenneth Rose, *Superior Person*, p. 111
4 Consuelo Vanderbilt Balsan, op. cit., pp. 119–20
5 J. G. Ruffer, *The Big Shots: Edwardian Shooting Parties*, pp. 97–8
6 Earl of Carnarvon, *No Regrets*, p. 15
7 Lord Grantley, op. cit., pp. 22–3
8 Ibid., p. 144
9 Earl of Carnarvon, *Ermine Tales*, pp. 71–2
10 Quentin Crewe, *The Frontiers of Privilege*, p. 19
11 Earl of Carnarvon, op. cit., p. 135
12 Consuelo Vanderbilt Balsan, op. cit., p. 63
13 Earl of Carnarvon, op. cit., p. 140
14 James Lees-Milne, *Ancestral Voices*, p. 188
15 Ibid., p. 232
16 Diana Cooper, *The Rainbow Comes and Goes*, pp. 34–7
17 Ronald Blythe, *Akenfield*, pp. 112–4
18 Ibid., p. 229
19 Consuelo Vanderbilt Balsan, op. cit., p. 68
20 Duke of Manchester, op. cit., p. 83
21 J. V. Beckett, op. cit., p. 348
22 J. G. Ruffer, op. cit., p. 11
23 Kenneth Rose, op. cit., p. 66
24 Lord Home, *Border Reflections*, p. 24
25 J. V. Beckett, op. cit., pp. 346–7
26 Robert Lacey, op. cit., p. 17
27 Duke of Bedford, op. cit., p. 226

Chapter 7: The Middling People

1 John Seed, 'From "Middling Sort" to Middle Class in Late Eighteenth- and Early Nineteenth-century England', in M. L. Bush, ed., *Social Orders and Social Classes*, pp. 114, 115
2 Greg Hadfield and Mark Skipworth, *Class: Where Do You Stand?*, pp. 155, 164–6
3 Lawrence and Jeanne Stone, op. cit., p. 424
4 Paul Fussell, op. cit., p. 39
5 Quoted in Lawrence and Jeanne Stone, op. cit., pp. 408–9
6 Alexis de Tocqueville, op. cit., pp. 70–2
7 G. E. Mingay, op. cit., p. 265
8 R. H. Tawney, op. cit., pp. 101–2, 107–8
9 Harold Perkin, op. cit., pp. 81–2
10 Greg Hadfield and Mark Skipworth, op. cit., pp. 59–60
11 Mark Bence-Jones and Hugh Montgomery-Massingberd, *The British Aristocracy*, pp. 4–5

Chapter 8: The Great and the Good

1 *Spectator*, 23 September 1955
2 *New Statesman*, 8 August 1953
3 Jeremy Paxman, op. cit., pp. 12–13
4 Hippolyte Taine, op. cit., p. 179
5 Quoted in Jeremy Paxman, op. cit., p. 6

6 Kingsley Martin, *The Crown and the Establishment*, pp. 84–5
7 Brian Sedgmore, *The Secret Constitution*, pp. 11–12
8 *Sunday Times*, 17 September 1995
9 Tony Benn, *Conflicts of Interest*, entry for 3 May 1978, pp. 297–8
10 Rupert Wilkinson, *The Prefects*, p. 23
11 Stephen Fay, *Portrait of an Old Lady*, pp. 21, 52
12 Victor Sandelson, 'The Confidence Trick', in Hugh Thomas, ed., *The Establishment*, p. 139
13 Philip Stanworth and Anthony Giddens, 'An Economic Elite: Company Chairman', in Stanworth and Giddens, op. cit., pp. 82–3
14 Greg Hadfield and Mark Skipworth, op. cit., p. 79
15 Julian Paget, op. cit., pp. 191–3
16 Quoted in David Pannick, *Judges*, p. 143
17 Alexis de Tocqueville, op. cit., p. 42
18 David Pannick, op. cit., p. 145
19 Simon Lee, *Judging Judges*, pp. 33–4
20 Ibid., p. 33–4
21 *The Times*, 18 May 1996
22 David Cannadine, op. cit., p. 23
23 Jane Austen, *Mansfield Park*, chapter 11
24 F. M. L. Thompson, op. cit., p. 71
25 Roy Perrott, op. cit., p. 191
26 Quentin Crewe, *Well, I Forget the Rest*, p. 246
27 Jessica Mitford, op. cit., pp. 21–2

Chapter 9: Officers and Gentlemen

1 Corelli Barnett, *Britain and Her Army*, p. 137
2 J. V. Beckett, op. cit., pp. 409–10
3 Corelli Barnett, op. cit., pp. 227–8
4 Quoted in Corelli Barnett, op. cit., pp. 236–7
5 J. V. Beckett, op. cit., p. 409
6 Corelli Barnett, *The Story of Sandhurst*, p. 309
7 Seymour Becker, *Nobility and Privilege in Late Imperial Russia*, p. 111
8 Quoted in Corelli Barnett, *Britain and Her Army*, p. 346
9 J. V. Beckett, op. cit., p. 409
10 Lord Carnarvon, op. cit., pp. 34–5
11 John Masters, *Bugles and a Tiger*, pp. 49–50
12 Andrew Sinclair, op. cit., p. 69
13 Evelyn Waugh, *Letters*, letter to Laura Waugh, 10 December 1939, p. 129
14 *The Times*, 23 January 1997
15 Ibid.
16 Corelli Barnett, op. cit., p. 488
17 Antony Beevor, *Inside the British Army*, pp. 68–70

Chapter 10: The Identity Crisis of the Working Class

1 *The Times*, 13 April 1996
2 *Independent*, 14 April 1996
3 F. M. Martin, 'Some Subjective Aspects of Social Stratification', in D. V. Glass, ed., *Social Mobility in Britain*, pp. 59–61
4 Richard Hoggart, *The Uses of Literacy*, p. 21
5 Robert Roberts, *The Classic Slum*, p. 6
6 Ibid., pp. 9, 11, 16
7 Harold Perkin, op. cit., p. 107
8 *Independent on Sunday*, 18 August 1996
9 Tony Benn, *The End of an Era*, entry for 4 May 1988, p. 542

10 William Cobbett, *Rural Rides*, p. 379
11 G. Stedman Jones, *The Languages of Class*, p. 237
12 Ross McKibbin, *Ideologies of Class*, p. 4
13 Ibid., p. 11
14 Robert Roberts, op. cit., pp. 67–8
15 Ibid., pp. 178–9, 185
16 Richard Hoggart, op. cit., pp. 62–3
17 Stephen Reynolds and Bob and Tom Woolley, *Seems So!: A Working-Class View of Politics*, pp. 85–6
18 David Martin and Colin Crouch, 'England', in Margaret Scotford Archer and Salvador Giner, op. cit., pp. 271–2
19 Anthony Crosland, *The Future of Socialism*, p. 66
20 Quoted in Tony Benn, op. cit., entry for 28 October 1980, p. 42
21 Richard Crossman, *The Backbench Diaries*, entry for 21 October 1959, p. 794
22 Richard Crossman, *The Diaries of a Cabinet Minister*, Vol. 1, entry for 3 April 1966, p. 493
23 R. H. Tawney, op. cit., p. 28
24 R. H. Tawney, *Commonplace Book*, entry for 1914, p. 80
25 Anthony Crosland, *The Conservative Enemy*, pp. 119–20
26 Tony Benn, op. cit., entry for 12 December 1980, p. 59

Chapter 11: Broken Biscuits Sold Here

1 Patrick Joyce, op. cit., p. 8
2 G. Stedman Jones, op. cit., p. 184
3 Ibid., pp. 225, 230
4 *Independent on Sunday*, 5 May 1996
5 John and Elizabeth Newson, *Infant Care in an Urban Community*, pp. 165–7

6 Jilly Cooper, *Class*, pp. 36–7
7 Robert Roberts, op. cit., p. 66
8 Harold Perkin, op. cit., pp. 425–6
9 Eric A. Nordlinger, *Working Class Tories*, p. 180
10 Robert McKenzie and Allan Silver, op. cit., p. 157
11 Ibid., pp. 197–8
12 Interview with the author
13 Eric A. Nordlinger, op. cit., pp. 13, 115, 175, 176
14 Hippolyte Taine, op. cit., p. 232
15 Quentin Crewe, *The Frontiers of Privilege*, p. 73
16 Ibid.
17 R. H. Tawney, op. cit., p. 5
18 Jessica Mitford, op. cit., p. 19
19 Ibid., p. 57
20 Louis Heren, *Alas, Alas for England*, p. 113
21 Freya Stark, *Letters*, Vol. 2, letter to Venetia Buddicom, 23 January 1934, p. 171

Chapter 12: Overclass and Underclass

1 *Sunday Times*, 1994
2 *Sunday Times*, 27 August 1995
3 In Ruth Lister, ed., *Charles Murray and the Underclass*
4 Ibid., p. 82
5 Ibid., p. 37
6 Ibid., p. 115
7 *British Medical Journal*, 20 April 1996
8 *Independent on Sunday*, 30 June 1996
9 G. E. Mingay, op. cit., p. 276

Chapter 13: Majesty

1 Walter Bagehot, *The English Constitution*, 1867
2 Kenneth Rose, op. cit., p. 141

3 Quoted in Richard Crossman, *The Diaries of a Cabinet Minister 1966–1968*, entry for 26 July 1967, p. 442
4 J. V. Beckett, op. cit., p. 473
5 Jeremy Paxman, op. cit., p. 65
6 Richard Crossman, op. cit., entry for 20 September 1966, pp. 43–4
7 Tony Benn, *Office Without Power*, entry for 22 October 1969, pp. 207–8
8 Consuelo Vanderbilt Balsan, op. cit., p. 47
9 James Pope-Hennessy, *Queen Mary*, pp. 404–5
10 David Cannadine, op. cit., pp. 83–90
11 Julian Paget, op. cit., p. 43
12 Ibid., p. 45
13 Sir Edward Cadogan, op. cit., pp. 88–90
14 Richard Crossman, op. cit., entry for 24 October 1967, p. 534
15 Ibid.
16 Diana Cooper, op. cit., pp. 197–8
17 Ibid.
18 Duke of Bedford, op. cit., p. 119
19 James Pope-Hennessy, op. cit., p. 471
20 Kingsley Martin, op. cit., p. 57
21 Barbara Castle, *The Castle Diaries 1964–1970*, entry for 28 November 1967, p. 331.
22 Richard Crossman, *The Diaries of a Cabinet Minister*, Vol. 1, entry for 22 October 1964, p. 29
23 Tony Benn, *Against the Tide*, entry for 3 November 1975, pp. 453–4
24 Quoted in R. K. Massie, Introduction to J. Finestone, *The Last Courts of Europe*, p. 33
25 Quoted in Kingsley Martin, op. cit., p. 27
26 Quoted in Roy Jenkins, *Sir Charles Dilke*, p. 70

27 Caroline Benn, *Keir Hardie*, pp. 123, 170
28 Harold Nicolson, *Diaries and Letters 1930–1939*, entry for 12 May 1936, p. 260
29 Richard Crossman, *The Diaries of a Cabinet Minister 1968–1970*, entry for 11 November 1969, pp. 723–4. However, in a letter to the author, Roy Jenkins points out that Crossman was not accurate and that he is, instead, 'a cool royalist . . . regarding the present arrangements as a more convenient form of providing a head of state than would be the election of a president'.
30 Kenneth Rose, op. cit., pp. 382–3
31 *Sunday Times Magazine*, 21 April 1996
32 Kingsley Martin, op. cit., pp. 137–8
33 Shirley Green, *Who Owns London?*, pp. 9–17
34 R. K. Massie, Introduction to J. Finestone, op. cit., p. 33
35 Ibid.
36 *The Times*, June 1953
37 *The Times*, 12 August 1996
38 *New Statesman*, 23 August 1996

Chapter 14: Laws of Heredity: The House of Lords

1 House of Lords Information Office
2 *The Times*, 22 April 1996
3 Jeremy Paxman, op. cit., p. 92; Donald Shell, *The House of Lords*, p. 39
4 J. V. Beckett, op. cit., p. 470
5 Donald Shell, op. cit., p. 39
6 Ibid.
7 Hugh Montgomery-Massingberd, *Debrett's Great British Families*, p. 117
8 *The Times*, 1 March 1996

9 Kenneth Rose, op. cit., pp. 140–1
10 *Sunday Times*, 15 May 1994
11 House of Lords Accounts Office
12 *The Times*, 11 January 1996
13 Lord Longford, *A History of the House of Lords*, pp. 10–12
14 Donald Shell, op. cit., pp. 203–4
15 M. L. Bush, *The English Aristocracy*, p. 19
16 J. V. Beckett, op. cit., p. 412
17 Quoted in Kenneth Rose, op. cit., p. 141
18 Lord Longford, op. cit., pp. 138–9
19 Quoted in David Cannadine, op. cit., p. 156
20 Duke of Bedford, op. cit., pp. 20–1
21 Lord Longford, op. cit., p. 140
22 Jessica Mitford, op. cit., p. 21
23 M. L. Bush, op. cit., pp. 151–2
24 Donald Shell, op. cit., pp. 10–11
25 Duke of Sutherland, *Looking Back*, pp. 137, 139
26 Michael De La Noy, op. cit., p. 96
27 Kenneth Rose, op. cit., pp. 142, 144
28 Lord Longford, op. cit., p. 170
29 Barbara Castle, op. cit., p. 309
30 Richard Crossman, *The Diaries of a Cabinet Minister 1966–1968*, entry for 15 November 1967, p. 575
31 Donald Shell, op. cit., pp. 18–20
32 Lord Longford, op. cit., pp. 182–3
33 Tony Benn, *Conflicts of Interest*, entry for 2 April 1979, pp. 482–3, 486–7
34 Jeremy Paxman, op. cit., p. 94
35 *Sunday Times*, 8 October 1995
36 *Independent on Sunday*, 20 August 1995
37 *Guardian*, 5 February 1996; *The Times*, 8 February 1996
38 *Sunday Times*, 11 February 1996
39 Ibid.
40 Danny Danziger, *Eton Voices*, p. 285
41 *The Times*, 13 February 1996
42 *The Times*, 5 December 1995
43 *The Times*, 8 February 1996
44 Hugh Montgomery-Massingberd, *Debrett's Great British Families*, p. 22
45 *The Times*, 5 July 1996
46 Alexander Pope, *Essay on Man, III*: lines 203–4
47 *Independent on Sunday*, 20 August 1995
48 *The Times*, 5 July 1996
49 *The Times*, 3 July 1996
50 Richard Crossman, *The Diaries of a Cabinet Minister, Volume 2*, entry for 7 September 1967, p. 468
51 Tony Benn, op. cit., entry for 12 December 1979, pp. 562–3
52 Barbara Castle, op. cit., entry for 26 June 1974, pp. 121–2
53 *The Times*, 8 February 1996
54 Robert Lacey, op. cit., p. 214
55 BBC Radio 4, 3 February 1996

Chapter 15: The Honours Market

1 Kenneth Rose, op. cit., p. 33
2 Quoted in James Margach, *The Abuse of Power*, p. 48
3 Lord Longford, op. cit., p. 167
4 Tony Benn, *The End of an Era*, entry for 27 February 1986, p. 439
5 *The Times*, 13 May 1997
6 *The Times*, 18 November 1995
7 Charles E. Timberlake, 'The Middle Classes in Late Tsarist Russia', in M. L. Bush, ed., *Social Orders and Social Classes in Europe since 1500*, pp. 86–90
8 Hugh Montgomery-Massingberd, *Debrett's Great British Families*, p. 8
9 Julian Paget, *The Pageantry of Britain*, pp. 169–70
10 Roy Perrott, op. cit., p. 81
11 Richard Crossman, *The Diaries of a*

Cabinet Minister, Vol. 2, entry for 22 September 1966, p. 47

12 Barbara Castle, op. cit., entry for 11 May 1967, p. 255

13 Jeremy Paxman, op. cit., pp. 69–70

14 Michael De La Noy, op. cit., pp. 102, 117

15 Ibid., p. 135

16 *The Times*, 14 June 1996

17 *Observer*, 13 April 1997

18 *Sunday Times Magazine*, 21 April 1996

Chapter 16: The Elastic Season

1 Lord Cadogan, op. cit., p. 15

2 Lord Carnarvon, *Ermine Tales*, pp. 34–5

3 Karl Heinz Abshagen, *King, Lords, and Gentlemen*, p. 17

4 Jessica Mitford, op. cit., p. 75

5 Lord Grantley, op. cit., pp. 187–8

6 *Independent*, 18 June 1996

7 *The Times*, 21 May 1884

8 Quoted in Godfrey Smith, *The English Season*, p. 90

9 The Duke of Manchester, op. cit., pp. 75–9

10 Ibid., pp. 75–9

11 Ibid., pp. 75–9

12 *Sunday Times*, 20 October 1996

Chapter 18: Education: Diversity and Inequality

1 Rupert Wilkinson, op. cit., p. 65

2 Lawrence and Jeanne Stone, op. cit., p. 27

3 M. L. Bush, *The English Aristocracy*, p. 162

4 Paul Johnson, 'The Education of an Establishment', in G. M. Fraser, ed., *The World of the Public School*, pp. 21–2

5 Quoted in Bernard Darwin, *The English Public Schools*, p. 21

6 Bernard Darwin, op. cit., pp. 26–7, 67

7 Harold Perkin, op. cit., pp. 367–8

8 Hippolyte Taine, op. cit., p. 110

9 Quentin Crewe, *Well, I Forget the Rest*, p. 29

10 Rupert Wilkinson, op. cit., pp. 38–9

11 Quentin Crewe, op. cit., pp. 29–30

12 M. L. Bush, op. cit., pp. 158–9

13 C. A. R. Crosland, op. cit., p. 174

14 A. H. Halsey, A. F. Heath and J. M. Ridge, *Origins and Destinations: Family, Class and Education in Modern Britain*, pp. 206–7

15 Jeremy Paxman, op. cit., p. 156

16 Richard Ollard, op. cit., p. 182

17 Jeremy Paxman, op. cit., pp. 78, 167

18 Anthony Sampson, *The Changing Anatomy of Britain*, p. 127

19 Richard Ollard, op. cit., p. 183

20 Mark Bence-Jones and Hugh Montgomery-Massingberd, op. cit., p. 42

21 Quoted in Danny Danziger, op. cit., p. 165

22 G. M. Fraser, ed., op. cit., pp. 1–2

23 Quoted in Danny Danziger, op. cit., p. 45

24 David Martin and Colin Crouch, 'England', in Margaret Scotford Archer and Salvador Giner, op. cit., p. 256

25 Quoted in Anthony Sampson, op. cit., p. 124

26 R. H. Tawney, op. cit., pp. 157–8

27 Giles and Esmond Romilly, *Out of Bounds*, pp. 96–7, 107

28 Hugh Thomas, 'The Establishment

and Society', in Hugh Thomas, ed., *The Establishment*, p. 20

29 *Prospect*, October 1996, pp. 36–7
30 Ibid.
31 Ibid.
32 John Rae, *The Public School Revolution*, pp. 54–5
33 *Sunday Times*, 28 January 1996
34 *Sunday Times*, 8 October 1995
35 Harold Perkin, op. cit., p. 370
36 *The Times*, 3 January 1997
37 Ibid.

Chapter 19: Snobbery: Lackeys and Parasites

1 Jessica Mitford, op. cit., pp. 53–4
2 Peregrine Worsthorne, 'Boy Made Man', in G. M. Fraser, op. cit., p. 92
3 Ibid., p. 92
4 Harold Nicolson, *Diaries and Letters 1939–1945*, entry for 13 January 1940, p. 57
5 James Lees-Milne, op. cit., pp. 186–7
6 James Lees-Milne, *Another Self*, pp. 77–8
7 Duchess of Sermoneta, *Sparkle Distant Worlds*, p. 37
8 *Times Magazine*, 16 September 1995
9 *Evening Standard*, 2 June 1994
10 *Independent*, 25 June 1994
11 *Sunday Times*, 21 April 1996
12 Anthony Powell, *Infants of the Spring*, p. 181
13 Cynthia Asquith, *Diaries*, entry for 21 July 1916, p. 194
14 Andrew Sinclair, op. cit., pp. 233–4

15 Quoted in Kenneth Rose, op. cit., p. 48
16 Michael De La Noy, op. cit., pp. 28–9
17 James Lees-Milne, *Ancestral Voices*, entry for 2 March 1943, p. 163
18 Ibid., entry for 11 September 1942, p. 100
19 Quentin Crewe, *Well, I Forget the Rest*, p. 167
20 Paul Fussell, op. cit., p. 41
21 Ibid., pp. 56–7
22 Mark Bence-Jones and Hugh Montgomery-Massingberd, op. cit., pp. 14–15
23 Dick Leith, *A Social History of English*, p. 55
24 Quoted in K. C. Phillips, op. cit., p. 50
25 Harold Perkin, op. cit., pp. 267–8
26 Evelyn Waugh, *Letters*, letter to Nancy Mitford, 1 September 1955, p. 452
27 Nancy Mitford, *Letters*, 24 May 1971, p. 505
28 Mark Bence-Jones and Hugh Montgomery-Massingberd, op. cit., p. 234

Chapter 20: Class Dismissed

1 *Sunday Times*, 22 October 1995
2 Greg Hadfield and Mark Skipworth, op. cit., p. 2
3 Ibid., pp. 21–2
4 Ibid., p. 172
5 Ibid., p. 175
6 *Sunday Times*, 21 April 1996
7 Ibid.

BIBLIOGRAPHY

Abshagen, Karl Heinz, *King, Lords and Gentlemen*, trans. E. W. Dickes, London: William Heinemann, 1939

Acton, Harold, *More Memoirs of an Aesthete*, London: Methuen, 1970

Archer, Margaret Scotford and Giner, Salvador, eds, *Contemporary Europe: Class, Status and Power*, London: Weidenfeld & Nicolson, 1971

Asquith, Lady Cynthia, *Diaries 1915–1918*, ed. E. M. Horsley, New York: Knopf, 1969

Balsan, Consuelo Vanderbilt, *The Glitter and the Gold*, London: Heinemann, 1953

Barnett, Correlli, *Britain and her Army 1509–1970*, London: Allen Lane, 1970

Barzini, Luigi, *From Caesar to the Mafia*, London: Hamish Hamilton, 1971

Baynes, J. C. M., *The Soldier in Modern Society*, London: Eyre Methuen, 1972

Beaton, Cecil, *The Parting Years: Diaries 1963–74*, London: Weidenfeld & Nicolson, 1978

Becker, Seymour, *Nobility and Privilege in Late Imperial Russia*, Dekalb, Ill.: Northern Illinois University Press, 1985

Beckett, J. V., *The Aristocracy in England 1660–1914*, Oxford: Blackwell, 1986

Bedford, John, Duke of, *A Silver-Plated Spoon*, London: Cassell, 1959

Beevor, Antony, *Inside the British Army*, London: Chatto & Windus, 1990

Bell, Florence, Lady, *At the Works*, London, 1911

Bence-Jones, Mark and Montgomery-Massingberd, Hugh, *The British Aristocracy*, London: Constable 1979

Benn, Caroline, *Keir Hardie*, London: Hutchinson, 1992

Benn, Tony, *Years of Hope: Diaries, Letters and Papers 1940–1962*, London: Hutchinson, 1994

    Office Without Power: Diaries 1968–72, London: Hutchinson, 1988

    Against the Tide: Diaries 1973–76, London: Hutchinson, 1989

    Conflicts of Interest: Diaries 1977–80, London: Hutchinson, 1990

    The End of an Era: Diaries 1980–90, London: Hutchinson, 1992

Blythe, Ronald, *Akenfield: Portrait of an English Village*, New York: Delta, 1969

Brandon, Ruth, *The Dollar Princesses*, London: Weidenfeld & Nicolson, 1980

Buckle, Richard, ed., *U and Non-U Revisited*, London: Debrett's, 1978

Bush, M. L., *The English Aristocracy*, Manchester: Manchester University Press, 1984

    The European Nobility: Rich Noble, Poor Noble, Manchester: Manchester University Press, 1988

Bush, M. L. ed., *Social Orders and Social Classes in Europe Since 1500*, London and New York: Longman, 1992

Cadogan, Sir Edward, *Before the Deluge*, London: John Murray, 1961

Cannadine, David, *Aspects of Aristocracy*, New Haven and London: Yale University Press, 1994

Carnarvon, [6th] Earl of, *No Regrets*, London: Weidenfeld & Nicolson, 1976
Ermine Tales, London: Weidenfeld & Nicolson, 1980

Carr, Raymond, *Spain 1808–1939*, Oxford: Oxford University Press, 1966

Carr, William, *A History of Germany 1815–1945*, London: Edward Arnold, 1969

Carr-Saunders, A. M., and Wilson, P. A., *The Professions*, Oxford: Clarendon Press, 1933

Castle, Barbara, *The Castle Diaries 1964–70*, London: Weidenfeld & Nicolson, 1984
The Castle Diaries 1974–76, London: Weidenfeld & Nicolson, 1980

Chorley, Katharine, *Manchester Made Them*, London: Faber & Faber, 1950

Clare, John, 'The Parish', in *The Early Poems of John Clare*, ed. Eric Robinson and David Powell, Oxford: Clarendon Press, 1989

Clemenson, Heather A., *English Country Houses and Landed Estates*, London: Croom Helm, 1982

Cobbett, William, *Rural Rides*, ed. G. D. H. and Margaret Cole, 3 vols., London: Peter Davies, 1930
The Opinions of William Cobbett, ed. G. D. H. and Margaret Cole, 1944

Cooper, Lady Diana, *The Rainbow Comes and Goes*, London: Hart-Davis, 1958
The Light of Common Day, London: Hart-Davis, 1959

Cooper, A. Duff, *Old Men Forget*, London: Hart-Davis, 1953

Cooper, Jilly, *Class*, London: Eyre Methuen, 1979

Crewe, Quentin, *The Frontiers of Privilege*, London: Collins, 1961
Well, I Forget the Rest, London: Hutchinson, 1991

Critchley, Julian, *Westminster Blues*, London: Elm Tree, 1985

Crosland, C. A. R., *The Conservative Enemy*, London: Jonathan Cape, 1962
The Future of Socialism, London: Jonathan Cape, 1956

Crossman, Richard, *The Backbench Diaries*, ed. Janet Morgan, London: Hamish Hamilton and Jonathan Cape, 1981
The Diaries of a Cabinet Minister, Vol. 1: *1964–1966*, New York: Holt, 1976
The Diaries of a Cabinet Minister, Vol. 2: *1966–1968*, London: Hamish Hamilton and Jonathan Cape, 1976
The Diaries of a Cabinet Minister, Vol. 3: *1968–1970*, New York: Holt, 1977

Dahrendorf, Ralf, *Class and Class Conflict in Industrial Society*, London: Routledge & Kegan Paul, 1959

Danziger, Danny, *Eton Voices*, London: Viking, 1988

Darwin, Bernard, *The English Public Schools*, London and New York: Longman Green, 1931

De La Noy, Michael, *The Honours System*, London and New York: Allison & Busby, 1985

Duby, Georges, *The Three Orders: Feudal Society Imagined*, trans. Arthur Goldhammer, Chicago and London: Chicago University Press, 1980

Earle, Peter, *The Making of the English Working Class*, London: Methuen, 1989

Eliot, T. S., *Letters*, Vol. 1: *1898–1922*, ed. Valerie Eliot, London and New York: Harcourt Brace Jovanovich, 1988

Fay, Stephen, *Portrait of an Old Lady*, London: Viking 1987

Fidler, John, *The British Business Elite*, London: Routledge & Kegan Paul, 1981

Finestone, Jeffrey, *The Last Courts of Europe*, London: Dent, 1981

FitzGerald, Brian, *The Anglo-Irish*, London: Staples, 1952

Foster, John, *Class Struggle and the Industrial Revolution*, London: Weidenfeld & Nicolson, 1974

Franklin, M. N., *The Decline of Class Voting in Britain*, Oxford: Clarendon Press, 1985

Fraser, George Macdonald, ed., *The World of the Public Schools*, London: Weidenfeld & Nicolson, 1977

Furbank, P. N., *Unholy Pleasure, or The Idea of Social Class*, Oxford: Oxford University Press, 1985

Fussell, Paul, *Caste Marks*, London: William Heinemann, 1984

Giddens, Anthony, 'Elites in the British Class Structure', in *Elites and Power in British Society*, ed. Philip Stanworth and Anthony Giddens, Cambridge: Cambridge University Press, 1974

Glass, D. V., ed., *Social Mobility in Britain*, London: Routledge & Kegan Paul, 1954

Gould, Bryan, *Goodbye to All That*, London: Macmillan, 1995

Grantley, Lord, *Silver Spoon*, London: Hutchinson, 1954

Green, Shirley, *Who Owns London?*, London: Weidenfeld & Nicolson, 1986

Hadfield, Greg and Skipworth, Mark, *Class: Where Do You Stand?*, London: Bloomsbury, 1994

Halsey, A. H., Heath, A. F., and Ridge, J. M., *Origins and Destinations: Family, Class and Education in Modern Britain*, Oxford: Clarendon Press, 1980

Henderson, Nicholas, *Mandarin: The Diaries of an Ambassador 1969–1982*, London: Weidenfeld & Nicolson, 1994

The Private Office, 1984

Heren, Louis, *Alas, Alas for England*, London: Hamish Hamilton, 1981

Growing Up Poor in London, London: Hamish Hamilton, 1973

Hignett, Sean, *Brett*, London: Hodder & Stoughton, 1984

Hitchens, Christopher, *Blood, Class, and Nostalgia: Anglo-American Ironies*, London: Chatto & Windus, 1990

Hoggart, Richard, *The Uses of Literacy*, London: Chatto & Windus, 1957

Home, Lord, *Border Reflections*, London: Collins, 1979

Jacobs, Eric, and Worcester, Robert, *We British Under the Moriscope*, London: Weidenfeld & Nicolson, 1990

Jenkins, Roy, *Sir Charles Dilke*, London: Collins, 1958

Joyce, Patrick, *Visions of the People. 1991*, Cambridge: Cambridge University Press, 1991

Kelly, Sir David, *The Ruling Few*, London: Hollis & Carter, 1952

Koditschek, Theodore, *Class Formation and Urban-Industrial Society*, Cambridge: Cambridge University Press, 1990

Kohn-Bramstedt, Ernst, *Aristocracy and the Middle Classes in Germany*, London: King, 1937

Lacey, Robert, *Aristocrats*, London: Hutchinson, 1983

Lee, Simon, *Judging Judges*, London: Faber & Faber, 1988
Lees-Milne, James, *Another Self*, London: Hamish Hamilton, 1970
  Ancestral Voices, London: Chatto & Windus, 1975
Leith, Dick, *A Social History of English*, London: Routledge & Kegan Paul, 1983
Lewis, Roy and Maude, Angus, *Professional People*, London: Phoenix House, 1952
Lister, Ruth, ed., *Charles Murray and the Underclass*, London: IEA Health and
  Welfare Unit, 1996
Loane, M., *Neighbours and Friends*, London: Edward Arnold, 1910
Longford, Earl of, *A History of the House of Lords*, London: Collins, 1988
Ludovici, Anthony M., *A Defence of Aristocracy*, London: Constable, 1933
McKay, Malcolm, *The Origins of Hereditary Social Stratification*, Oxford: BAR, 1988
McKenzie, Robert, and Silver, Allan, *Angels in Marble: Working Class Conservatives
  in Urban England*, London: Heinemann, 1968
McKibbin, Ross, *Ideologies of Class*, Oxford: Clarendon Press, 1990
Manchester, Duke of, *My Candid Recollections*, London: Grayson & Grayson, 1932
Margach, James, *The Abuse of Power*, 1978
Martin, F. M., 'Some Subjective Aspects of Social Stratification', in D. V. Glass,
  Social Mobility in Britain
Martin, Kingsley, *The Crown and the Establishment*, London: Hutchinson, 1962
Massie, Robert K., Introduction to J. Finestone, *The Last Courts of Europe*
Masters, Brian, *The Dukes*, London: Blond & Briggs, 1977
Masters, John, *Bugles and a Tiger*, London: Michael Joseph, 1956
Mingay, G. E., *English Landed Society in the Eighteenth Century*, London: Routledge
  & Kegan Paul, 1963
Mitford, Jessica, *Hons and Rebels*, London: Victor Gollancz, 1960
  A Fine Old Conflict, New York: Alfred A. Knopf, 1977
Mitford, Nancy, *The Letters of Nancy Mitford*, ed. Charlotte Mosley, London:
  Hodder & Stoughton, 1993
Moncreiffe, Sir Iain, 'The Expectancy and Rose of the Fair State', in Buckle, ed., *U
  and Non-U Revisited*
Montague-Smith, Patrick, 'The Peerage and the Aristocracy', in Buckle, ed., *U and
  Non-U Revisited*
Montgomery-Massingberd, Hugh, *Debrett's Great British Families*, Exeter: Webb
  & Bower, 1988
Moorhouse, Geoffrey, *The Diplomats*, London: Jonathan Cape, 1977
Moser, C. A., and Hall, J. R., 'The Social Grading of Occupations', in D. V. Glass,
  Social Mobility in Britain
Murray, Charles, *The Growing British Underclass*, London: IEA Health and Welfare
  Unit, 1990
Newson, John and Elizabeth, *Infant Care in an Urban Community*, London: Allen
  & Unwin, 1963
Nicolson, Harold, *Letters and Diaries 1930–1939*, ed. Nigel Nicolson, London:
  Collins, 1966
  Letters and Diaries 1939–1945, ed. Nigel Nicolson, London: Collins, 1967
Nordlinger, Eric A., *The Working Class Tories*, London: MacGibbon & Kee, 1967
Ollard, Richard, *An English Education*, London: Collins, 1982

Ossowski, Stanislaw, *Class Structure in the Social Consciousness*, trans. Sheila Patterson, London: Routledge & Kegan Paul, 1963

Paget, Julian, *The Pageantry of Britain*, London: Michael Joseph, 1979

Pannick, David, *Judges*, Oxford and New York: Oxford University Press, 1987

Paulin, Tom, *A New Look at the Language Question*, 1983

Paxman, Jeremy, *Friends in High Places*, London: Michael Joseph, 1990

Perkin, Harold, *The Rise of Professional Society*, London and New York: Routledge & Kegan Paul, 1989

Perrott, Roy, *The Aristocrats*, London: Weidenfeld & Nicolson, 1968

Phillips, K. C., *Language and Class in Victorian England*, Oxford: Blackwell, 1984

Pilkington, Peter, 'End Egalitarian Delusion: Different Education for Different Talents', London: Centre for Policy Studies, 1991

Pincon, Michel and Monique, *Grandes Fortunes*, Paris: 1996

Pope-Hennessy, James, *Queen Mary*, London: Allen & Unwin, 1959

Powell, Anthony, *Infants of the Spring*, New York: Holt Rinehart Winston, 1976

Rae, John, *The Public School Revolution*, London and Boston: Faber & Faber, 1981

Raven, Simon, *The English Gentleman*, London: Blond, 1961

Reissman, Leonard, *Class in American Society*, London: Routledge & Kegan Paul, 1960

Reynolds, Stephen, and Woolley, Bob and Tom, *Seems So!: A Working-Class View of Politics*, London: Macmillan, 1911

Roberts, Robert, *The Classic Slum: Salford Life in the First Quarter of the Century*, Manchester: Manchester University Press, 1971

Robinson, John Martin, *Buckingham Palace: Official Guide*, London: Michael Joseph, 1966

Romilly, Giles and Esmond, *Out of Bounds*, London: Hamish Hamilton, 1935

Rose, Kenneth, *Superior Person: A Portrait of Curzon and His Circle in Late Victorian England*, London: Weidenfeld & Nicolson, 1969

Ruffer, J. G., *The Big Shots: Edwardian Shooting Parties*, Debrett, 1977

Sampson, Anthony, *The Changing Anatomy of Britain*, London: Hodder & Stoughton, 1982

Sedgemore, Brian, *The Secret Constitution*, London: Hodder & Stoughton, 1980

Sermoneta, Duchess of, *Sparkle Distant Worlds*, London: Hutchinson, 1947

Shell, Donald, *The House of Lords*, Oxford: Philip Allan, 1988

Shepperd, Alan, *Sandhurst*, London: Country Life Books, 1980

Sinclair, Andrew, *The Last of the Best: The Aristocracy of Europe in the Twentieth Century*, London: Weidenfeld & Nicolson, 1969

Smith, George Davey, 'Income Inequality and Morality', *British Medical Journal*, 20 April 1996

Smith, Godfrey, *The English Season*, London: Pavilion, 1987

Smith, Sydney, *Selected Writings*, ed. W. H. Auden, New York: Farrar, Straus & Giroux, 1956

Stanhope, Henry, *The Soldiers: An Anatomy of the British Army*, London: Hamish Hamilton, 1979

Stanworth, Philip, and Giddens, Anthony, 'An Economic Elite: A Demographic Profile of Company Chairmen', in *Elites and Power in British Society*, ed. Philip

Stanworth and Anthony Giddens, Cambridge: Cambridge University Press, 1974

Stanworth, Philip, and Giddens, Anthony, eds., *Elites and Power in British Society*, Cambridge, Cambridge University Press, 1974

Stark, Freya, *Letters*, Vol. 2, Tisbury: Compton Russell, 1975

Stedman Jones, Gareth, *Languages of Class*, Cambridge: Cambridge University Press, 1983

Sternberg, Cecilia, *The Journey*, London: Collins, 1977

Stone, Lawrence, and Stone, Jeanne C. Fawtier, *An Open Elite? 1540–1880*, Oxford: Clarendon Press, 1984

Strong, Roy, *et al.*, *The Destruction of the Country House*, London: Thames & Hudson, 1974

Sutherland, Duke of, *Looking Back*, London: Odhams, 1957

Sykes, Christopher, 'Clothes: The Well-Dressed Man', in Buckle, ed., *U and Non-U Revisited*

Taine, Hippolyte, *Notes on England 1872*, trans. Edward Hyams, London: Thames & Hudson, 1957

Tawney, R. H., *Commonplace Book*, ed. J. Winter and D. M. Joslin, Cambridge: Cambridge University Press, 1972

Thackeray, W. M., *The Book of Snobs*, London: Smith Elder, 1869
Equality, London: Allen & Unwin, 1931, new edn, 1952

Thomas, Hugh, ed. *The Establishment*, London: Blond, 1959
The Story of Sandhurst, London: Hutchinson, 1961

Thompson, E. P., *The Making of the English Working Class*, revised edn, London: Penguin, 1977

Thompson, F. M. L., *English Landed Society in the Nineteenth Century*, London: Routledge & Kegan Paul, 1963

Thompson, Kenneth, 'Church of England Bishops as an Elite', in *Elites and Power in British Society*, ed. Philip Stanworth and Anthony Giddens

Tocqueville, Alexis de, *Journeys to England and Ireland*, trans. George Lawrence and K. P. Mayer, ed. J. P. Mayer, London: Faber & Faber, 1958

Wagner, Sir Anthony, *A Herald's World*, London, 1988

Waugh, Evelyn, *The Letters of Evelyn Waugh*, ed. Mark Amory, London: Weidenfeld & Nicolson, 1980

Wilkinson, Rupert, *The Prefects*, London and New York: Oxford University Press, 1964

Wydenbruck, Nora, *My Two Worlds*, London: Longman, 1956

INDEX